Song:
Anatomy, Imagery, and Styles

ANATOMY

Song

IMAGERY, AND STYLES

BY *Donald Ivey*

THE FREE PRESS · New York

COLLIER-MACMILLAN LIMITED · London

To Helen

*Who has kept alive
the song in my heart*

ML
3815
.I 94

The Free Press
A Division of The Macmillan Company,
866 Third Avenue, New York, New York 10022

COLLIER-MACMILLAN CANADA LTD., Toronto, Ontario

Library of Congress Catalog Card Number: 77–80470

printing number
1 2 3 4 5 6 7 8 9 10

Contents

Preface

S ONG IS a hybrid, and like any hybrid it owes its existence and its effectiveness to a successful amalgamation of the various elements that enter into it. In this sense, any satisfactory experiencing of song must involve the whole rather than a series of parts. To draw an analogy: in the eating of a nectarine, at what point is one aware of the peach and at what point of the plum? So it is with song. Assuming that the amalgam of poetry and music is meaningful, the listener is rarely aware of the elements, but only of the results of true synthesis.

At the same time, any attempt at discussion must begin with parts. But it must be continually kept in mind that the functions of poetry and music in the song enterprise cannot in reality be fragmented clearly and cleanly. Overlaps and interactions are constantly at work: melody is often closely related to harmony and rhythm; musical meter and rhythm encroach upon one another and upon their poetic counterparts; poetry in both its denotative and connotative aspects is frequently intertwined with musical expression. Only on paper can they be segregated for purposes of discussion. With these limitations in mind, however, it is possible to indicate at least partially the varying and sometimes conflicting factors that, working simultaneously, culminate in song.

This book is directed primarily (but not exclusively) to singers, teachers of singing, and to that large body of music lovers for whom the song is a source of pleasure and inspiration. Because of its nature as a short, intimate type of expression and one that appears uncomplicated, both performers and audiences tend to react quite spontaneously to it and to base whatever evaluations they may make largely upon whether or not they like the tune. Among singers in particular there is a general apathy about the relationship between text and tone. This means that in many cases the performer is almost unaware that the words, of themselves, have first existed in poetic form and with a poetic expressiveness that does not necessarily require the addition of music in order to complete its effectiveness. Frequently a singer has looked upon text repetitions as an aid to memorization rather than as an indication of the composer's orientation toward musico-poetic elements. Barbarisms in accentuation or in musical attention to unimportant words or syllables have often gone unnoticed, simply because singer and audience alike have thought of the words (or accepted them without thinking) as subsidiary to the melody rather than as factors that determine it. In many cases the words have been seen solely as vehicles for the production of vocal sound.

This book is written in the hope that a discussion of some of the musico-poetic aspirations and implications in song will aid in a deeper understanding of the genre. Although there are several fine surveys of the history of song in existence,[1] there is no single volume addressed to the interrelationships of word and tone and how these have affected stylistic variations in different periods and places. The most searching discussions often appear as prefaces to song collections or as isolated portions of studies devoted to the work of individual composers.[2] Many of these are extremely scholarly, but unfortunately their widest circulation has been among scholars, not performers. In the course of this book there are frequent references to such discussions, principally in an attempt to bring under one cover a sampling of the insights that others have brought to bear upon the subject.

The discussion is limited to the song repertoire that has served, and still serves, as the heart of the performing literature, although this does not include even the bulk of existing song in the music of the Western world. At the same time, other song will be considered when it has been influential in shaping ideologies that have found a reflection in the more widely performed repertoire.

It has become traditional to arrange recitals so that the first portion is devoted to Italian or English song of the seventeenth and/or eighteenth centuries, the second portion to German *lieder*, the third to French *mélodies*, and the last to folk or contemporary English music. Although there are departures from this format, of course, including the insertion of operatic arias or music from Spain, Russia, or other countries, the procedure as I have outlined it is standard and a change from it is notable because it *is* a departure.

There is good reason for such a format, since it reflects the chronological development of song style. There are similarly reasons (which will be clarified in the course of the following discussions) why the seventeenth and eighteenth centuries are usually represented by repertoire from Italy and England and the nineteenth century by songs chosen from the German and French repertoire. In general, the evolving and ever-changing ideologies that affect the relationship between word and tone are not found consistently within the music of one country. They are truly international,

---

1 Two of the most widely circulated books in English are:
Denis Stevens (ed.), *A History of Song* (London: Hutchinson and Co., Ltd., 1960). James H. Hall, *The Art Song* (Norman: University of Oklahoma Press, 1953).

2 For example, two of the best discussions of the lute song are to be found in the prefaces of Edmund Fellowes' collection, *The English School of Lutenist Song Writers* and in the Introduction to Noah Greenberg's *An Elizabethan Song Book*.

in the sense that Italy, Germany, France, and England have contributed in differing ways at different periods while at the same time retaining certain characteristics individual to their own language and to their own musical orientation. Although countries other than these have also developed their own traditions, it is as those traditions and styles relate to song from the standard repertoire that they take on meaning for both performer and audience. It is possible and practical, therefore, to discuss the song as a type without going beyond the representative literature as it appears regularly on recital programs.

Any discussion must have a point of departure and this is often an arbitrary one. Because so little attention has been given to musico-poetic relationships, I have chosen to begin by briefly describing those relationships in two of their most important aspects. The first is the mechanical correspondences between poetry and music—the ways in which music can reflect or reinforce the "surface" of the poem. The first part of the book is devoted to that characteristic as it appears in songs of all the representative countries from the seventeenth century to the present. The second portion of the book discusses the role of music as an aid to expression, to enhancing or heightening the emotional or connotative implications of the poetry. This division of mechanical and expressive is an arbitrary one and many good arguments against it have been put forward by thoughtful commentators. Nevertheless, it seems to me to have certain advantages that make such a division usable as a basis for discussion.

The final portion of the book is devoted to a survey of the stylistic principles that have been most significant in the chronological development of song style since the advent of what is ordinarily called the monodic revolution in Western music—a development that is intimately involved with the musico-poetic relationships considered in the first two parts of the book. It should not be inferred from this reference to chronology that the later songs are better just because they are more recent. No value judgments at all can be made on the basis of when a song was written. But the songs of the nineteenth century are different from the songs of the seventeenth, and the difference is in part a matter of changed attitudes toward the relative roles of word and tone. It is to these fluctuating relationships that the third part of the book is addressed.

My greatest hope is that the reader of this book will be encouraged to investigate further the musico-poetic factor in the songs he sings or hears. No study of this type can be completely exhaustive because each individual song is an entity that carries its own rationale, processes, and justification. The only way to cover the ground fully would be to discuss *every* song, which is patently impossible. But there are also defensible generalizations. In those that I attempt to make in the course of this book, the individual reader may perhaps find a point of departure that will lead him to a deeper awareness of the nature as well as the complexities of the song as a unique medium of expression.

D. I.

Acknowledgments

I SHOULD like to extend my gratitude to the following publishing houses for their cooperation in granting permission to quote passages from music for which they control the copyrights:

Editions Salabert, Paris, France
Alfred A. Knopf, Inc., New York
Edwin F. Kalmus, Huntingdon Station, New York
Stainer & Bell, Ltd., London
Carl Fischer, Inc., New York City
Summy-Birchard Company, Evanston, Illinois
Boosey and Hawkes, Inc., New York City
Theodore Presser Company, Bryn Mawr, Pennsylvania
Galaxy Music Corporation, New York City
G. Schirmer & Co., New York City
Edward B. Marks Music Corporation, New York City
Franco Colombo, Inc., New York City
Wilhelm Hansen Musik-Forlag, Copenhagen, Denmark

In addition I should like to extend my particular appreciation to the International Music Company of New York City for their kind blanket permission to quote from any of their publications, including the use of their translations of foreign song texts. Their editions have taken the lead in providing exact line-by-line translations of most of the significant song repertoire—certainly that portion which appears with greatest frequency and consistency on the recital stage. Their kindness has greatly eased the burden of extensive illustration and quotation.

I appreciate also the assistance of Dr. Jacob Adler, University of Kentucky, who gave gracious advice in helping me untangle some knots in poetic scansion, and of Dr. Gordon Kinney, University of Kentucky, in providing professional insight and information on several composers and some particular musical problems. To Miss Phyllis Jenness, Michael Sells, and Jacob Ayers I owe a very special debt for their continuing interest in the book and their willingness to read and discuss large portions of it with me. None of them are responsible, however, for any misinformation or misinterpretations. For these I have only myself to thank.

Song:
Anatomy, Imagery, and Styles

I

Musico-poetic Synthesis— The Surface

Meter in German and English Song

I N SONGS from the German and English repertoire, one of the most recognizable correlatives between poetry and music is the use of some type of metrical organization.[1] However, the correlation is not an exact one from a functional standpoint. An overemphasis of the metrical characteristics of poetry can be destructive to a sensitive reading. On the other hand, to disregard the demands of meter in music is to invite a breakdown of one of the most important principles of its rhythmic organization in most of the song from the "common practice period."

Poetic meter involves the arrangement of verbal syllables into groups of stressed and unstressed elements in a more or less regular pattern, *i.e.,* so many strong to so many weak. The structural component here is the metric foot, and for practical purposes it is almost always composed of one accented syllable followed or preceded (and sometimes both) by one or more unaccented syllables. There are notable exceptions, however. In actual poetic practice one often encounters a foot of two equally stressed syllables (spondaic) or similarly two unstressed syllables (pyrrhic). However, these usually occur as variations in a context of other meters. Although many commentaries on versification give several more, for the purposes of this study the metric classifications can be limited to the following (in which the dot represents the unstressed element and the diagonal line the stressed):

Iambic: Un-til / the moon / has ris'n / a-gain

Trochaic: Now the / stream is / run-ning / ful-ler,

Anapestic: At the end / of the side- / walk we found / it a-gain,

Dactylic: Old Mis-sus / Mil-li-gan / drink-ing her / fill a-gain,

Amphibrachic: The wind in / the wil-lows / is rust-ling / in whis-pers.

1 The versification principles of French and Italian do not rely upon meter as an organizational factor and songs in those languages will be discussed separately.

These examples are my own and I hope they will not inaugurate a decline in the art of prosody. The types represented are far and away the most commonly met in poetry that has been set to music for the solo voice. It should be emphasized that the division of verse into metric feet is a mechanical, artificial device, useful in analyzing the syllabic organization but with limited application to recitation. If adhered to rigidly in reading, it can reduce any poem to a mere jingle.

In a book that assumes a considerable musical vocabulary already at hand for the reader it should not be necessary to discuss musical meter. However, one need only consult three or four of the standard reference works on music to discover the astounding confusion that exists both in the definitions and in the use of meter and rhythm and allied terminology. In the light of such confusion it seems best to define clearly the meanings that will be assigned these terms here.

In music, meter is one of several devices by means of which rhythm is organized. To clarify this fully, it is necessary to discuss rhythm itself: to give such a discussion meaning in the context of this study, application must be made to both poetry and music. In both arts—indeed in life itself—rhythm is the ordering of movement in time. As such it includes such things as accent, meter, phrasing, and pauses. In music rhythm itself begins with a regularly recurring impulse and it is the structuring of sound phenomena around that impulse which allows for a definition of rhythmic characteristics. For instance, the impulse may be divided and subdivided at will, a musical sound may be extended through several impulses, a profusion of accentual variations may be assigned to the impulses. But always the relatively regular impulse underlies musical rhythm—it is most commonly referred to as the "beat." Although it is not always audible, it must be *felt* in order to bring order to the musical movement. This regularity of impulse is not present in poetry other than the most trite variety; thus, although rhythm in both music and poetry is concerned with movement, there is no real common denominator for its regulation.

One way to regulate the rhythmic beat in music is by means of meter. There seems to be little doubt that, given a regularly recurring sound of any sort (a clock's tick is the usual example), the listener will instinctively group the sounds according to patterns of stressed and unstressed elements. As I use the term in this book, meter is that patterning. It determines the number of impulses in a group as well as which impulse is felt to be strongest under normal circumstances. In music the metrical unit is the bar, and the first note regularly carries the greatest accentual importance. Unremitting overemphasis of the accent coarsens the music, but where metric regularity is one of the factors in the organization, to ignore that accent or to frustrate its reasonably regular arrival usually results in chaos. It should be acknowledged here that not all music is metrically regular. That of the twentieth century, for example, utilizes considerable metric variation in order to achieve rhythmic complexity. But meter, where it is used at all, functions as the organizer of rhythmic impulses into numerically definable groups with certain accentual characteristics.

To recapitulate, then: meter is one of the means by which stressed and unstressed elements are organized. In poetry the elements are verbal syllables; in music they are recurring beats or pulses. In poetry the meter is a means to analysis and is mechanical and artificial; in music it is functional and meaningful to most of the repertoire we shall be discussing, in terms of its regularity or complexity, its presence or absence, its strength or weakness, and it is one of the important ways of ordering rhythm.

Although an undue emphasis on meter does an injustice to poetry, there has been a great amount of literal transfer from poetic to musical meter, which has not been restricted to any particular period. The attraction has evidently been in terms of the "swing" that results from a conscious awareness of this element of poetic organization. It must be stressed, however, that when the transfer is literal, the musical meter imposes upon the poetic meter a regularity of occurence in time that is not ideal for poetic utterance. The examples that follow are given, not as an illustration of the great kindness that music can render poetry but only as evidence that the condition of transfer does exist and that it has been a continuing factor in song composition. None of the works cited is complete—enough has been excerpted to illustrate the principles.

IAMBIC

The following lines by James Stephens are in regular iambic meter:

> As down | the road | she wam- | bled slow,
>
> She had | not got | a place | to go:
>
> She had | not got | a place | to fall
>
> And rest | her-self, | no place | at all!

Since the concern at this point is with metric transfer only, the musical realization is given in note values alone, without regard to melodic contour or harmonic punctuation, although these things are of great importance to a song's effectiveness. Samuel Barber's setting of Stephens's lines (*Bessie Bobtail*) are as follows:

She had   not got   a place   to fall

And rest   her-self, no   place   at   all!

A more regular realization could hardly be imagined. In this case the content of the lines strongly suggests just such regularity as that which Barber utilizes. In this instance, then, the choice of meter itself serves an expressive purpose over and above its purely mechanical utility. But in terms of the relationship between poetry and music in the most literal sense, the important factor is that each accent of the poetic meter has been treated as an accentual factor in the musical meter.

An example of iambic meter in German is found in these opening lines from a poem by Goethe:

> Im Fel- | de schleich | ich still | und wild,
> Ge-spannt | mein Feu- | er-rohr,

Franz Schubert, in his *Jägers Abendlied*, sets the lines:

Im Fel - de schleich ich still und wild,

Ge-spannt mein Feu - er-rohr,

Some explanation of my rhythmic notation is in order here. Because of melodic considerations, a composer will sometimes assign several notes to a single syllable. In such cases, as in this and the following illustrations, the sum of their rhythmic values is given as a single note. For instance, Schubert actually writes in the first line:

Im Fel - de schleich ich still

In the examples used here the durational values of all syllables are reproduced as the composer wrote them, although the actual number of notes may not be the same. To return to the song itself, it can readily be seen that the poetic and musical meters stand in exact relationship to one another.

Such literal transfers as those represented by these excerpts are not the usual ones in song composition, although in certain styles and during certain periods their occurrence is strikingly consistent. This characteristic of controlled transfer from poetry to music is one of the distinguishing marks of the German *continuo lied* and the later *volkstümliches lied*, for instance. In these two types of song it was an indication that the composer was concerned with a simplification of both poetic and musical factors and sometimes even that the poets themselves were attempting to structure their poetry in conformity with one of the most basic principles of music. Unfortunately, this sort of literalism discourages both poetic and musical subtlety and may help to account for the fact that neither the *continuo* nor *volkstümliches lied* has continued to hold the interest of singers or public.

Frequently a composer utilizes a secondary accent within the bar to augment the possibilities offered by the primary accent of the first beat. Thus, in $\frac{4}{4}$ meter, the third beat will frequently carry the poetic accent successfully because of its relationship to the weaker second and fourth. In the same sense, compound meters carry stress points on beats other than the initial one of the bar, and utilization of these metric stresses allows a composer a wider variety of choice in meters than if he were restricted to the first beat alone, accentually speaking.

In this context, the following lines by Sedley offer an interesting illustration of a primarily iambic lyric which shifts gears at several strategic spots, thus posing something of a problem to a composer.

> "Hears not | my Phil- | lis how | the birds,
>
> Their feath- | er'd mates | sa-lute,
>
> They tell | their pas- | sion in | their words,
>
> Must I | a-lone | be mute?"
>
> Phil-lis | with-out | a frown | or smile,
>
> Sat | and knott- | ed all | the while.

The problem is in the final two lines and a word should be said about the idiosyncrasies of poetic scansion. Unless the lines are extremely regular, there are very apt to be several possible solutions in diagramming them, all of which may have merit. What is given above is a traditional solution. Substitution of a trochaic foot in an otherwise iambic line (as in line five) is not at all unusual—it relieves what might be unbearable monotony and it contributes strongly to the poem's rhythmic interest. The last line is more troublesome; it could be scanned:

> Sat and | knott-ed | all the | while.

In this scheme, the last foot would be construed as truncated, consisting of a defective trochee and this is not unusual. In the scansion given, however, the first syllable is the defective one and the balance of the line regains the iambic continuity established in the opening of the strophe. This seems more consistent with the practices of a typical seventeenth-century poet. Similar problems present themselves constantly in the mechanics of poetic scansion. When apparent ambiguities do occur, probably the important factor is their presence rather than the need for a solution that might be universally acceptable, especially in the light of continually changing theories of poetic practice. Varying solutions obviously present themselves to composers, as well as to academicians, and thus represent a conflict that must be resolved in composition. In the discussions that follow, therefore, there will be no further apology or defense for the scansion. I will give what seems the most reasonable solution for whatever conflicting possibilities happen to be involved.

Henry Purcell's setting, *The Knotting Song,* uses this rhythmic scheme:

Again a few words about my rhythmic realization, this time in relation to text repetitions. Where they do not vary the metric scheme or the accentual pattern, I have deleted them. Purcell, like many of his contemporaries in the baroque period, was much given to repetition, but often the rhythms as well as the words are reiterated in identical fashion. When this is the case, a measure or two of repeated patterns may be omitted without destroying the relationship between poetry and meter, although it would eradicate a very charming feature of this song.

Purcell seems to have solved the metric problems of the final two lines by changing his own meter. This may not have been the sole consideration, however. It is possible that he was also resorting to text illustration of a relatively subtle sort so that the rocking motion of the meter would suggest that Phyllis was rocking as well as knotting. Such tone-painting devices were part of the stock-in-trade for composers of the period and constitute an important element in the definition of baroque vocal style.

Sometimes it is necessary to take in an extra syllable of poetic text rather than compensating for a missing one. Such a situation is illustrated in these lines by Goethe:

Ich bin | der wohl- | be-kann- | te Sän-ger,

Der viel- | ge-rei- | ste Rat- | ten-fän-ger,

In his setting, *Der Rattenfänger*, Hugo Wolf uses primary and secondary accents to retain the poetic meter:

Innumerable musically regular solutions are possible for any poetic meter, of course, and the purpose here is not to illustrate or suggest all or even most of them. The examples are intended only to show that at times it suits a composer's purpose to respond quite exactly to the meter of the poem. At this point the correlation between important organizational principles of poetry and music is very precise. Even within the limits of literalism the variety of responses is a significant factor in helping to understand a composer's resourcefulness in declamation.

TROCHAIC

Metrically regular examples of trochaic organization are numerous; here is one by Goethe:

Tie-fe | Stil-le | herrscht im | Was-ser,

Oh-ne | Re-gung | ruht das | Meer,

Und be- | küm-mert | sieht der | Schif-fer

Glat-te | Flä-che | rings um- | her.

Schubert in his *Meeres Stille* responds to the regularity:

The effect is almost hypnotically static, as may frequently be the case when a literal metric transfer is effected. In this particular song, however, much more than accent is at stake, for the poetic content itself is hypnotic.

> Deep calm prevails over the water.
> The sea rests motionless,
> And anxiously the sailor scans
> The smooth surface all around

> Translation from International Music Company edition.

As suggested earlier, poetic metric schemes are susceptible to many rhythmic solutions. Thus a trochaic pattern of striking regularity, such as represented by these lines by Rochlitz:

> *Lei-ser, | lei-ser, | klei-ne | Lau-te*
>
> *Flü-stre, | was ich | dir ver- | trau-te,*
>
> *Dort zu | je-nem | Fen-ster | hin!*

may readily be absorbed into a compound metric format essentially as lyric as the poem itself. This version is Schubert's *An die Laute*.

Although both Goethe and Rochlitz employ the same poetic meter, the moods of their poems are sharply contrasted. It is a tribute to Schubert's skill that he was able, by means of his choice of musical meter, to capture this difference. Other factors are important, of course, but the meter in *An die Laute* is undeniably a gently lyric one. The frequent use of compound and triple meters to accompany poems that are highly lyric or that suggest rocking, lullabies, or similarly gently flowing motion or mood, must be recognized as having some basis in the inherent expressive qualities of those meters. Here mechanics and content are closely intertwined. The translation of Rochlitz's lines reveals the aptness of Schubert's realization.

> Gently, gently, little lute,
> Whisper what I entrust to you,
> To that window there.

> Translation from International Music Company edition.

Of the numerous examples of trochaic meter in English song, I have chosen two that have been set by composers widely separated in time. The first occurs in a song by John Dowland, possibly on his own text. Of the song literature in the performing repertoire, the work of Dowland and his contemporaries in lutenist song composition was among the first to concentrate upon the relationship between text and music. Metrical regularity was not a feature of this particular school, primarily because the application of the bar line and musical meter itself were jointly in a period of transition from the largely unbarred music of the Renaissance toward the consistent metrical barring of the later baroque. The following piece is of special interest because the tune seems to have been borrowed from a folk song, "the frog galliard." Its relationship to the dance has some bearing on the relative rhythmic regularity. But Dowland, though retaining the metric consistency, has replaced the mood of gaiety typical of the galliard with one of sad lamenting.

> Now, O | now, I | needs must | part,
> Part-ing | though I | ab-sent | mourn.
> Ab-sence | can no | joy im- | part,
> Joy once | fled can- | not re- | turn.

And the rhythmic scheme:

The fourth line demands some attention. Poetically there is no metric change from the three preceding lines. The musical feeling, however, shifts suddenly to what feels like groups of duple rather than triple impulses. There is no *accentual* change—the movement continues in alternate stressed and unstressed elements. But the relative values of the accented syllables are affected, and the metric feeling as well. In this case accent is not solely responsible for the metric division—duration plays a part. One important factor in the expression here is that the sudden change of metric arrangement, emerging from a previously static context, adds a vitality that calls attention to the text.

An equally regular poetic metric scheme is found in these lines from a poem by George Herbert:

> Come, my | Way, my | Truth, my | Life:
>
> Such a | Way, as | gives us | breath:
>
> Such a | Truth, as |ends all | strife:
>
> Such a | Life, as | kil-leth | death.

Setting the lyric in his *Five Mystical Songs*, Ralph Vaughan Williams provides this pattern:

There are similarities between the Dowland song and this. In both the musical rhythm is unrelievedly repetitious, closely following the metric accentuation, until the final lines of the poems. In this respect the poetic meter is translated with extreme literalism until an expressive point that suggests a departure. In Dowland's song the departure takes the form of a complete shift of metric emphasis. In Vaughan Williams's there is an expressive extension of the significant word, *death*. It is worth noting that trochaic meter tends to proceed more consistently than most other types, frequently resisting the substitution of other metric feet. In itself this can pose something of a problem for the composer, who runs the risk of monotony if he gets too firmly caught in the scheme of accentuation. As indicated earlier this does an injustice to both the poem and the musical realization. Rhythmic and/or metric adjustment (as in Dowland) and syllable extension (as in Vaughan Williams) are examples of typical compositional devices that relieve this regularity. The sudden release from the initial static quality of the rhythm heightens the expression very effectively. There are a myriad other devices, of course; the perceptive performer will recognize them and take full advantage of them in fulfilling the expressive possibilities.

As a general rule, disyllabic organization, *i.e.*, two syllables to a foot, seems to be relatively stable. Trisyllabic feet appear to be more troublesome to poets and composers alike. The lyricism that seems inherent in triple meters would suggest a ready point of contact for word and tone, but in actual practice this has not been the case. In poetry the occurrence of disyllables in German and English far outnumbers that of trisyllables. But of the two languages, German, when it employs trisyllabic organization, tends to be more consistent and stable than English. Perhaps because of this relative stability there are more examples of literal transfer from poetry to music in German than in English, although even in the former they are relatively infrequent.

DACTYLIC

These lines from a poem by Rückert are typical of *dactylic* meter:

> Lách-en und | Wéi-nen zu | jég-li-cher | Stún-de,
>
> Rúht bei der | Líeb auf so | mán-cher-lei | Grún-de.

Schubert's realization in *Lachen und Weinen* is rhythmically as well as metrically regular:

Lach - en und Wei - nen zu jeg - li - cher Stun - de,

Ruht bei der Lieb auf so man-cher - lei Grun - de.

As in the transfer of disyllables, composers have frequently utilized the secondary as well as the primary metrical accents. A case in point is Schubert's use of these lines from a poem by Stollberg:

> Mít-ten im | Schím-mer der | spíe-geln-den | Wél-len
>
> Gléi-tet, wie | Schwä-ne, der | wán-ken-de | Káhn;
>
> Ách, auf der | Fréu-de sanft- | schím-mern-den | Wél-len
>
> Gléi-tet die | See-le da- | hín wie der | Káhn;

Schubert's rhythmic-metric pattern in *Auf dem Wasser zu singen* is:

Mit - ten im Schim-mer der spie-geln-den Wel-len

Glei - tet, wie Schwä-ne, der wan-ken-de Kahn;

Ach, auf der Freu - de sanft schim-mern-den Wel-len

Glei - tet die See-le da - hin wie der Kahn;

As in some of the previous examples, the expressive quality of the musical meter itself is apparent here.

> Amid the shimmer of the mirroring waters
> Glides, like a swan, the rocking boat;
> Ah, on gently shimmering waves of joy
> The soul also glides away, like the boat.
>
> Translation from International Music Company edition.

Schubert has been criticized for his often literal adoption of poetic meter, and it is true that, particularly during the early stages of his development, he was sometimes unduly attracted to this and other elements of poetic structure. In this song, a product of his more mature command of musical materials, the literalism does not in any way intrude upon either the musical mood or the poetic content, but rather implements them both. Defective feet (usually occurring at line endings) are taken in gracefully by the simple expedient of rhythmic adjustment.

The use of dactylic meter does not always reflect a graceful or lyric poetic mood. A sense of great weariness and sorrow pervades these lines from a poem by Scheffel:

> *Kampf-müd' und | sonn-ver-brannt,*
>
> *Fern an der | Hei-den Strand,*
>
> *Wald-grü-nes | Thü-ring-land,*
>
> *Denk' ich an | dich.*

> Battle-weary and sun-scorched,
> On a distant pagan shore,
> Green-wooded Thüringland,
> I think of thee.
>
> Translation from International Music Company edition.

The heaviness of Hugo Wolf's rhythmic realization is entirely in keeping with the lyric.

The use of a defective final foot in the last line adds a great deal of weight and is important to the cadential feeling as well as for the expressive importance it gives to the line.

ANAPESTIC

Of the three trisyllabic types, the anapest is by far the most infrequent in German and appears almost always in a context that is relatively irregular. Its insertion creates considerable strain in the scansion and it is questionable whether an academic solution is defensible or even desirable. The following example is chosen for two reasons. It demonstrates the instability of metric texture where the anapest is involved; it also demonstrates Brahms's characteristic tendency to smooth out with music the troubled waters of poetic complexitty. The poem is an arrangement by Scherer of a traditional verse:

> Gu-ten | A-bend, | gut' Nacht, | mit Ro- | sen be-dacht,
>
> Mit Näg'- | lein be-steckt, | schlupf' un- | ter die Deck';
>
> Mor-gen | früh, wenn | Gott will, | wirst du wie- | der ge-weckt.

I have been unable to locate the original version of the poem but one may be certain that Scherer's arrangement does not smooth out any wrinkles in the metric scheme, whatever other virtues it may have. Brahms was never inhibited by poetic subtleties, a facet of his work which does not seem to have depressed his popularity. His beloved *Wiegenlied*, based upon this poem, reveals both his musical charm and his disregard for poetic niceties. While it may not illustrate a fussy attempt to stress declamation, it is wonderfully appropriate to the demands of a lullaby.

Gu-ten A-bend, gut' Nacht, mit Ro-sen be-dacht,

Mit Näg'-lein be-steckt, schlupf' un-ter die Deck';

Mor-gen früh, wenn Gott will, wirst du wie-der ge-weckt.

AMPHIBRACHIC

Some of the finest lyrics in German song involve the use of the amphibrach, particularly during the romantic flowering of the nineteenth century, and they appear with relative stability. The following lines by Uhland are illustrative:

Ich hör' mei- | nen Schatz,

Den Ham-mer | er schwin-get,

Das rau-schet, | das klin-get,

Das dringt in | die Wei-te,

Wie Glo-cken- | ge-läu-te,

Durch Gas-sen | und Platz.

Brahms's *Der Schmied* responds with a rhythmic organization of such strong metric proportions that one cannot help feeling the lusty blows of the blacksmith's hammer:

Although metrically much the same, a more impetuous poetic mood is found in this excerpt from a Heine lyric:

Die Ro-se, | die Li-lie, | die Tau-be, | die Son-ne,

Die liebt ich | einst al-le | in Lie- | bes-won-ne.

Ich lieb' sie | nicht mehr, | ich lie-be | al-lei-ne

Die Klei-ne, | die Fei-ne, | die Rei-ne, | die Ei-ne;

Robert Schumann was certainly a lyricist, but usually less addicted than Schubert to metric literalism. In this instance, however, the on-going surge of the setting in his song cycle *Dichterliebe* takes full advantage of the poetic meter.

As a purely mechanical process, the only variety in Schumann's rhythmic scheme occurs in exact correspondence to the two metric substitutions in Heine's verse. In both cases the substitution is that of an iamb in the otherwise consistent amphibrachic structure (lines two and three). In the first instance, at *Liebeswonne*, the missing syllable needed to fill out the metric foot is compensated for by the addition of a dot to the eighth note. The rest Schumann uses in the third line not only compensates for the missing syllable but also articulates musically the caesura one feels in the middle of the line.

An amphibrachic organization in a different poetic mood is found in these lines from a poem by Heyse:

Nun wan-dre, | Ma-ri-a, | nun wan-dre | nur fort.

Schon krä-hen | die Häh-ne | und nah ist | der Ort.

Nun wan-dre, | Ge-lieb-te, | du Klein- | od mein,

Und bal-de | wir wer-den | in Beth-le- | hem sein.

Hugo Wolf, relying strongly on secondary metric accents, sets the text as follows:

Nun wan-dre, Ma-ri-a, nun wan-dre nur fort.

Schon krä-hen die Häh-ne und nah ist der Ort.

Nun wan-dre, Ge-lieb-te, du Klein-od mein,

Und bal-de wir wer-den in Beth-le-hem sein.

The adoption of eighth notes as rhythmic equivalents of unstressed poetic syllables becomes in this case the substitution of rests of that value for defections in the final feet of the first three lines. Likewise, at the iambic foot in line three, the first syllable of the word *Kleinod* is extended in order to compensate for the missing metrical element.

As even these few examples illustrate, there is some consistency in trisyllabic meters in German poetry. This is less true in English. Shapiro and Beum point out that the dactyl and its companion trisyllable, the anapest, "are difficult to manage in serious English verse," and are found most frequently in contexts that involve relatively extensive substitution of other metric types.[2] This is borne out, although with slightly different emphasis, by McAuley, who states:

> . . . trisyllabic feet combine easily to give a sort of generalized trisyllabic metre. In addition disyllabic feet can be freely introduced. . . . In such mixed verse, with multiple substitutions, it can become doubtful whether we are dealing with a trisyllabic metre with frequent disyllabic substitutions or the other way round.[3]

The point seems to be that the unrelieved use of a single type of trisyllabic meter presents major functional problems to the English poet, except perhaps in a very limited format of the jingle variety. This is reflected in song. Representative of the problem is this lyric from Henry Purcell's *The Indian Queen*, on a libretto by Dryden and Howard:

I at-tempt | from Love's sick- | ness to fly | in vain,

Since I | am my-self | my own fe- | ver and pain.

No more | now, fond heart, | with pride | no more swell,

Thou canst | not raise for- | ces e-nough | to re-bel.

This poem is certainly not highly irregular, but five metric substitutions in four lines are more than a composer can overlook. Purcell succeeded for the most part in absorbing the slight irregularities into a fairly regular musical scheme:

I at-tempt from Love's sick-ness to fly in vain,

Since I am my-self my own fe-ver and pain.

No more now, fond heart, with pride no more swell,

Thou canst not raise for-ces e-nough to re-bel.

2 Karl Jay Shapiro and Robert Beum, *A Prosody Handbook* (New York: Harper & Row, 1965), p. 33.

3 James P. McAuley, *Versification: A Short Introduction* (East Lansing: Michigan State University Press, 1966), p. 21.

But when the metric construction is even this irregular, other factors tend to assume more significance. For instance, although the word *Love* in the first line is metrically weak both poetically and musically, it cannot justifiably be treated lightly from the standpoint of verbal import. Purcell does give some emphasis by providing a musical melisma on the word; although this helps, it is only partial compensation.

Complications are much more in evidence in this lyric from the libretto written by Betterton for Purcell's *Dioclesian*:

> What shall I | do to show | how much I | love her?
> How ma-ny | mil-lions of | sighs can suf- | fice?
> That which wins | oth-er's hearts | ne-ver can | move her;
> Those com-mon | me-thods of | love she'll des- | pise.

What I have given is a traditional scansion—it is obvious that this does not begin to give adequate attention to the contextual importance of a number of the words. One of the problems is the profusion of monosyllabic words, several of which vie for attention apart from their normal accentual significance. Caught up in the poetic scansion, Purcell provides a very regular realization.

An expressive reading of the lines would almost certainly emphasize the word *much* in the first line, the first syllable of *many* in the second, the words *wins* and *hearts* and possibly even *her* in the third, and the first syllable of *common* in the fourth. All of these are weak metrically, however, and the literal transfer of the poetic meter into musical meter simply reinforces the weakness. In order to regulate such a series of irregularities, so to speak, a great deal more rhythmic flexibility would be required. But though rhythmic maneuverability was definitely a part of Purcell's equipment and vocabulary, the relatively inflexible metric drive that characterized much of the music of the period may have exerted more control over him than the demands of poetic subtlety. An additional factor was the important distinction between recitative and aria in Purcell's day, a distinction that included considerable declamatory emphasis in the former and decidedly less in the latter. In the aria the main concern was vocal and melodic attractiveness rather than the skillful avoidance of barbarisms.

More hazardous in every way is the following excerpt from a 1661 collection entitled *Wit and Drollery*:

> The life of | a shep-herd | is void of | all care-a,
>
> With his bag | and his bot- | tle he mak- | eth good | fare-a,
>
> He ruf-fles, | he shuf-fles | in all ex- | treme wind-a,
>
> His flock | some-times | be-fore him, | and some-times | be-hind-a.

The futility of scansion (which has led to so much discontent with this device in recent years) is immediately apparent. This rollicking, carefree lyric was never meant to be so fussily documented! Surely, to do the piece justice, one would simply have several feet with more than the academic number of unaccented syllables. Thus:

> With his bag and | his bot-tle | he mak-eth | good fare-a,

and possibly:

> His flock some- | times be-fore him, | and some-times | be-hind-a.

It is even likely that the last line was originally meant to be read (or sung, in the event that it was the text of a folk song to begin with) as:

> His flock some- | times 'fore him, | and some-times | be-hind-a.

Any of these concessions would alleviate the academic problems, at least. In musical terms, Peter Warlock, using the poem for his *The jolly shepherd*, simply responded to the general mood of devil-may-care and provided the lyric with its own best swing.

A more direct, happy-go-lucky approach would be hard to imagine—and a few rhythmic manipulations take care of those pesky unaccented syllables as directly as possible.

Highly irregular meters have been one of the identifying features of much poetry written in the last hundred years. Fortunately, the musical vocabulary, rhythmic and otherwise, has become increasingly flexible, so that composers have been able to meet metrical and rhythmic complexities in poetry with a correspondingly complex musical texture. One example is this portion of a poem by Thomas Hardy:

Here is | an an- | cient floor,

Foot-worn | and hol- | lowed and thin,

Here was | the form- | er door

Where the | dead feet | walked in.

Scansion in this context is almost superfluous—but rhythm and accent are of great significance. Gerald Finzi, setting the poem as a portion of his cycle *Before and After Summer,* treats the lyric in the following manner:

Making use of secondary accents, the musical transfer is exact. Even the pyrrhic and the spondee in the last line are accounted for, the first by metrically weak musical rhythms and the second by syncopation which gives due emphasis to the word *feet.*

Equally stimulating but problematical is the metrical flux in this portion of *Velvet Shoes* by Elinor Wylie:

Let us walk | in the | white snow

In a sound- | less space;

With foot- | steps qui- | et and slow,

At a tran- | quil pace.

There have been numerous settings of this appealing poem; the musical realization given by Mary Howe in *Let Us Walk in the White Snow* demonstrates the use of metric change to compensate for the fluctuations of verse meter.

Whether this amount of metric manipulation is necessary may be open to question, but the accentual relationship between music and poem is evident. The musical weakness allowed on the word *white* is difficult to justify, but in all other respects the declamation is quite sensitive.

SUMMARY

The metric strength of English and German poetry has apparently exercised some influence in the musical setting of texts in these languages. The degree of that influence varies from composer to composer, but it is a useful clue to some elements of individual style. Some of the differences in rhythmic flexibility between Schubert and Wolf, for instance, are based upon their responses to poetic meter. One has only to read the poetry that Schubert set to the rhythms he provided in order to realize that much of it consists of a strikingly regular transfer of the poetic meter, an indication that this factor was a significant motivating force in much of his song composition. The same thing cannot usually be said for Wolf, although he was always careful to accent properly. At the same time, his choice of rhythms *within* a metrical framework tended to be more diverse, to move more freely, and to rely less upon metrical accent than upon rhythmic flexibility. Thus a rhythmic reading of his song texts can closely resemble a sensitive recitation of the poetry itself. By the same token, Purcell was generally more inclined to regulate the poetic rhythm through his musical treatment than were the composers of the lutenist school. The reasons for these variations will be made clear in the third section of this book; they are important in achieving full understanding of the differing demands in declamatory sensitivity that the work of these composers places upon the performer.

Versification in Italian and French Song Texts

ITALIAN

V ERSE types in Italian depend less upon regular accentuation patterns than upon the construction of lines according to the number of verbal syllables. Accent is important, but its occurrence is often quite irregular. While this sounds simple on the surface, the matter is complicated by several factors. For the purposes of this book it is not necessary to go deeply into all the poetic types nor the numerous exceptional poetic practices; it is enough to state the general principles and give illustrations of how they function in song.

Italian verse of the baroque period, which is the source of most of the song repertoire in this language, allows for lines that vary in length from four to eleven syllables, although in actual practice other possibilities are represented.[1] Within any given line, depending upon the number of syllables present, there are one or more syllables which carry a stronger accent than those preceding and following them. Thus, in a line of four syllables, the third will carry the only regular accent. In a line of five, the fourth will be accented. In a line of six syllables, the fifth will carry the principal accent, but there is normally a secondary accent on the second syllable. As the number of syllables increases the accentual possibilities become more profuse. For instance, in a line of eleven syllables, where the tenth regularly carries the principal accent, secondary accents may occur on the sixth, on the fourth and eighth, or on the fourth and seventh.

To complicate matters still further, lines with eight or more syllables

1 Much of the information in this discussion is drawn from: Putnam Aldrich, *Rhythm in Seventeenth-Century Italian Monody* (New York: W. W. Norton & Company, Inc., 1966). For those who are interested enough to demand a complete and well-illustrated consideration of musico-poetic factors, particularly of a rhythmic nature, there is no better source in my opinion.

usually contain a caesura after the secondary accent or the syllable immediately following it. Much of the nature of Italian versification may be traced to the characteristics of the language itself, which is true of any sort of prosody, of course. The majority of Italian words, when they contain more than one syllable, have feminine endings, which is to say that the penultimate syllable carries the accent. This is so overwhelmingly the case that poetic structure assumes feminine line endings as a regular occurrence, and in those cases where there is not actually an unaccented syllable, the line is counted as though there were one. In addition, if there happen to be two unaccented syllables ending a line, only one of them is considered in the count. Naturally, all of these possibilities have names. To indicate just a few: a five-syllable line is a *quinario*, a six-syllable line is a *scenario*, a seven-syllable line a *settenario*. Any reader familiar with Italian can probably add the rest or come pretty close. Verses that carry the accent on the penultimate syllable are known as *piano*; those ending on an accented syllable are known as *tronco* (the relationship to the truncated line in English verse is apparent); if two unstressed syllables occur at the line ending, the verse is known as *sdrucciolo*.

The counting of syllables is complicated by the problem of elision and other related factors. Ordinarily, when one word ends with a vowel and the following word begins with a vowel, the two vowels are elided and counted as one syllable. This is normally the case within a word also. However, often for accentual reasons, there are cases in which two succeeding vowels are pronounced separately and in these instances the syllables are likewise considered separately. The word *trivïa* is counted as three syllables, for instance, and here a helpful clue is the double dot over one of the vowels. Furthermore, when a word ending in two or more vowels occurs at the *end* of a poetic line the vowels are counted separately, whereas when such a word occurs in the *middle* of a line the vowels are considered as being only one syllable. Other exceptions occur when adjacent vowels carry accents for reasons other than those already cited; in such cases they are counted as separate syllables. Normally, when three vowels occur together a division of accent breaks the combination into two syllables.

All of this seems highly mechanical and arbitrary and it is. As in German and English, versification principles, if allowed full reign, can reduce poetry to a mere academic problem and can intrude upon expression to an alarming degree. Nevertheless, they do form a vital and controlling force in prosody and all thoughtful composers take them into consideration. Italian versification allows inherently for movement across an often extended number of unaccented syllables, which can closely approximate normal speech patterns. The lack of arbitrary division into short metric feet encourages a lyricism that in German and English is won only with much effort and skill on the part of poet, reader, and singer.

To clarify all this description, let us take a close look at the poem used by Alessandro Scarlatti in *Se Florindo è fedele*. Although the piece is an aria rather than a song, the principles of versification are the same and the poem is interesting enough to afford good illustration. Accents are underlined and elisions are indicated by slurs under the affected vowels.

> *Se Flo-rin-do̲ è fe-de-le*
>
> *Io m'in-na-mo-re-rò*
>
> *Po-trà ben l'ar-co ten-de-re*
>
> *Il fa-re-tra-to̲ ar-cier*
>
> *Ch'io mi sa-prò di-fen-de-re*
>
> *D'un guar-do lu-sin-ghier.*
>
> *Pre-ghi, pian-ti̲ e que-re-le*
>
> *Io non a-scol-te-rò*
>
> *Ma se sa-rà fe-de-le*
>
> *Io m'in-na-mo-re-rò*

This is an example of *settenario* verse, regularly a seven-syllable line with accents on the sixth syllable and on one of the first four. As may be seen, many of the principles discussed at the beginning of this section are at work in this lyric. Although in general the accentuation pattern follows the prescription for this type of verse structure, there are several places where more than one secondary accent is present (lines three, four, and five). Lines one, seven, and nine are *piano*, carrying the accent on the penultimate syllable. Lines two, four, six, eight, and ten (all the even-numbered lines) are *tronco*, ending with an accented syllable. These lines contain only six syllables but are counted as though the expected unaccented syllable were actually there. Lines three and five are *sdrucciolo*; they contain eight syllables but the last one is ignored in counting.

The advantages that favor lyricism in such a verse are apparent. At the same time the difficulties of accommodating the poem to a metrically regular musical scheme are equally obvious. Scarlatti's setting abounds in barbarisms, as a matter of fact; the piece is too widely known to require illustration. The inconsistencies between poetic and musical accentuation help to account for the fact that, beginning with the baroque period, Italian concentration in solo vocal music centered almost exclusively upon opera. The medium was one in which melody rather than careful declamation was the controlling factor until well into the nineteenth century. Particularly in its Neopolitan heyday, during the eighteenth century, opera was a vehicle for vocal pyrotechnics and the poetry furnished only a generalized guide for what was primarily a musical expressiveness. Paradoxically, most of the presently performed Italian repertoire from the period is excerpted from opera or cantata—it is not true song. As the pieces appear in most available editions, however, they are relatively brief and song-like, largely because they contain no suggestion of the ornamentation and extemporization to which they were subjected in baroque performance. They therefore deserve attention in any discussion of musico-poetic relationships.[2]

Some of the versification schemes carry with them an accentual pattern so regular that it can lend itself quite readily to metric stability in music. One such is the *scenario*, the six-syllable line accenting the second and fifth syllables. The relationship to amphibrachic verse is quite exact, and sometimes settings of *scenario* poetry do have the same sort of swing as settings of amphibrachic. One example is Giovanni Legrenzi's *Che fiero costume*.

Che fie-ro co-stu-me

D'a-li-ge-ro nu-me,

Che a for-za di pe-ne

Si fac-cia a-do-rar.

The musical rhythm provided by Legrenzi is metrically strong and matches the poetic accentuation with great integrity.

This is a happy situation, of course, but frequently (as in *Se Florindo è fedele*) there is not the same consistency. One very unhappy situation, poetically speaking, is found in Scarlatti's *O cessate di piagarmi*. (He seems to be our whipping boy here but his contemporaries are equally at fault.) The verse is *ottonario* with several *tronco* lines, but it is not necessary to quote much of it to reveal the basic problem.

O ces-sa-te di pia-gar-mi,

O la-scia-te-mi mo-rir!

2 It is an unfortunate fact that practically all the available performing editions of Italian solo vocal music of the seventeenth and eighteenth centuries fail to indicate the sources of the compositions. Neither, for the most part, do they acknowledge poets. Tracking down such information might be helpful, but does not fall within the scope of a book such as this.

The accents fall regularly on the third and seventh syllables, which is to be expected in *ottonario* verse from this period. The musical rhythm completely frustrates this element of the poetic intention.

As is so often the case, the problem is not limited to secondary accents. It includes the creation by musical means of a metric pattern that imposes accents which do not properly belong to the language. In the two lines quoted above, neither of the syllables occurring on the strong first beats of measures two and four should carry even a hint of verbal accent.

The following excerpt from a song by Andrea Falconieri further documents this peculiarity of baroque vocal style. The song is entitled *Occhietti amati*; these are the first four lines:

> *Oc-chiet-ti_a-ma-ti*
>
> *Che m'in-cen-de-te,*
>
> *Per-chè spie-ta-ti*
>
> *Or-mai più sie-te?*

The verse is *quinario*, with the primary accent normally on the fourth syllable and a secondary (very light) one, if present at all, on the second. The musical rhythm from Falconieri's setting is:

The difficulty arises with the very first word and continues to some degree throughout the song.

Despite the barbarisms that exist in this body of Italian vocal repertoire, one cannot and should not dismiss the vast wealth of song and aria from the baroque period on the basis of its sometimes cavalier disruption of versification principles. In almost all cases, the music by melodic and harmonic means does reflect some facet of the poetic intent. Many of the accentual problems derive from the convention of taking dance forms and rhythms into the aria repertoire, a practice that encouraged metric regularity. The main point is that, from a declamatory standpoint, poetry that is not metrically oriented is bound to suffer somewhat when it is put to music that utilizes relatively strong metric stability as one of its organizing principles. Although more attention will be given later to the stylistic and historical aspects of song in the baroque, one broad generalization is possible at this point.

Emphasis at the turn of the seventeenth century was upon the careful musical delineation of poetic expression. Although composers alleged a deep concern for text, that concern was never reflected in really careful accentuation. Two of the greatest compositions of the early period, Monteverdi's *Lasciatemi morire* and Caccini's *Amarilli*, are laced with barbarisms. In spite of this, they are immensely expressive in terms of a heightening of poetic imagery.

This initial involvement with expressiveness subsided as increasing interest in the musical stage drew attention away from the text toward a more dramatic, colorful, and almost totally *musical* expression. This interest in theatrics naturally favored the larger forms of opera, cantata, and oratorio and it was not until late in the nineteenth century that an interest in song composition awoke once more in Italy. Even then, it was only in isolated cases that these latter-day composers were much concerned with declamation. Like their predecessors, they concentrated their expression upon melodic and harmonic sensitivity—and an abounding respect for the voice as a vehicle for lyric beauty. Whether in song or more extended types, the musico-poetic enterprise in Italian vocal music has consistently disregarded mechanics, compensating for this meanwhile by its wealth of tunefulness and vocal excitement.

FRENCH

In dealing with a poetic language as highly sophisticated and stylized as French, it seems almost frivolous to attempt generalizations that might serve as guides to understanding the relationship between music and versification principles. Nonetheless, a few brief observations can be made, which provide a starting point for understanding, even though in a minimal sense, some of the elementary problems of musico-poetic interplay. This discussion, however, must be understood as skeletal only. The best reference work in English to come to my attention is that by Frederic O. Musser, and the reader interested in exploring more deeply is urged to consult it.[3]

To begin with first principles, French verse is identified and characterized by the number of syllables it contains, much like Italian. The

3 Frederic O. Musser, *Strange Clamor* (Detroit: Wayne State University Press, 1965).

nomenclature is not difficult. For instance, an eight-syllable line is an octosyllable, a ten-syllable line is a decasyllable, etc. The commonest line of French verse is the Alexandrine, a line of twelve syllables, which is used for most serious poetry. However, other types are numerous, and it is not uncommon to find combinations of varying line lengths within a poem, so that there might be an alternation of alexandrine and octosyllable lines as a structural feature.

The syllable count is complicated by the character of the mute *e*. The simplest guide is the following, though there are enough exceptions to make it troublesome in actual application: mute *e*'s occurring before or after another vowel are not counted; those occurring between pronounced consonants *are* counted. In the following line the pronounced (and counted) mute *e*'s are underlined and the unpronounced (and uncounted) one is identified by a subscript *x*:

Abeilles d'or qu'attire un invisible miel;

This is an alexandrine verse. One thing more about mute *e*'s: they are *not* counted when they occur at line endings.

Another point to be mentioned is the function of the caesura, especially in alexandrine verse. The normal procedure is to provide a caesura following the sixth syllable, thus separating the line into two equal segments of six syllables each. Other line lengths apparently do not segment so equally, and many contain no caesura at all. The normal rhythmic movement is not from accent to accent as in metric verse and even in Italian, but rather toward line endings or caesuras. This is partly because of the unaccented nature of the French language, which does not divide into stressed and unstressed elements but rather moves to cadence points in prose as well as in poetry. In poetry, these cadences usually occur at line endings, but subsidiary ones result from caesuras.

One of the characteristics of French poetry is the convention of alternating feminine with masculine line endings. Sometimes the scheme is not actually in alternates but in pairs of alternates, or even with lines one and four masculine and lines two and three feminine. Still more elaborate variations are possible without departing from the basic principle. The following are all considered proper end-rhymes:

. . . *folie*	. . . *retour*	. . . *réclame*
. . . *vent*	. . . *roses*	. . . *âme*
. . . *cueillie*	. . . *mi-closes*	. . . *charmants*
. . . *rêvant*	. . . *jour*	. . . *darmants*

The process of alternation is so common that other procedures are considered definite variants, though they occur fairly frequently in song texts. This may be because so many of the poets set by the song composers of the late nineteenth and the twentieth centuries (and this literature forms the bulk of the current performing repertoire in French) were relatively experimental in all respects.

There is one additional factor: Normally each counted syllable in the poetry will be given a corresponding note in the musical setting. The one exception is the final mute *e* (or its equivalent in verb endings) of a poetic line. Although this is neither counted nor pronounced in reading French poetry, it has traditionally been given a separate note in music. This is true even in folk and cabaret song and I have been unable to determine the justification for it, or find a reasonable explanation for the tradition. There are a few exceptions in recent French song literature, but they are so decidedly exceptional that they cannot be interpreted as establishing a new trend.

An excellent example of a musically regular realization of alexandrine verse is found in the second stanza of Fauré's *Aurore* on a poem by Armand Silvestre. Elisions are indicated by slurs under the affected syllables.

Du jar-din de mon cœur qu'un rê-ve lent en-ivre,

S'en-vo-lent mes dé-sirs sur les pas du·ma-tin,

Comme·un es-saim lé-ger qu'à l'ho-ri-zon de cuivre,

Ap-pelle·un chant plain-tif, é-ter-nel et loin-tain.

The musical rhythm is as follows:

The feminine line endings (one and three) are given an additional note, even though in reading the poem these final syllables would not be sounded. At the midpoint in each line there is a regular rhythmic pause that corresponds exactly to the poetic caesura at these places. Other rhythmic variations serve partially as aids in refining the delivery of key words or syllables, but the musical caesuras can be interpreted as a response to a conventional element of poetic form.

Alexandrine verse sometimes appears in variant forms, while still retaining the general principles that help to identify it. The following lines from a poem by Paul Verlaine are regularly alexandrine in the grouping of their thought in the expected twelve-syllable format. However, the appearance on the page suggests that the syllabification follows an alternating pattern of eight-syllable and four-syllable lines. When read, the effect is of an alexandrine verse with a caesura occurring regularly after the eighth syllable rather than after the sixth. In addition, there is a subsidiary caesura following the third syllable of every other line. The poetic rhythm is certainly not complex and there is a recurring cadence that is not unlike the regular tolling of the bell referred to in the fifth and sixth lines.

> *Le ciel est, par-des-sus le toit*
>   *Si bleu, si calme,*
> *Un ar-bre, par-des-sus le toit,*
>   *Ber-ce sa palme;*
> *La clo-che, dans le ciel qu'on voit,*
>   *Dou-ce-ment tinte,*
> *Un oi-seau, sur l'ar-bre qu'on voit,*
>   *Chan-te sa plainte.*

Fauré, setting the poem as *Prison*, maintains the phrasing of the alexandrine verse pattern while providing for the strongest caesuras, those that mark the line endings. There is no similar provision for the slighter caesuras that occur in the middle of lines. Incidentally, though this is only the first of Verlaine's three strophes, the same form is used throughout the poem and Fauré's cadential pattern is equally consistent.

It should not be inferred, however, that all song texts follow the alexandrine or other traditional forms. There are innumerable variations and departures. The Jean Richepin poem, *Au Cimetière*, is an example of verse form that uses neither the alexandrine format nor the convention of alternating masculine and feminine line endings. The insertion of two-syllable lines that belong syntactically to the line preceding or following them creates an added rhythmic interest.

> *Heu-reux qui meurt i-ci,*
>   *Ain-si*
> *Que les oi-seaux des champs!*
> *Son corps près des a-mis*
>   *Est mis*
> *Dans l'herbe et dans les chants.*

The formal arrangement continues throughout the poem. Fauré's setting tends to eradicate the subtleties of the poetic rhyme and rhythm and to phrase according to syntax.

$\frac{3}{4}$

Heu - reux qui meurt i - ci,

Ain - si que les oi-seaux des champs!

Son corps, près des a - mis,

Est mis dans l'herbe et dans les chants.

Although much of what Fauré provides in these and similar settings derives from the structural aspects of the poetry he uses, he is apt to pay less attention to the rhythmic subtleties of poetic utterance. In some cases, he even commits barbarisms, as in the second line of *Au Cimetiére*, where he emphasizes the word *les* because of the metrical accent. The result is often a regularization and regimentation of the poetic rhythm rather than an evidence of concern for its fluid quality.

Such regularization was, in fact, a characteristic feature of French song until the time of Debussy. Some of Debussy's earlier songs utilize a relatively free rhythmic style that conforms not only to the poetic form but to its inflection and movement as well. The following lines are taken from a poem by Charles Baudelaire, *Recueillement*, and are in the conventional alexandrine format.

Sois sa-ge, ô ma dou-leur, et tiens-toi plus tran-quille.

Tu ré-cla-mais le soir; il des-cend, le voi-ci:

Debussy's setting, given in Example 2.1, observes all the poetic subtleties without clinging slavishly to a metric scheme which would inhibit the rhythm of the verse. Among the many important factors are the interplay between voice and accompaniment, the speechlike rhythms of the vocal line, and the pauses which help to correlate the musical declamation with the poetic declamation.

Later Debussy developed a style of declamation that was even more fluid rhythmically and even less committed to melodic tunefulness. This facet of French song will be discussed fully in Part III of the book.

While it would be possible to illustrate other types of French verse, many of a decidedly esoteric nature, it would not be profitable in the context of this study. The principal guideline in dealing with the surface elements of musico-poetic relationships in French song is simply that accents as such do not play a role similar to their function in German and

EXAMPLE 2.1

English. From the performing standpoint nothing does quite so much
harm, therefore, as a rigidly metrical emphasis. It is fortunate that a composer such as Debussy has left a body of song that is so skillful in its
declamatory practices. For those who are familiar with French pronuncia-
tion only (as contrasted with those who speak the language fluently), a
careful reading of his song texts, using the rhythms he provided, will help
in developing a sensitivity toward all French poetry. A further bonus will be

far greater understanding of the significance of the composer himself in the development of French song style

SUMMARY

To the extent that meter is less functional in French and Italian poetry than in German and English, the imposition of musical meter can be a very real hazard to declamation. Because of this, the incidence of barbarisms is considerably higher in songs written in the first two languages than in the others. The stabilization of musical meter during the baroque period imposed a sense of accentual regularity on both Italian and French song, a regularity that was to some extent a disservice to the poetic intent. Despite this, the musical characteristics of Italian song in particular proved sufficiently ingratiating for much of the literature to remain an important segment of the performing repertoire. It was not, however, until the advent of Debussy in France and his fellow Impressionist in Italy, Respighi, that the fluid movement of poetic utterance found a counterpart in the speech-like rhythms of song.

Melody, Harmony, Rhythm

THE FURTHER one departs from the barest mechanics of poetic construction—the choice of meter and syllabification—the more perilous it becomes to attempt an identification of independent musical devices as they relate to text delineation. Melody involves more than a mere tune; rhythmic elements enter strongly into its character. Accompaniment functions harmonically as well as illustratively, sometimes contributing to the declamation independently of the vocal line, sometimes joining hand in hand with the voice, and sometimes furnishing nothing more than the barest and most generalized musical background. In spite of the peril, however, it is still possible to categorize to some extent, so long as it is acknowledged at the outset that such categorization tells only a part of the story. The following discussion, then, will deal with melody, harmony, and rhythm as they are related to the articulation of the text. The orientation is toward mechanics, but there is considerable overlap with expressive techniques, particularly in the area of harmony.

MELODY

Probably the closest mechanical coincidence of melodic style and verbal delivery is effected when the melody is primarily syllabic, avoiding an excess of sustained notes and/or melismas. Even here, however, concessions must be granted, because the pitch inflections in any but the most limited melody will exceed those encountered in normal speech or recitation. But beyond this, a wide choice of rhythmic and melodic manipulation is available to the composer—a choice that often produces a style closely approximating many aspects of speech. Example 3.1, from a song by Henry Cowell, based upon a poem by Robert Frost, is illustrative of such an approach.

Of importance here is the relatively rapid musical movement, which correlates in a general way with speech tempo and which makes rhythmic concessions at such significant points as the words *stop*, *leaves*, and *clear*. The musical phrasing bears a strong relationship to the poetic phrasing in that the cadences occur at places where the poetic movement would be naturally marked by pauses. Although the melodic range far outreaches even the most highly inflected speech, it can be seen as a heightened delivery

EXAMPLE 3.1

I'm go-ing out to clean the pas-ture spring; I'll

on-ly stop to rake the leaves a-way (And wait to watch the wa-ter clear, I

may): I shan't be gone long.— You come too._____

The Pasture—Music by Henry Cowell. © Copyright 1964 Edward B. Marks Music Corporation; used by permission. Text by Robert Frost from *Complete Poems of Robert Frost*, Copyright 1930 and 1940 by Henry Holt & Company, Inc., used by permission of Holt, Rinehart and Winston, Inc. and Jonathan Cape, Ltd.

that enlarges upon the impulsive nature of the text. Especially in this sort of pseudo-recitative style, this is not an unusual form of expressive license. The treatment of the final poetic line:

> I shan't be gone long. You come too.

is particularly effective both in its melodic inflection and in its use of suitable rhythms.

This type of melodic style is closely associated with the true recitative. The inclusion of recitative itself as well as melodies that are derived from it is not a recent development in song. Much of the medium's history, particularly during the period of its greatest flowering in the nineteenth century, reflects the attempt to refine recitative so that it might successfully be taken into a lyric context. The work of Schubert, for instance, reveals considerable struggle in this regard, as Kramarz indicates.[1] The composer's early songs frequently resort to recitative, often in contexts where the dramatic emphasis apparently takes precedence over the lyric demands.

[1] Joachim Kramarz, *Das Rezitativ im Liedschaffen Franz Schuberts*. Inaugural Dissertation (Berlin: Frei Universität Berlin, 1959).

Thus, in Example 3.2, at the climactic point of *Erlkönig* we find:

EXAMPLE 3.2

After 1819, however, Schubert's tendency is to work the declamatory
elements successfully into a more lyric format, so that a song like *Der
Leiermann* meets the requirements of both speech and song, as Example 3.3
illustrates:

EXAMPLE 3.3

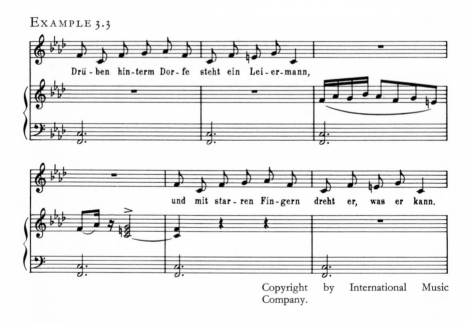

Schumann, always greatly concerned with musico-poetic relationships,
carries the approach still farther, sometimes forsaking the tune almost

completely in favor of recitation that adheres closely to the inflections of speech. Example 3.4 is taken from the fourth song of his cycle *Dichterliebe*:

EXAMPLE 3.4

Wenn ich in dei - ne Au - gen seh, so schwin - det all mein Leid und Weh;

At times, Schumann uses the approach not only to approximate the mechanics of speech but also to aid in interpreting the poetic substance. In the opening line of the final song from *Frauenliebe und Leben*, for instance, a less careful composer could easily have been drawn into the metric scheme and responded to the scansion in a pedantic way. Schumann ignores the poetic meter, which is iambic and suggests a weak treatment of the first word:

Nun hast | du mir | den er- | sten Schmerz | ge-than . . .

His musical realization draws attention to the importance of the word *nun* (now), not only as this song relates to the others in the cycle, but also as the death of the singer's husband relates to their life together.

EXAMPLE 3.5

Adagio.

Nun hast du mir den er - sten Schmerz ge - than

In some cases where the voice is assigned a largely "reciting" role, a contrasting lyricism is provided in the accompaniment so that the "singing" character, so important in song, is not forsaken entirely. Hugo Wolf, in his setting of *Was soll der Zorn*, provides an example of such a situation.

EXAMPLE 3.6

Even more striking is this example from Beethoven's pioneering song
cycle *An die ferne Geliebte*:

EXAMPLE 3.7

The accompaniment in this section is devoted to a complete reiteration of
musical material, the melody of which was assigned to the voice in the
preceding stanza. In contrast, the vocal line in the quoted passage merely
recites the entire poetic strophe in a rhythm compatible with the accompaniment. Thus the musical significance is channeled exclusively into the

piano, while the voice is left free to declaim the text—or at least as free as Beethoven's rhythm allows.

As early as the seventeenth century the French were demonstrating an unusual concern for the relationship of word and tone, a concern that was brought into sharp focus by the operatic "reforms" of Lully. The eventual culmination of this interest was the declamatory style of Debussy, whose opera *Pelléas et Mélisande* is a landmark in the fusion of vocal recitative and harmonic illustration of mood. The same composer's mature song style displays a similar interest in the declamatory aspects of the text. Passages such as Example 3.8, from *Le Tombeau des Naïades*, abound in his later songs:

EXAMPLE 3.8

Debussy has been criticized for the "fussiness" of his melodic style and for his lack of vocal lyricism in contexts such as that illustrated in Example 3.8. Martin Cooper, commenting on the vocal style of this period in Debussy's development, writes that such procedures are

. . . perfect realizations of Debussy's method, subtle dramatic and poetic unities. But a modern listener is struck by the poverty, the over-discretion, of the writing for the voice. . . . In the songs there is a strong hint of the French tendency to treat singing as a form of heightened declamation, as Lully and Rameau treat it.[2]

Nevertheless, Debussy's skill in musically approximating the poetic delivery cannot be lightly dismissed. A reading of Charles Baudelaire's poem *Recueillement* (a portion of which was quoted on p. 33) is included in an excellent recorded anthology edited by Georges Guy.[3] A comparison of M. Guy's reading and the musical rhythm provided in Debussy's setting of the poem reveals a remarkable concordance in many particulars. This sort of concession to the melodic suggestion of the text cannot be brushed aside because of the lack of "tune" in Debussy's song. It might be argued that the lyricism is, after all, in the poem itself; in this case the composer simply supplies musical illustration in the accompaniment without disrupting the poetic delivery by the voice.

Like Debussy, the Italian impressionist Ottorino Respighi frequently incorporates recitative-like passages in his songs, focusing attention on the text through the melodic style, but also providing an appropriate continuo-like accompaniment. A typical example is this brief quotation from *La fine*, one of a set of five songs on texts by various poets, this one a translation from Tagore.

EXAMPLE 3.9

e do-man-de - rà: "Dov'è il nos-tro pic - ci - no,   so - rel-la?"

© Copyright 1918 by G. Ricordi & Co. Milan.

2 Martin Cooper, *French Music* (London: Oxford University Press, 1961), p. 97.
3 *An Anthology of French Poetry,* Vol. II. Period Records: FRL 1523.

It is not unusual for a composer to distinguish even more sharply between lyric and declamatory sections, particularly when setting a text of some length. Such a distinction is made by Samuel Barber in his setting of Matthew Arnold's justly famous poem, *Dover Beach*, where the clearly recitative section in Example 3.10 is interpolated between extended passages of a much more tuneful nature.

EXAMPLE 3.10

The section serves to bridge the transition from the extremely reflective opening of the poem to the more impulsive, urgent expression that succeeds the recitative. But it also functions on the mechanical level as a translation into musical terms of what is certainly the most proselike and explicatory portion of Arnold's poem.

Ned Rorem, perhaps the most prolific of contemporary American song composers, often makes striking use of lyric recitative. Example 3.11 is a portion of the *Interlude*, based on a poem by Theodore Roethke, which Rorem uses as a formal pivot point in the cycle *Poems of Love and the Rain*. It is effective not only because of its focal significance in the organization of the songs as a group, but also because of the emphasis accorded the text by the melodic style and by the lack of accompaniment.

EXAMPLE 3.11

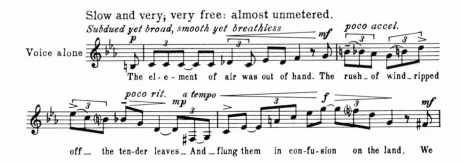

On some occasions composers have been drawn to song texts that are actually prose rather than poetry. Charles Ives, the American experimentalist, often used excerpts from public documents or speeches, and sometimes even provided his own words, as in Example 3.12:

EXAMPLE 3.12

In this case, from *An Election,* such a direct declamatory approach seems particularly appropriate. It should not be implied, however, that prose texts are universally or even preferably handled in this manner. Of many exceptions that might be cited, one well-known one is Brahms's use of Biblical verses for his *Vier ernste Gesänge*, in which the musical realization is often extremely lyrical.

The use of recitative or recitative-like melodic outlines, then, represents the most specific general concession that composers have granted to the demands of declamation. Whether such passages occur only spasmodically within a more lyric framework or whether the total melodic fabric tends toward speech-oriented material seems to depend upon a composer's general response to the declamatory demands of the poem at hand.

A more common melodic response is to provide a tune that will stress important words and phrases within the poem. In many cases, the importance is further underlined by the use of striking harmonic color and the provision of a rhythmically extended note. Example 3.13, from John Dowland's *Come again! Sweet love doth now invite*, shows all three factors (melody, harmony, and rhythmic extension) working together to reflect the poetic climax.

EXAMPLE 3.13

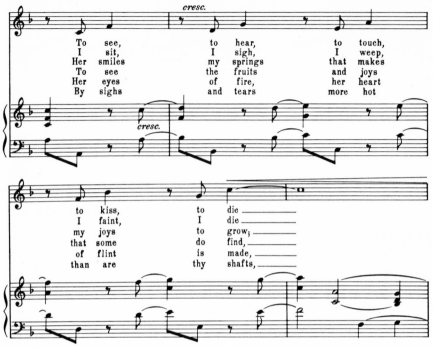

Here the movement is heightened by the mounting melodic line as well as by the dialogue between voice and accompaniment and by a harmonic progression that mounts steadily upward toward the culminating cadence on the tonic. The elongation of the word *die* adds musical significance to this climax of the poetic expression.

The device of melodic climax has had a continuing popularity in song as in opera. Every singer has his favourites, of course; one of mine is the exciting passage from one of Schubert's most passionate outbursts, *Rastlose Liebe*, given in Example 3.14; in this case he fulfills all the demands of declamation as well as of musical ecstasy.

EXAMPLE 3.14

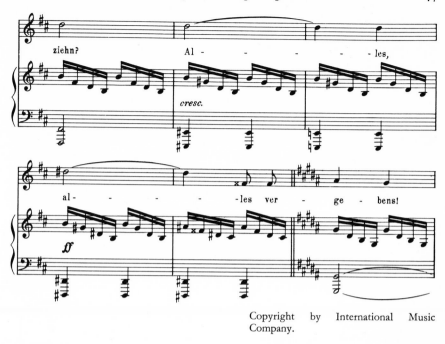

Schubert's propensity for melodic beauty does not always do so much justice to the declamation and he has been criticized because of this. The brief excerpt in Example 3.15 from *Heidenröslein*, with its awkward accentuation of *Heiden*, is one of the many instances in which the tune intrudes.

EXAMPLE 3.15

In this ever popular song even the most capable singers are faced with the problem of trying to handle the phrase without sounding as though they were in the middle of a hiccup.

Working in the same tradition of consummate lyricism, Brahms often mistreats words too. In setting Daumer's lyric, *Wie bist du, meine Königin*, Example 3.16, he writes:

EXAMPLE 3.16

durch sanf - te   Gü - te won-ne - voll!_   Du läch - le

The melodic rise to the middle syllable of *wonnevoll* is completely out of character with the accent of the word, and although it occurs on the weakest portion of the weakest beat of the measure, it cannot but receive an emphasis that is inappropriate. Here the musical demands and the declamatory requirements come into direct conflict. The note functions musically as an upbeat to the next measure, and if the passage were played on a cello, for instance, it would be entirely satisfying.

This type of tone-word misdirection is not infrequent in Brahms. An even more bizarre example is Example 3.17, a passage from the cycle *Vier ernste Gesänge*, where the last phrase of the last song contains:

EXAMPLE 3.17

die   Lie - be   ist   die grö - - -   sse - ste

un - ter ih - nen.

Again, the misaccentuation of the last syllable of *grösseste*, brought about by the melody alone, has a musical justification only—it functions as a musical upbeat to the succeeding measure. This passage is far more difficult to handle convincingly than the one from *Wie bist du, meine Königin*, however. The average performer is forced to break the phrase at this point for a breath, which brings the declamatory problem into focus and at the same time destroys the musical justification by obliterating the pick-up feeling. Unfortunately, Brahms's magnificent arching melodies were not always conceived with the limitations of the human lungs in mind!

Many of Brahms's barbarisms must be seen in the light of his commitment to the music itself. The phrase in Example 3.18, from *Die Mainacht*, has often been used to illustrate the undue significance that he sometimes gives to unimportant words—in this case *und*:

EXAMPLE 3.18

und die ein - sa - me Trä - - -

espress.

The sustained *und*, bad as it may be as declamation, must be viewed in its context as a part of the entire musical phrase. The first two measures actually function as an extended upbeat to the first syllable of *Träne*, which receives its appropriate melodic and declamatory significance largely because of the measures that precede it. The phrase is beautifully integrated harmonically as well as melodically, in that the movement is a prolonged cadential progression from the tonic $^6_4$ through a series of complementary chords to the dominant seventh chord, reaching its fruition only after the vocal phrase has cadenced. Viewed in this way the over-sustained *und* becomes considerably less annoying.

Despite the traditional French attention to words, similar difficulties appear in much French song before the time of Debussy. The beginning of Fauré's *Les Berceaux*, given in Example 3.19, could not be cited for exemplary declamation.

EXAMPLE 3.19

Although the general melodic shape of the phrase is suitable to the poem's content, especially as it relates to the rocking motion of the accompaniment, the emphasis given to *le* and *que* is completely inappropriate. At a later point in the song, Fauré redeems himself with an effective melodic climax that does full justice to the expressive high point of the poem (Example 3.20).

EXAMPLE 3.20

In spite of these and many other inconsistencies, however, composers have generally correlated important words with significant melodic configurations. If individual syllables and words have sometimes been sacrificed to musical considerations, such slips have usually been overlooked in favor of a pervasive expressive content, both poetically and musically. It is possible to make the rather broad generalization that those composers who have been the greatest lyricists have, perhaps because of that, fallen most readily into careless declamation. It must be recognized, too, that song literature would be infinitely poorer were we to delete all the compositions by Schubert, Brahms, Fauré, and others, that contained questionable verbal stresses because of their emphasis upon melody. It is safe to assume, I think, that such songs have persisted in popularity because they have a musico-poetic expressiveness that is rich enough to overcome a few mechanical problems of accentuation.

Particular melodic devices have also come in for their fair share of exploitation by composers. One such is the appoggiatura, a figure that combines the forces of both melody and harmony, which has been utilized expressively as well as to aid declamation. It was so prevalent throughout the baroque period that it has assumed a rhetorical significance as far as the relationship between word and tone is concerned. Example 3.21, from Purcell's *When I am laid in earth*, is typical of its application to a poetic situation of some poignancy and expressive depth.

Example 3.21

The use of the appoggiatura, not always employed exclusively for expressive purposes, continued throughout the eighteenth and nineteenth centuries, so long as tonality persisted in any sense that would allow nonharmonic tones to function meaningfully. Wagner in particular exploits the device extensively, as do those composers who come most directly under his influence—Liszt, Wolf, Mahler, *et al.* As is so often the case with Wagner there may even be an overemphasis, so that in *Träume*, for instance, there are at least twenty-four appoggiaturas in the voice line alone, and this within a space of only fifty-two measures. All of them are justifiable from the standpoint of declamatory emphasis as well as of expressive import, but they do become somewhat wearisome as melodic factors. There are others, many others, in the accompaniment.

Often the appoggiatura functions as an aid to declamation alone, giving an appropriate weight to the strong syllable of a word. This is its most mechanical application, but it is a relatively frequent one. Example 3.22, a brief excerpt from *Der Fichtenbaum* by Robert Franz, will serve to illustrate.

EXAMPLE 3.22

In other contexts, particularly during the eighteenth-century period of musical classicism, the appoggiatura is little more than a style mannerism, employed most frequently at cadential points for its purely musical interest and often with no relationship at all to musico-poetic synthesis.

A close relative of the appoggiatura is the suspension, and this has been used in varying contexts to focus attention upon words of some importance to the poetry as well as to heighten some expressive element. Example 3.23, a portion of *Caldi sospiri* by Raffaello Rontani, uses a brief succession of suspensions very effectively.

EXAMPLE 3.23

In time the suspension principle was applied in an even more dramatic manner by assigning the voice a long sustained note under which the harmony fluctuated, often quite expansively. The device was a special favorite of the romantics—Brahms used it with great effectiveness in *Die Mainacht*, a portion of which was quoted in Example 3.18. Hugo Wolf, too, found it useful, as in this excerpt, Example 3.24, from *Anakreons Grab*:

EXAMPLE 3.24

In this case the movement actually culminates in an appoggiatura, not an unusual situation in this sort of context, and the phrase continues to still another appoggiatura on *bepflanzt*. Such profusion simply indicates the usefulness of this sort of melodic-harmonic manipulation in calling attention to the most expressive words of the text.

Perhaps the most deliberate melodic device of all is the use of patterns that are meant unashamedly as pictorializations of individual words, phrases, or elements of the poem. Although such patterns are often quite expressive, they function most effectively as a musical counterpart to some purely surface aspect of the text, and are therefore largely objective in nature. The use of tone painting or text illustration, as the device is variously described, has had a long history in song. The period of greatest emphasis was the baroque, during which it was one of the definitive features of musical style in all media, but especially in vocal compositions. There was a genuine attempt to express the general mood of the poetry, but just as often the representation was applied to individual words. One instance that will be familiar to all is Purcell's extensive melisma given to the voice on the word *fly* in *I Attempt From Love's Sickness To Fly*. In that song the application is to an act, but similar figures were used to depict things. Example 3.25 comes from a composition almost totally devoted to musical illustration, Da Gagliano's *Valli Profonde*:

EXAMPLE 3.25

The intention here is an obvious structuring of the melody to imitate the slithering and winding motion of the snake as well as form a picture on the musical page that would *look* like a snake. Apparently unable to devise a similar illustration for *lupi* (wolves), Da Gagliano allowed the word to speak for itself without musical representation.

Although the procedure was a baroque convention, it is much in evidence in all musical periods. Part of the charm of Haydn's oratorio, *The Creation*, lies in its use of imitative musical movements that suggest the "flexible tiger," "sinuous worm," and other picturesque creatures mentioned in the libretto.

In the same vein, composers of all periods have often seized upon the sounds suggested by the text and attempted to re-create them in musical terms. Thus Schubert, in his last great cycle *Winterreise*, supplies the bark of the dogs in *Im Dorfe* (Example 3.26):

EXAMPLE 3.26

Throughout the cycle, as in much of his earlier song composition, he seems strongly drawn to use musical counterparts for such sounds of nature as the crowing of roosters, the splashing of water, or the gallop of horses' hooves. In many cases he is able to work such passages into the general fabric of the musical material (as in *Im Dorfe*), but sometimes they tend to intrude and to disrupt the musical continuity to some extent.

The use of tonal pictures is still prevalent in the twentieth century. Samuel Barber's leading motive in *Dover Beach* is a musical representation of the ebb and flow of waves against the shoreline. Benjamin Britten, in his *Charm of Lullabies*, continually utilizes rocking motives in the accompaniment and even an obvious imitation of the drone of bagpipes in appropriate places during the Scottish lullaby. The suggestion of bells has appeared frequently in song; one of the most graphic representations occurs in Arthur Honegger's setting of *Les Cloches*, an excerpt from Apollinaire's *Alcools*. The imitation of bird song has also proven irresistible to many composers, crossing both period and nationalistic style barriers. Example 3.27 is a rather amusing passage from *Beneath a Weeping Willow's Shade* by the first American composer of secular music, Francis Hopkinson:

EXAMPLE 3.27

More subtly treated but just as patently illustrative is the bird call, Example 3.28; in Douglas Moore's *Old Song*:

EXAMPLE 3.28

The greatest synthesis of poem and music that still remains within the limits set by true tone painting is found in cases where a figure is provided that will reflect both the act or thing indicated and the mood represented. In Example 3.29 Purcell, in an excerpt from *Since from my dear*, seems to want us to feel the "sinking into death" as well as the sighing expiration of breath and the fading of life itself.

EXAMPLE 3.29

The actual mechanics of tone painting have varied from period to period and from composer to composer. But the basic principle has always been the musical reflection of the sound or characteristic mood or action or thing suggested by a particular word or phrase—and sometimes even by a total poetic content. The process, though largely oriented toward one or more of the most obvious poetic factors, represents one of the continuing means by which composers have attempted to arrive at a reasonable musico-poetic integration.

HARMONY

Of the three most important musical elements (rhythm, melody, harmony) and their derivatives, harmony is the most difficult to describe as a mechanical device apart from its expressive significance. It serves in a meaningful way as an aid to articulation of phrases, of course, which could be considered at least partially mechanical; it combines with melody and rhythm to enhance movement, including tension and release—another function that could be related somewhat to mechanics. Harmony is helpful as a defining factor in the description of form, still another area of objectification. But as it has been used in song from the baroque period onward, it has almost always appeared in contexts that suggest an expressive as well as a mechanical application. Because of this the descriptions that follow will in many cases anticipate the subject matter of Part II, although every attempt will be made to indicate the relevance of harmonic treatment to the construction of song, in addition to its word-tone function.

The employment of different key centers in order to distinguish the parts of a song is one of the most practical uses to which harmony may be put. Among the early forms that became highly stylized in this respect is the *da capo* aria, where the center section always uses a key center closely related to the tonic of the *da capo* section. Although there are indications that this change of tonality was originally meant to reflect a change in poetic imagery, it is often simply a conventional device to introduce an element of variety into the musical fabric. In an era in which expressive devices were themselves meticulously categorized, it was entirely natural that such a convention should be used by musicians as a means of heightening the content of the text, and that poets in turn would structure their sentiments to fit logically into the formal design. Despite this obeisance to expression, however, the rigidity of adherence to the pattern indicates a basic orientation toward the exigencies of tonal contrast rather than any overwhelming commitment to emotional content.

The song form most closely related to the *da capo* aria is, of course, the three-part song. The normal procedure here is to cast the middle section in a key closely related to the tonic of the piece, much as in the more elaborate aria form. Beethoven's *In questa tomba oscura* is typical; so is his *Ich liebe dich*. Brahms is particularly fond of the smaller song forms and in most cases uses not only melodic contrast but key change as well to define his parts. The popular *Minnelied* in *aaba* form is an example, and in this case the change of tonality has an expressive as well as a structural significance. In *Erinnerung* the implications of expression are not quite so strong, the choice of *ababa* simply serving to provide a musically cohesive format that bears some relationship to the stanzaic arrangement of the poem. Another example of the five-part song that uses the same sort of key contrast is Martini's *Plaisir d'amour*. Of the many others that might be mentioned Fauré's *Chanson d'Amour* has been consistently popular. All of these formal arrangements bear upon the concordance of poetic strophe with musical realization—which will be enlarged upon later.

Harmonic movement itself, as opposed to the establishment of tonal centers, is given one of its strongest impetuses by the employment of dissonance in a context where a resolution is suggested or demanded. It is at this point that it is most difficult to differentiate between harmonic movement in its purely musical sense and in its musico-poetic sense. In most cases the attempt to make a firm distinction becomes mere quibbling. Example 3.30, a passage from a song by Francesco Cavalli, is typical.

EXAMPLE 3.30

E l'a - spre mie pe - ne Nar - ra - te-gli un po - co

The piece is called *Sospiri di foco* and much of it is given to a sort of sighing melodic contour. In the quoted portion the musical movement is of a modulatory nature, but the sharpest dissonance is given to the word *pene* (anguish), which is certainly no coincidence.

In the course of developing a wider range of harmonic color as material for musical expressiveness, it was natural that when words were involved, the full harmonic vocabulary would be applied to text illustration. Mozart is constantly drawn to the diminished seventh chord as a harmonic device. In his vocal works it always functions within a framework that helps to strengthen the tonality, of course, but it also serves to punctuate the text. In his setting of Goethe's *Das Veilchen*, perhaps his best-known song, the three measures quoted in Example 3.31 are certainly not unusual harmonically, although in a general way the use of the leading-tone seventh chord creates a more compelling aural image than would the dominant.

EXAMPLE 3.31

"Ach!" denkt das Veil - chen,___ "wär' ich

The same chord is even more dramatically and insistently used in Example 3.32, a later section of the song, this time applied to the subdominant.

EXAMPLE 3.32

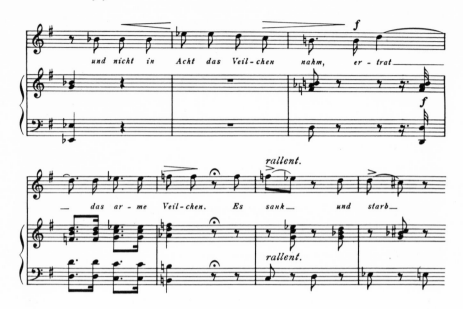

und nicht in Acht das Veil-chen nahm, er - trat

rallent.

das ar - me Veil-chen. Es sank____ und starb____

rallent.

The drama of the passage is heightened through the use of an augmented sixth chord for the word *starb* (died), a dissonant complex that was to increase in popularity throughout the romantic century in both vocal and instrumental music.

Schubert is particularly adept at combining harmonic movement and text illustration. He, like many of his contemporaries, is fond of using a series of applied dominants to accompany sequential melodic passages, and often this reflects a kind of uncertainty in the text. Example 3.33, a section from *Danksangung an den Bach*, is illustrative:

EXAMPLE 3.33

meint? Zur Mül - le - rin hin! so lau - tet der Sinn.

The use of this type of sequence is common in instrumental music, being one of the favorite devices for the extension or development of a motive. In this song, however, it serves a word-tone purpose as well, in underlining the questioning of the poem. The distinction between musico-poetic expression and strictly musical expression becomes difficult if not impossible to make in such a context. Some sort of harmonic progression is called for in all music that is not monophonic; without it the result would be utter stagnation. At the same time, when a harmonic sequence is given the additional function of fusing poetic and musical imagery, as in the Schubert excerpt just quoted, such a synthesis adds another dimension to the work—one that identifies this composer as a master of the song.

This command of synthesis played an increasing role in composition throughout the nineteenth century. Schumann, in his search for psychological emphasis, uses it constantly. In *Ich kann's nicht fassen*, the third song of his cycle *Frauenliebe und Leben*, the harmonic uncertainty of Example 3.34 is in exact concordance with the text.

EXAMPLE 3.34

war's ich träu-me noch im-mer, es kann ja nim-mer so sein,—

Is this simply a typically romantic modulatory passage to the relative major? It is, of course. But its extensive use of dissonances of the most inconclusive sort, including the insistence upon augmented sixth chords, gives it a musico-poetic emphasis, too. There is little doubt that Schumann chose this particular texture not merely as a means of moving into the relative major for the outburst of the succeeding line, but for psychological illustration as well. Where form and content become so inextricably intertwined, any attempt to pick at them as individual facets is futile and destructive.

In our own century, where a generally dissonant texture is so often the norm, there are instances of the use of simple triadic harmony to serve the purpose of harmonic punctuation. An adroit use of consonance in such a context is made by Marc Blitzstein in his setting of an E. E. Cummings poem *Jimmie's got a goil*, where the composer establishes an initial rollicking and raucous mood with this pattern (Example 3.35):

EXAMPLE 3.35

Vivo ♩ = 152   *mf*

Jim-mie's got a goil goil goil,

Later, when Cummings turns his attention to a description of the lady's most appealing attribute, we find Example 3.36:

EXAMPLE 3.36

The consonance, emerging without warning from a primarily dissonant texture, proves to be as striking in attracting the listener's attention as was the use of dissonances in the music of earlier centuries. The passage does not appear to be illustrative in any way (except perhaps rhythmically) nor is it directed toward expression; it simply spotlights the words.

Like most other harmonic devices, the deceptive cadence often serves a dual purpose. Perhaps its most practical use is as a tool for introducing an extension. In this context it has appeared repeatedly just before text repetition, often at the close of strophes. Beethoven is especially fond of this procedure and beyond the purely formal significance there is often a truly expressive one. In Example 3.37, *Vom Tod* from the *Lieder von Gellert*, for instance, even though the deceptive cadence just before the repetition of the final poetic line serves as introduction to and preparation for a musical extension, it also falls on an extremely important word:

EXAMPLE 3.37

Conceived and utilized at first as a movement from the dominant to the submediant, the deceptive cadence was later extended to include any progression that frustrated the implied resolution of dissonance. As such it contributed frequently to text illustration in the nineteenth century. In Wolf's *Ich hab' in Penna einen Liebsten* the entire harmonic fabric is one of repeated harmonic deception. In one sense this simply encourages the on-going movement of the song, but it also contributes to a characterization of the singer—giddy, flirtatious, and extremely fickle.

To recapitulate briefly, harmony plays a role as a formal factor in song, just as it does in any musical medium. But its greatest contribution has been in the area of expressive emphasis. The use of major-minor contrast, for instance, has occupied composers for three centuries, but their concern has been directed largely toward mood. This and other ramifications of harmonic color will be discussed in Part II.

RHYTHM

Although it is possible to draw some reasonably defensible relationships between poetic meter and musical meter, this can seldom be done with rhythm as a whole. Poetic rhythm depends upon the pace of speech, including not only qualitative accent (the weight of a syllable or word), but quantitative accent (the duration of a syllable or word). There is some semblance of conformity between verbal and musical accents of a qualitative kind; there is almost none in terms of quantity. When set to a tune, almost all syllables and words last longer than they do in speech. It is only relative quantity that can be represented, and, as a general rule, most composers have structured their rhythms to musical values rather than to poetic ones. Among the notable exceptions are Wolf, Debussy, and, in our own day, Ned Rorem. In a significant number of their songs these composers have made a real attempt to carry over into song a sense of the rhythmic subtleties of the poetry they use. It seems unnecessary to illustrate this point here—some attention has already been given to it in connection with Debussy's melodic style. A reading of these composers' songs (just the rhythms and words) will reveal that they tend to provide a closer rhythmic ratio between song and speech rhythms than do most of their fellows.

However, even when the rhythms are flexible enough to suggest speech, the result is still only a relative concordance, in the same sense that melodic rise and fall has only the merest semblance of speech inflections. It is in the inflections that melody imposes upon poetic speech and in the movement that musical rhythm imposes upon poetic rhythm that poetry has conceded most and perhaps lost most of its individual power in song.

Aside from these general considerations, much of the discussion in preceding chapters has involved rhythmic manipulation in one way or another. Meter, for instance, is inseparable from rhythm, and melody itself is strongly reliant upon rhythm for many of its distinguishing characteristics. The important thing is the diversity, which is often an identifying element of style. The complexities of much modern song (such as Schuller's *Meditation*, illustrated on page 77) are simply reflections of similar complexities in most of the newer poetic and musical idioms. They are not, in other words, peculiar to song. Similarly the rhythmic stability of classicism and the metric relentlessness of the late baroque are reflections of the general musical temper of those periods.

At the same time there are rhythmic devices of a specific nature that composers have brought to bear in emphasizing certain aspects of the text. It would be fruitless to catalogue them, but several may be mentioned as typical. One such is syncopation.

Although the free metrical style of the lutenists does not encourage the sort of accentual expectancy that is essential for a full realization of syncopation, there are instances in which the rhythmic relationship between voice and accompaniment suggests its presence, especially to modern ears attuned to such possibilities. Example 3.38, from Thomas Ford's *Fair Sweet Cruel*, for instance, has a certain rhythmic urgency throughout and a very definite sense of syncopation at the reiteration of "Why dost thou fly me?"

EXAMPLE 3.38

By permission of the copyright holder, Stainer & Bell Ltd., London.

By the mid-seventeenth century the strengthening of the metrical accent encouraged the frequent employment of syncopation, as in Example 3.39, from Purcell's *An Evening Hymn*:

EXAMPLE 3.39

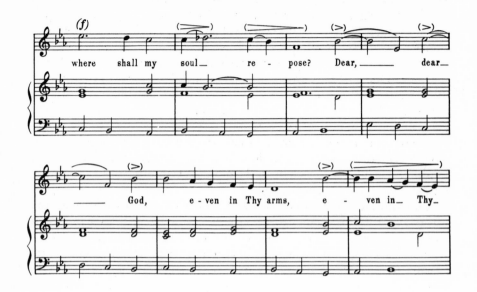

The device of syncopation gained in favor and became a favorite means
of strengthening declamation. Those composers who gave their careful
attention to a meaningful articulation of the text were especially drawn to
it. Example 3.40, from Wolf's *Schlafendes Jesuskind* is typical of the meticulous accentual and expressive treatment that is characteristic of this composer's word setting—and syncopation plays a vital role.

EXAMPLE 3.40

Like syncopation, dotted rhythms seem to have functioned in an often specific way for many composers, and in varying relation to the text. In Purcell's *An Evening Hymn* (which was partially quoted earlier) the use of dotted rhythms in Example 3.41 not only serves to give the word *Hallelujah* an appropriate accentuation but lends something to the jubilant character as well.

EXAMPLE 3.41

In an obviously different expressive context, Example 3.42, a passage that occurs in *Selve amiche* by Antonio Caldara, seems equally appropriate but for different reasons. Here the rhythm is representative of the heart itself rather than the mood of the word.

EXAMPLE 3.42

Tone painting with rhythms is a favorite pastime in song and the responsibility is often given to the accompaniment. The insistent pounding triplets in Schubert's *Erlkönig* are the hooves of the horse but they also give a sense of haste and excitement. Both Dvořák and Brahms, among others, illustrate their settings of gypsy songs with what they felt to be rhythms associated with gypsy dances. The rhythmic pattern in the accompaniment of Fauré's *Les Berceaux* is an obvious representation of gently rocking boats; it also suggests the motion of the cradles that for the men of the poem have been replaced by boats.

Departures from the norm that has been established can also serve to draw attention to some facet of the text. The sudden introduction of triplets (Example 3.43) in Beethoven's setting of *Kennst du das Land?* is clearly meant to illustrate the "soft breezes":

EXAMPLE 3.43

ein sanf - ter Wind vom blau - en __ Him - mel __ weht,

Interestingly enough, Schubert resorts to the same rhythmic device at the same place in his setting of the poem. In many other particulars, the two settings reveal a striking similarity. The lyric has attracted a number of composers, among them Schumann, and although the latter's treatment is significantly different from those of Schubert and Beethoven, he does utilize a similar triplet figure to illustrate the breezes.

Rhythm, then, has been a useful tool for tone painting as well as for mood suggestion. As a melodic characteristic it has been put at the service of declamation, and the extreme diversity and pliability to which it is subject makes only the broadest generalizations possible. At the same time, an important part of any composer's song style must be described in terms of the imagination he brings to his use of rhythm.

SUMMARY

Melody, harmony, and rhythm serve a purely mechanical purpose in many songs. They are particularly useful in strengthening the declamation as well as in controlling the pace of delivery and the articulation of formal characteristics. To some extent they can combine forces in order to delineate a general type of song conception, such as lyric versus declamatory. In the broadest sense, however, they cannot really be separated from expressive intent. Their function as mechanical devices is far more apparent on the page and in description than in the actual performance of a song, where they usually serve merely as integrated elements in the expressive experience.

The Phrase and the Strophe

THE PRECEDING chapters have been devoted to the thesis that music can and does correlate to some extent with the metrical and syllabification devices of poetry and that its elements of melody, harmony, and rhythm may be brought to bear upon declamation and illustration. In a similar way music often relates to the larger components of poetic form—the phrase and the strophe.

Although there are many exceptions, particularly in recent years, the poetry chosen by song composers tends to be fairly regular in most regards. The rhyme scheme is often quite precise, usually coinciding with the ends of lines, and the lines most commonly consist of a complete phrase, or at least suggest a verbal cadence that can be reflected in musical terms. As a result, when the music is itself regular, it can be of considerable value in helping to articulate both the poetic phrase and the rhyme.

In the discussion of meter, reference was made to Purcell's setting of Betterton's libretto for *Dioclesian*, and the following stanza from one of the lyrics was quoted. It can serve as an illustration of the concordance of poetic and musical material in the service of formal clarity. The first stanza of the poem is as follows:

> What shall I do to show how much I love her?
> How many millions of sighs can suffice?
> That which wins others' hearts, never can move her,
> Those common methods of love she'll despise.

As was pointed out earlier, the musical meter and rhythm in Purcell's song match their poetic counterparts. In addition, the musical phrasing mirrors the poetic phrasing in that the musical cadences occur regularly at line endings, and the harmonic scheme used for the cadences even echoes the rhyme scheme. This is not at all unusual in song. The first and third lines (which are rhyming) cadence on the tonic, and the second and fourth on the dominant. The same process or a slight variation of it occurs in innumerable songs of all periods, although this must not be taken to imply that it is a consistent or standard procedure for *all* songs.

A similar situation is found in Schubert's *Der Leiermann*, where the organization of the poem is in five strophes. It is given below with each line representing both a poetic phrase and a musical phrase. The cadential harmony follows a definite rhyming pattern:

Drüben hinterm Dorfe steht ein Leiermann.	[tonic]
Und mit starren Fingern dreht er, was er kann.	[tonic]
Barfuss auf dem Eise wankt er hin und her,	[dominant]
Und sein kleiner Teller bleibt ihm immer leer.	[dominant]
Keiner mag ihn hören, keiner sieht ihn an.	[tonic]
Und die Hunde knurren um den alten Mann.	[tonic]
Und er lässt es gehen alles, wie es will,	[dominant]
Dreht, und seine Leier steht ihn nimmer still.	[dominant]
Wunderlicher Alter, soll ich mit dir gehn?	[tonic]
Willst zu meinen Liedern deine Leier drehn?	[tonic]

The only departure from this scheme is in the repetition of the fourth and eighth poetic lines, which are in the tonic. The total effect is a unification of the poetic phrase with the musical phrase, and the rhyme scheme is reinforced by the harmonic scheme.

An instance of melodic rather than cadential rhyme is found in Hugo Wolf's setting of Mörike's *Ein Stündlein wohl vor Tag*. Composed of three five-line strophes, the rhyme scheme in each stanza is *aabba*. Wolf provides a musical form that relates directly to the poem, except for minor modifications used to heighten the musical interest without interfering with the basic structure. All of the *a* lines employ the same melodic formula. All of the *b* lines are treated sequentially—the second *b* being a sequence of the first in each case. The slight melodic variation in the third stanza is for expressive purposes and does not disrupt the formal continuity. The result is a direct transfer of poetic form into musical form with strikingly similar characteristics. Inasmuch as Wolf's setting is strophic, the form of the entire poem is reflected in the song.

Of course, the verbal phrase does not always coincide with the poetic line, and in such cases the composer must make some adjustment in his materials. The most common departure poetically is the run-on line, where the syntax does not allow for a cadence at the line ending. One example that produced a most unhappy result is found at the very beginning of Heine's poem which Schumann set as *Die Lotosblume*, where the first two lines read:

Die Lotosblume ängstigt
Sich vor der Sonne Pracht.

Schumann, usually more careful in his treatment, writes, in Example 4.1:

EXAMPLE 4.1

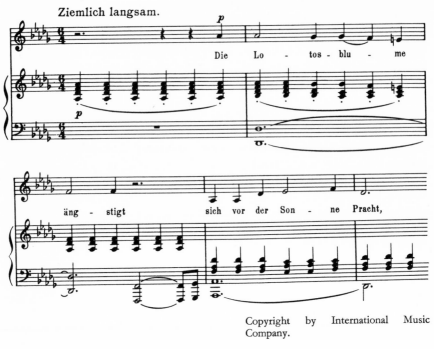

Absolutely no compensation can be made in performance for the gap in
syntax that is created by Schumann's rests in the vocal line at the end of the
third measure.

The problem occurs most frequently in a strophic setting, where each
poetic stanza is provided with identical musical material. Here, if the poetic
phrases are in keeping with individual lines throughout the first strophe,
the musical treatment is normally equally regular. If a subsequent stanza,
however, contains a run-on line, some compensation must be made by the
performer, and it frequently happens that this has to be done at some
sacrifice to the musical logic. Edward Purcell, setting a text used by
Thomas Ford in his *Musicke of Sundrie Kindes*, 1607, utilizes three of the
original six strophes. The first two are quite regular, and Purcell's music
is phrased with corresponding regularity. The third, however, presents a
problem:

> Cupid is wingéd and doth range
> Her country so my love doth change;
> But change she earth, or change she sky,
> Yet will I love her till I die.

Having set up a cadential pattern that relates to the line endings of the previous stanzas, there is no way to handle the bridge between lines one and two except to run across the cadence. Although this requires no excessive vocal skill, it does strain the musical form to some extent.

The poem has been a popular one. Ford's own setting, which is strophic, is as awkward as Purcell's in this stanza. Norman Dello Joio, also drawn to the lyric, avoids the problem altogether by omitting the two troublesome lines and substituting two from the first stanza. Peter Warlock set the poem twice, once using all six strophes and once only three. The shorter setting has a rest between lines one and two and thus is as awkward syntactically as the settings of other composers. The longer version makes no particular concessions to the run-on but because it is in a syllabic style throughout with almost no rhythmic breaks within the stanzas, it is possible to accommodate the variation in poetic phrasing without difficulty.

A related problem has been a continuing nuisance to composers when dealing with the strophic format. This is the occurrence in succeeding stanzas of relatively unimportant and inexpressive words in positions that have been assigned considerable significance in the first stanza. Of the many instances that might be singled out, Example 4.2, from Schubert's *Ständchen*, is typical:

EXAMPLE 4.2

des Ver - rä - ters feind - lich Lau - schen
rüh - ren mit den Sil - ber - tö - nen

Copyright by International Music Company.

The treatment of *des Verräters* is exemplary, of course, but the attention given to *mit* in the second stanza (and at the expense of the more expressive *rühren*) is out of keeping with its importance and is the result of Schubert's having designed this particular melodic passage because of his response to the first stanza.

Interestingly, the problem can work in reverse—musical material that is appropriate to all other stanzas may be inadequate for the first. This raises the question of whether, in such instances, the composer was willing to ignore the sins of the opening strophe because of the redeeming features of the succeeding ones. It seems more likely, though, that melodic intent simply takes precedence over textual idiosyncrasies. Schubert (who seems to have had more than his share of difficulty in such situations) is extremely bizarre in his treatment of the third and fourth lines of the first stanza of *Wasserflut* from his cycle *Winterreise*. The lines read:

> *Seine kalten Flocken saugen*
> *Durstig ein das heisse Weh.*

Not only does his setting separate *saugen* from *durstig ein* by a rest, but it goes farther and unforgivably repeats the last line as a musical extension. Thus the verb prefix is left dangling in the repetition, where it makes no sense whatever from the standpoint of syntax. Except in this one instance, the poem phrases at the line endings and Schubert's cadences and repetitions do no injustice to grammar.

These and related problems are among the motivations behind the practice of modification of one or more strophes, not only for expressive purposes but also in the interest of improvements in phrasing. Strophic modification was in use before Schubert's time, but the latter's skillful use of this type of song composition led the way for the refinements of later nineteenth-century composers. For the most part, Schubert tends to confine his modifications to changes of mode (major and minor contrast) rather than resorting to extensive melodic manipulation. Such variation primarily serves an expressive purpose rather than increasing the effectiveness of the declamation or treating more carefully other aspects of poetic form and phrasing. On the other hand, a composer like Wolf is more apt to rephrase while still largely retaining the melodic outline—all in order to shape a musical statement that will handle the poetic phrasing more adequately. The passages in Example 4.3, from the first and third stanzas of *Ach, des Knaben Augen* from the *Spanisches Liederbuch*, show clearly the type of modification of which Wolf was particularly fond, where the rhythmic variation aptly fits the changed poetic phrasing:

EXAMPLE 4.3

schie - nen, und ein Et - was strahlt aus ih - nen, das mein

Third Stanza

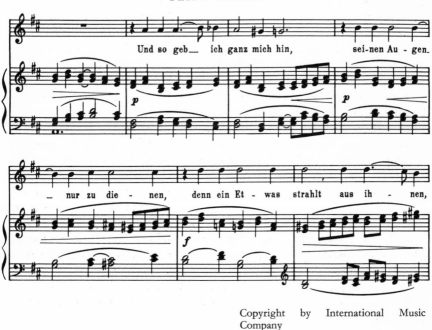

Und so geb— ich ganz mich hin, sei-nen Au - gen—

_ nur zu die - nen, denn ein Et - was strahlt aus ih - nen,

The accompaniment for both passages is identical; the modification is confined to the vocal line and serves exclusively to bring the words into a better rhythmic and melodic scheme.

Another type of modification that has been useful to composers is the supplying of a distinctly different accompaniment style as well as some variation in the melodic line. Henri Duparc, setting Gautier's poem as *Lamento*, provides the initial two strophes with a primarily chordal accompaniment that also uses several of the more striking chromatic melodic figures drawn from the vocal line. In the third stanza, although retaining the basic harmonic and melodic material of the other stanzas, the accompaniment becomes significantly more impulsive through the addition of sixteenth-note broken chord outlines. Here, too, the vocal melody is modified to some extent in keeping with the words, but enough of the skeletal material remains to identify the treatment as modified-strophic in principle.

An interesting modification device is employed by Ernst Krenek in his serial setting of John Donne's *The Flea*. The composer utilizes the material of his tone row in such a manner as to define the stanzas of the poem. The first strophe is set to the notes of the basic row itself, used melodically in the strict procedure for this idiom but with the usual rhythmic variations and interchanges of octaves. The second strophe is set with melodic material derived from a transposition of the row, and the final strophe uses a retrograde transposition. The total effect is rather academic, but in a certain sense the esoteric nature of this compositional technique serves as a foil for the highly sophisticated wit and symbolism of Donne. In any case, the musical material relates directly to the poetic strophes and is a modern version of the modified strophic principle of construction.

The most complete disruption of poetic form is apt to result from a compositional technique that has become known as through composition, that is, the providing of new musical material for each strophe of the poem. This procedure received its greatest impetus from Schubert, although, as in other song forms, he was not an innovator. Much of his original motivation toward through composition was a result of his attraction to texts that were highly developmental in nature, or in which there were very obvious changes of emotional or narrative content. Drawn in his early years to the dramatic ballad, he frequently matched the story's increasing intensity with musical material that provided a corresponding expressive crescendo. Perhaps his most famous song of this type is *Erlkönig*, although there are dozens more that are equally representative, some quite elaborate. The same format served him for *Gretchen am Spinnrade*, where there is no real story but rather a series of emotional episodes of varying character.

It is difficult to generalize about any composer's reaction to text as it relates to his choice of song form. A poem like Goethe's *Heidenröslein* would appear to invite a good deal of musical illustration, but Schubert responded with the utmost simplicity, not even attempting to exploit the dialogue that is involved. On the other hand, a poem by the same author, *Heiss mich nicht reden* (*Lied der Mignon I*), which is considerably more static in mood, was through composed by Schubert. Only tentatively, then, can it be said that he resorted to through composition when the poem was too dramatic or inconsistent in mood to be treated successfully within the confines of the strophic or modified strophic formats.

As for distinctions between the three main formal types, these are not always easy to make. How much modification of musical material is possible within the confines of the true strophic format? In Wolf's *Ein Stündlein wohl vor Tag* the material is almost identical for all three stanzas, but it is presented in three different keys. Strophic or modified strophic? It seems a question best left to theorists. Likewise, compositions such as Brahms's *Immer leiser wird mein Schlummer* and *O kühler Wald* and Wolf's *Fussreise* contain so much reiterative material from stanza to stanza and at the same time make so many significant departures that it is difficult to identify the songs definitely as either modified strophic or through composed. More important than a tag in such cases is the awareness that related musical material creates a synthesis of texture although it still allows for a constantly fluctuating treatment of the text. Of all the forms the strophic is the most difficult to handle convincingly, and it demands a poem either unashamedly folklike in nature or that sustains a poetic mood of great consistency. Through composition also has its perils, however, in the temptation to provide so much diversity of musical material that the continuity of the song is disrupted and the formal relationship between the poetic strophes is badly strained.

The experimental poetry of the twentieth century presents a serious challenge to the composer. The loosening of poetic form has taken away one of the restrictions, but it has taken with it a controlling factor that had served song writers well for many centuries—an obvious linear-phrase and strophe arrangement that could help guide the musical form. The work of Gertrude Stein has attracted some attention from song composers in recent years, for instance, and the extreme freedom of her utterance makes it difficult to bring the formal characteristics into focus. Fortunately, however, much contemporary music is itself so firmly rooted in formalistic principles that it can sometimes produce a salutory effect upon the feeling of poetic form. Gunther Schuller, setting Miss Stein's *Meditation*, catches the poet's verbal style in his compositional pointillism with quite successful results (Example 4.4).

EXAMPLE 4.4

I will   there - fore   of - fer   there - fore   I

Meditation—Music by Gunther Schuller.
© Copyright 1964 Edward B. Marks
Music Corporation; used by permission.
Text by Gertrude Stein; used by per-
mission.

Although this is only a brief excerpt, the approach is similar throughout
Schuller's song. The repetitive nature of the verse is suitably echoed in the
vocal intervals. The entire composition is characterized by the reiteration
of accompaniment as well as melodic fourths and minor seconds with
various inversions, and these are coupled with numerous rhythmic repetitions. As a result, there is considerable musical coherence, which imposes
a sort of formal clarity on the poem, a clarity that is not immediately self-
evident in the text itself.

Despite the continuing attempt to define song in terms of its formal
structure, however, the diversity of organization has been far more
pertinent to that definition than has any illusion of conformity. Certain
types tend toward extreme clarity and simplicity of organization, often
because of the aesthetic principles of the eras in which they were produced.
Thus one expects and finds more formal definition in the seventeenth and
eighteenth centuries than in the freer nineteenth. A poem during these
earlier periods tends to be set more as a series of episodes (usually the stanza)
than as a synthesized unit moving from beginning to end. This is partly a
reflection of available poetic types as well as of musical concepts; it will be
discussed more fully in succeeding sections of this study.

While music can and often does reiterate or even clarify in its own terms
the formal outlines of poetry, there are occasions when the song has had a
negative effect on the words. Some of these have been noted in passing, but
others need attention.

One of the most consistent criticisms of song composers has been directed
against their habit of repeating words, most frequently for purely musical
reasons rather than for poetic emphasis. Tennyson raised his voice against
the practice: "Why do these damned musicians make me say a thing twice
when I say it only once?" It is true that vocal composition from the baroque
to the present day has been overrun with text reiterations. Even Schumann,
in spite of his concern for the literary integrity of the poems he set, has a

habit of repeating the entire first stanza at the close of a song, very often using the same musical material as on its first presentation. The motivation can be interpreted as musical only—it is patently an attempt to round out the musical form. In many cases the repetition also involves extensions based on the principal material. *Intermezzo* from the *Liederkreis*; *Er, der Herrlichste von allen* from *Frauenliebe und Leben*; and *Widmung* all use this device, and there are countless others that could be cited. French song composers, particularly before 1900, are not guiltless, either. In Fauré's setting of Richepin's *Au Cimetière*, the final section of the song consists of a repetition of the first two stanzas of the poem. Richepin himself repeats the first stanza, but Fauré, to complete his musical thought, is forced into including the second as well. And, of course, Verlaine's *Mandoline* has no such series of *la, la*'s as those that conclude Debussy's setting and that are such a significant part of the song's form. In his setting of the same poem, Fauré repeats the entire first stanza, again in the interest of musical symmetry.

Word repetition within a stanza can be utterly destructive to the poetic form, of course, and it is this type of repetition that occurs most frequently. Even the lutenists in England, who were often poets themselves and dedicated to the closest amalgamation of musico-poetic elements, frequently indulge in repetition for musical reasons. The most frequently used device is the extension of a six-line strophe into an eight-phrase musical composition by the simple expedient of repeating the last two lines of the poem to identical music. The only logic behind such a procedure is a musical one, the creation of a balanced form. Purcell's songs are so often burdened with word and phrase repetitions that it becomes difficult to ferret out the basic poem as in, among innumerable others, *Since from my dear*. Goethe, criticizing Beethoven's setting of *Kennst du das Land?*, says: "By her very nature, Mignon can only sing a song, not an aria."[1] The criticism is equally applicable to other settings of the same poem, among them Schubert's, and has its basis not only in the elaborate musical style but in the many text repetitions, a characteristic of operatic expression.

One of the most dramatic examples of poetic form destruction through repetition is found in Schumann's setting of *Ich grolle nicht* from his *Dichterliebe* cycle. As Miller points out, there is little resemblance between the forms of the composer and Heine, the poet.[2]

At the opposite pole from repetition is the practice of deletion, and composers have freely omitted not only portions but entire poetic strophes when such a process suited their musical scheme. Among the many songs

---

1 Alfred Einstein, *Schubert* (New York: Oxford University Press, 1951), pp. 100–101.

2 Philip Miller, *The Ring of Words* (Garden City, New York: Doubleday & Company, Inc., 1963), p. 41. Besides providing excellent translations of much song literature, Mr. Miller is extremely informative about such things as word changes and deletions, stanza omissions, and settings of the same poem by different composers. A considerable portion of my discussion here is drawn from his invaluable notations.

that contain fewer stanzas than the poems from which they were derived
are *Die Stille* from Schumann's *Liederkreis*, Brahms's *Die Mainacht*,
Debussy's *Nuit d'Étoiles*, Duparc's *L'Invitation au Voyage*, Hahn's *Infidélité*,
and several from Fauré's cycle *La Bonne Chanson*. It is evident, even from
this very limited list, that the practice is relatively widespread and not
confined to a particular school, nation, or style. In many cases, the original
poem is longer than might be felt appropriate for the limited proportions of
the art song. In other instances, however, there seems no other reason than
the preference of the composer or the suitability of the verse to the musical
expression he has chosen.

More mischievous than the omission of a stanza, however, is the alteration or deletion of words or phrases within a stanza, since this can do
injustice to the poetic thought as well as to the versification scheme chosen
to express it. Unfortunately, the practice is not an unusual one.

Fauré, in his setting of Leconte de Lisle's *Lydia*, disrupts the syllabification scheme of the first stanza by omitting three words of the third line.
The poem, as De Lisle wrote it, begins:

> *Lydia, sur tes roses joues,*
> *Et sur ton col frais et plus blanc*
> *Que le lait, coule étincelant*
> *L'or fluide que tu dénoues.*

The lyric in Fauré's setting is as follows:

> *Lydia, sur tes roses joues*
> *Et sur ton col frais et si blanc,*
> *Roule étincelant*
> *L'or fluide que tu dénoues.*

The composer has thus evaded a run-on line but in the process he has
necessarily altered the versification scheme and deleted a meaningful poetic
image. There is no question that, although musically satisfying, the song
does some disservice to the poetic thought and form at this point.

A related instance is the deletion by Reynaldo Hahn of three syllables
from the last line of each of the poetic stanzas of Hugo's poem, *Si mes vers
avaient des ailes*. Hugo writes:

> *Des ailes comme l'oiseau.*
> . . . .
> *Des ailes comme l'esprit.*
> . . . .
> *Des ailes comme l'amour.*

In each stanza Hahn omits the words *Des ailes*, thereby altering the form
though not the sense of the poem.

One of the most common text alterations is the deletion of a poetic
syllable in order to accomodate the musical phrasing or rhythm. In
Schubert's setting of Goethe's *Wanderers Nachtlied, I*, the composer

contracts two words in order to regulate the scansion in conformity with his melody. Goethe's lines read:

> *Der du von dem Himmel bist,*
> *Alles Leid und Schmerzen stillest,*
> *Den, der doppelt elend ist,*
> *Doppelt mit Erquickung füllest,*
> *Ach, ich bin des Treibens müde!*
> *Was soll all der Schmerz und Lust?*
> *Süsser Friede,*
> *Komm, ach komm in meine Brust!*

Schubert changes *stillest* and *füllest* to *stillst* und *füllst*, thereby evening out the number of syllables in all four opening lines. He also changes the word *Erquickung* to *Entzückung*, which is a little more serious because the meanings are not the same. Wolf, setting the same text, takes the original syllabification very nicely into his musical phrasing, but feels compelled to repeat *Süsser Friede*, possibly in order to bring that shortened verse into line with the rest of the poetic lines. Like Schubert, he cannot resist repeating the final two lines in their entirety.

Even more eccentric is a change Schubert makes in *Der Wegweiser*, from the *Winterreise* cycle, where the poem in the third stanza reads:

> *Weiser stehen auf den Strassen,*
> *Weisen auf die Städte zu*
> *Und ich wandre sondern Massen,*
> *Ohne Ruh', und suche Ruh'.*

The composer changes the last word of the first line to *Wegen*, which does not alter the meaning appreciably but certainly annihilates the rhyme! He repeats the crime in *Das Irrlicht*, from the same cycle, by changing *Wehen* to *Leiden* in the second stanza.

In his *Zueignung*, Richard Strauss alters the penultimate line of the poem by repeating the first word in order to accommodate his exciting musical climax. The line originally reads:

> *Heilig an das Herz dir sank,*

This is a straightforward trochaic line, as are the others throughout the poem except for the shortened refrain, *Habe Dank*, which concludes each stanza. Strauss disrupts the meter entirely by his alteration to:

> *Heilig, heilig ans Herz dir sank,*

The result is such a glorious musical effect that one may be willing to overlook the tampering with poetic meter, but it is yet another example of manipulation of text for purely musical purposes.

Many similar text alterations might be cited, but the examples given are sufficient evidence that the poetic form is sometimes in peril when it passes into the hands of a composer. In most cases, of course, a suitable musical form is provided in substitution, and in any case it is virtually impossible to transfer intact to music the entirety of a poem's construction. Even though the syllabification is carefully maintained, the accentuation meticulously guarded, and excessively melismatic passages avoided, the final result bears little relationship to spoken poetry. The language of poetry has its own music; the addition of melody and harmony, musical meter and rhythm, add a new but different dimension. Valuable and expressive though it may be, a song is neither entirely music nor entirely poetry and, if the hybrid is to be successful, the formal elements of both must relinquish some of their antonomy.

Ned Rorem makes the problem clear in his delightfully witty and informative book, *Music from Inside Out*.[3] He points out that many poets of all eras have questioned and even forbidden the use of their poetry for song settings. Others have taken a more tolerant stance, sometimes colored by an attitude of *laissez-faire* like Apollinaire, whom Rorem quotes as remarking: "If the musicians are amused, let them go ahead, I have no objections!"[4] Still others have allowed only one or two favored composers to set their work. Underlying all the poets' reactions has been the realization that the form chosen for their own expressive purposes must in some sense be bent to the demands of music in song.

A word should be said about the use of poetic devices such as alliteration, assonance, and the like, as they relate to songsetting. By and large, such devices are allowed to fend for themselves in songs, possibly because composers have felt that they have an intrinsic expressive power that either does not demand musical illustration or does not even lend itself to musical enlargement. There are exceptions, one notable one being Roger Sessions's setting of a James Joyce lyric, *On the Beach at Fontana*. As shown in Example 4.5, this makes considerable musical provision for the more striking alliterative passages:

EXAMPLE 4.5

3 Ned Rorem, *Music from Inside Out* (New York: George Braziller, 1967).
4 *Ibid.*, p. 41.

On the Beach at Fontana—Music by Roger
Sessions. © Copyright 1964 Edward
B. Marks Music Corporation; used by
permission. Text by James Joyce; used
by permission.

Here the music supports the poetic alliteration admirably by its use of
melodic and rhythmic patterns that draw attention to the language. In this
case, the presence of a strong element of onomatopœia is also exploited by
Sessions to the advantage of both the poetry and the music.

Samuel Barber, too, responds to the strong verbal sounds in Joyce's
lyric *I hear an army*, when he sets the following passage:

EXAMPLE 4.6

The entire texture of the song is ideally suited to Joyce's violent and stirring poem, but the excerpt quoted seems particularly effective in graphically underlining the series of searing consonantal combinations that crowd upon one another in such close succession.

Not always, however, have composers been prepared to take advantage of sound play in poetry. The French poets have been quite adventurous in their use of word color, and the following lines from a poem by Jean Richepin would suggest some sort of musical response that might attempt to parallel the verbal music.

> *Il dort d'un bon sommeil*
> *Vermeil*
> *Sous le ciel radieux.*
> *Tous ceux qu'il a connus,*
> *Venus,*
> *Lui font de longs adieux.*

Richepin's entire poem is constructed along these lines, relying heavily upon the force of assonance and arresting syllabification. Fauré, in his setting *Au Cimetière*, however, provides no musical counterpart that would help to illuminate this element of the poetry.

Debussy is usually more concerned than most of his fellow French song writers with the meticulous enunciation of the poetic language. Possibly as a result of this, he sometimes brings its niceties into focus in his settings. In the well-known *Il pleure dans mon coeur*, for instance, where so much of the charm and color of Verlaine's poem relies upon the vowel sound *œ*, the composer allows the voice to linger on those vowels, bringing them into melodic prominence so that their importance to the expression cannot be minimized. In much the same vein, Example 4.7, a passage from Henri Sauguet's *Cloune étoilé*, the last song in his cycle *Cirque*, demonstrates a concern for the poetic suggestion. The use of a sequence is a simple enough device but it does bring the fleeting rime into line aurally.

EXAMPLE 4.7

le mil - le vi - sa - ges sa - ges

Such instances are unusual, however. The composers seem to have been more often concerned with general conformity to the poetic form and suggestion rather than with manipulating their materials to accomodate such subtleties.

Nor has there been a popular response to the more esoteric poetic types that have abounded in the twentieth century. This may be due as much to the subject matter as to the formal elements, as Arthur Jacobs suggests in his discussion of modern British song.

The taste of recital audiences became generally fossilized round Schubert, Schumann and Wolf. . . . Before seeking to capture such audiences, the living composer had to consider public reluctance to come to terms not only with modern music but with modern poetry—poetry which, from the 1930's, was often satiric, didactic, anti-romantic, and which no longer called sympathetically for music. . . .[5]

SUMMARY

The relation of musical form to poetic form is many sided. In those instances where there is an exact correlation in line for phrase and strophe for stanza, the music can aid in articulating the poetic structure. In cases of strophic modification and through composition, the musical variations are apt to be aimed rather at expressive intensification than at formal

5 Denis Stevens (ed.), *op. cit.*, p. 174.

considerations, although this is not exclusively the rule. Perhaps the greatest disruption of poetic form in song composition has been the result of repetition and/or deletion of words, phrases, and even entire stanzas in order to accommodate musical demands. The fact that many of the most beloved songs involve just this sort of disruption is evidence that performers and public alike have often been more sensitive to musical than to poetic clarity and continuity.

II

Musico-poetic Synthesis—
The Imagery

The Image—
Vehicle of Musico-poetic Expression

Part I has been devoted to the more mechanical correspondences shared by music and poetry in song. The primary concern has been to point out the role of music in relation to reinforcement of word-syllable accents, syllabification constructs, phrasing, and the like. These considerations are basically structural and are directed toward shape and weight, toward the "surface" of the work. There has been no attempt to compile an exhaustive catalogue of devices; it is questionable whether such a catalogue is possible or even desirable. The discussion has been illustrative only, pointing to some of the more frequently used tools; I have gone into the matter at all because it is an area to which very little attention has been given in previous discussions of song.

Fortunately for the song as an art form, it cannot be reduced to the mechanics of correlatives on the structural level alone. Surface compatibility between text and tone are necessary if the song is to communicate meaningfully, and to this extent the matters under discussion in Part I make a contribution to the expression of mood and emotion—to the content, as it is frequently designated. Without an articulate format of some sort, no expression is possible. However, to be entirely successful as a song, the music must be more than a mere servant to the externals of the poem. It must contribute something meaningful and compatible in the area of the poem's deeper, more expressive significance. Behind the impulse to create song, in fact, has been the continuing feeling and conviction that music *can* make such a contribution, that its powers of expression can be brought to bear directly upon the emotional content of the words—that it can heighten that content to some extent. In order to understand how this is possible, it is necessary to consider music as an entity, apart from its association with words in song.

The attempt to describe or to account for the expressive characteristics of music has occupied scholars for centuries. In general, two mainstreams of thought have been pursued. In one, the form and the content (expression) have been explained as separate elements, although closely related. In the other, the two have been inseparable—the form *is* the content, in other words. Although there have been interesting and instructive variations on these two themes, the themes themselves have been fairly consistent. It is not my intention to enter the controversy, although I am aware of the philosophical dangers of separating mechanics (form) and expression (content), even for purposes of discussion. Nevertheless, some position is necessary, and it will be helpful to review some of the thinking that has influenced my own conclusions. The very organization of this book in fact betrays my conviction that, at least to serve as a basis for illustration, the mechanism *can* be distinguished from the moods and emotions it may express.

The dichotomy between the two philosophical positions has been so well articulated by Leonard Meyer that a good beginning may be borrowed from his description.

> The first main difference of opinion exists between those who insist that musical meaning lies exclusively within the context of the work itself, in the perception of the relationships set forth within the musical work of art, and those who contend that, in addition to these abstract, intellectual meanings, music also communicates meanings which in some way refer to the extra-musical world of concepts, actions, emotional states, and character. Let us call the former group the "absolutists" and the latter group the "referentialists."[1]

In his invigorating study, Meyer develops the thesis that both meanings are interrelated and interactive in music and that the absolutist and the referentialist are therefore not necessarily at odds. Adopting the psychologist's position that emotion results from the inhibition of some sort of expectancy, Meyer concludes that, by purely musical means, a situation is established whereby the listener is led to expect certain consequences. When, again by purely musical means, these expectancies are frustrated, an emotional reaction occurs in the listener. This response gives the music its meaning. Thus, although the format and its result may be analyzed separately, in the actual performance of and response to music they are completely unified.

The application, as Meyer demonstrates, may be extended to include melodic, harmonic, and rhythmic material, assuming the listener has been sufficiently conditioned by experience, training, or indoctrination to grasp the stylistic implications of the music. It would be tempting to go all the way with Dr. Meyer, the more so because his presentation is magnificently documented and illustrated. It seems to me, however, that some musical situations do not respond to his analysis. The emotional satisfaction of complete fulfillment (as at the return of the tonic following a digression)

[1] Leonard B. Meyer, *Emotion and Meaning in Music* (Chicago: The University of Chicago Press, 1956), p. 1.

may be just as strong as the emotional disturbance resulting from frustration (as at a deceptive cadence). Meyer would argue, if I follow him correctly, that in such an instance there is no emotional response involved because there was nothing frustrating to react to. I can only counter that fulfillment of expectation is emotionally oriented, for me at least. Nonetheless, his thesis accounts for much of music's power of expression, especially in such areas as movement, excitement, or anticipation.

Paul Farnsworth, discussing the same problem of emotional response to music, and basing his arguments upon experiments involving many listeners, arrives at somewhat similar conclusions.[2] Seeking musical configurations that would elicit significantly similar responses among his auditioners, and that could be described in extramusical terms, he found that although other elements are of importance, the two factors that seem most to affect the assignment of meaning to music are tempo and mode. Both Farnsworth and Meyer are insistent that the musical sophistication of the listener is of great importance in the response. And both men attack the position taken by C. C. Pratt[3], who makes a sharp distinction between the emotional character as being an objective quality of the music itself (which is Pratt's position), and the emotional character as being a subjective response within the listener.

In still another study attempting to define the musical elements that account for expression, Deryck Cooke proposes an extensive rhetoric of musical patterns that, because of their inherent quality and their historical associations in Western music, have been used as expressive material in definite contexts. In terms of the vocabulary that he sets up, for instance, the ascending major scale from the tonic to the dominant is used to "express an outgoing, active, assertive emotion of joy."[4] Other emotional expressions are attributed to other configurations, the basis of the vocabulary always being the existence of various intervallic tensions that have a peculiar significance for each pattern or a variation of it. Although the study is profusely illustrated, the danger of such categorization is in its reduction of the materials of music to a mere catalogue of melodic devices, which it certainly is not. It also reduces the composer's role to one of manipulative variation, no matter how original, rather than recognizing it as one of imaginative creation. Cooke's thesis is attacked incisively by Donald Ferguson, who insists that such configurations are not *elements* of expression (as Cooke defines them), but rather *instances* of expression.[5] Ferguson himself contends, again in opposition to Pratt, that the structure

2 Paul R. Farnsworth, *The Social Psychology of Music* (New York: The Dryden Press, 1958).

3 C. C. Pratt, *The Meaning of Music* (New York: McGraw-Hill, Inc., 1931).

4 Deryck Cooke, *The Language of Music* (London: Oxford University Press, 1959), p. 115.

5 Donald N. Ferguson, *Music As Metaphor* (Minneapolis: University of Minnesota Press, 1960), Appendix.

of music, the tension and relaxation of melody, harmony, and rhythm, arouse an emotional response in the listener and therefore operate as expressive factors. Thus he is able to absorb Meyer's inhibitory function, Farnsworth's tempo and mode, and Cooke's intervallic tensions, and to allow all of music's materials to work decisively within the framework of his thesis.

Underlying the thought of all psychologists and aestheticians who have studied the problem is the awareness that music *does* relate somehow to emotion, and that it *does* function expressively. The lack of a complete and universally accepted explanation of *why* and *how* has been the relationship between the structure and the expression, between the form and the content. Like most of the commentators I have cited, my own conviction is that the structure embodies numerous acoustical complexes that encourage the perceptive listener to react. But I would add another dimension to the musical experience: the orientation of the auditor at the particular time. Only by such an area of differentiation would analysis or description be possible, for if the response were always in terms of emotion, no intelligent discussion could be undertaken. On the other hand, if the listener is involved exclusively in aural analysis, the possibilities of expressive communication are significantly reduced.

The difference in posture is rather well expressed by G. Révész.[6] In defining the musical response, he suggests that it is on two distinct levels, and he seems to propose that the listener can himself be somewhat selective. For Révész the physical vibrations of music influence the sensory mechanism of the listener, thus promoting a sensual-psychological-emotional response. This, for the author, must be distinguished from a musical-aesthetic response, which is available only to those who can repress the psychic excitations and associative reactions and "let the work exert its influence unimpeded, in the full beauty of its aesthetic form."[7] The aesthetic attitude is regarded as being on a higher level than the merely emotional. The reason for this is that the emotional response is not peculiarly musical— the emotions are not exclusively musical, in other words, and can be aroused by other than musical means. On the other hand, the aesthetic response, by its confinement to the work itself in all its formal unity, is a distinctly musical one and therefore artistically oriented. Only when the listener adopts the aesthetic attitude can analysis take place; conversely, only when he is armed with analytical ability, aesthetic intuition, knowledge, and a feeling for style, can the aesthetic response occur.

In modification of Révész's thesis, I would simply suggest that there is no qualitative difference, but only a difference appropriate to the occasion. The form must be experienced on a primarily intellectual basis, the content on a primarily emotional basis, and each are valid depending upon the need

6 G. Révész, *Introduction to the Psychology of Music* (Norman, Oklahoma: University of Oklahoma Press, 1954).

7 *Ibid.*, p. 242.

or desire of the moment. Furthermore, each may operate in almost total isolation from the other at different times for the same individual, again depending upon the occasion. Révész seems to want the two responses simultaneously:

Music is a world unto itself, a specific autonomous domain of human activity, an expressive form that is independent of all others. It represents a unique harmony between the sensuous and the intellectual. No other branch of art is able to achieve the synthesis to an equivaent degree.[8]

Perhaps this is true. But the end result of analysis is always desynthesis, and so I must adopt the attitude here that the form furnishes the vehicle for the expression, although the two factors are not identical in kind and must be approached differently. In the ensuing discussion of the expressive role of music in song, it must be understood that the descriptions of musical structures are not given in order to identify the musical expression itself. They are merely meant to describe the contexts within which lie the possibilities for expression. Only when such possibilities meet with an emotional response in the listener can expression actually take place. To be musically satisfying, the listener's emotional reaction must bear a reasonable relationship to the expressive possibilities in the music—he will not want to dance, for instance, when he hears a lullaby.

It should be possible, given the assumptions above, to state unequivocally that in song the expression contributed by the music, of a general emotional nature only (excitement, peace, tension, etc.), may be given a specific nature by the words of the poem. Max Schoen states as much: "Vocal music, due unquestionably to the words, has greater power to arouse a definite emotional response than has instrumental music."[9] The same assertion, in somewhat more detail, is made by Robert Bridges:

A certain disposition of ideas in words produces a whole result quite out of proportion to the parts: and if it is askt what music can do best, it is something in the same way of indefinit suggestion. Poetry is here the stronger, in that its suggestion is more definitely directed. Music is the stronger in the greater force of the emotion raised. It would seem therefore that music could hav no more fit and congenial task than to heighten the emotion of some great poetic beauty, the direction of which is supply'd by the words.[10]

8 *Ibid.*, p. 245.

9 Max Schoen (ed.), *The Effects of Music* (New York: Harcourt, Brace & World, Inc., 1927), p. 159.

10 Quoted in Calvin Brown, *Music and Literature* (Athens, Georgia: The University of Georgia Press, 1948), p. 49. Bridges (1844–1930) was Poet Laureate of England from 1913 until his death. Much of his life was spent in virtual seclusion, his only public interest being in the Society for Pure English, the purpose of which was to foster, among other things, a movement toward a revision of spelling. This fact accounts for the unusual spelling found in the quotation.

The two statements, Schoen's based upon experimental research and Bridges's upon observation and experience, seem clearly defensible, and it should be possible to proceed with illustrations of exactly how these relationships work. However, some extremely penetrating observations have been contributed by other scholars, observations that seem to contradict these assumptions, and some acknowledgment of them must be made.

In Chapter 10 of her monumental work on aesthetics, Susanne Langer presents her theory of the relationship between word and tone, a theory that argues for the complete assimilation of text by music.

When words and music come together in song, music swallows words; not only mere words and literal sentences, but even literary word-structures, poetry. Song is not a compromise between poetry and music, . . . song is music.[11]

And again: "When a composer puts a poem to music, he annihilates the poem and makes a song."[12]

What Mrs. Langer is driving at is something resembling an essential truth in song: the emotional impact—the expressive burden, if you will—is very often carried on musical shoulders. Even the form of a song, although sometimes closely related to the poetic form that inspired it, is nevertheless essentially a musical form. The phrasing is essentially musical phrasing. The rhythms, the harmonies, the meters, the tunes—all these are musical and the words are for the most part simply superimposed upon them. This theory goes a long way to explain why when one asks, "How does *The Star Spangled Banner* begin?", the response is almost always in terms of the melody rather than the poem. To this extent the music has indeed "swallowed" the words.

On the other hand, it is questionable whether in actual performance, the listener gives his attention *only* to the music, without concern of any sort for the text. Mrs. Langer's point is that, in song, the words become musical elements rather than verbal elements, and she offers instances in which the melody and its accompanying harmony, played on a nonvocal instrument, are as artistically satisfying as when sung with the text. In many cases this is undoubtedly true—I have heard Fauré's *Après un Rêve* performed by cello and piano and the result was fulfilling in every respect. But this is more a clue to Fauré's particular approach to song than it is to song as a genre. Schubert's *Erlkönig* could not possibly be as electrifying as an instrumental solo as when sung, and most of Debussy's later songs (the *Chansons de Bilitis*, for instance) are nothing short of ludicrous without the text—well enunciated, too.

Michael Tippett, writing the concluding chapter of *A History of Song*,

11 Susanne K. Langer, *Feeling and Form* (New York: Charles Scribner's Sons, 1953), p. 152.
12 *Ibid.*, p. 153.

goes nearly as far as Mrs. Langer in attempting a similar definition of the relationship between text and music.

> The moment the composer begins to create the musical verses of his song, he destroys our appreciation of the poem as poetry, and substitutes an appreciation of his music as song. . . . As soon as we sing any poetry to a recognizable melody we have at that instant left the art of poetry for the art of music.[13]

In continuing to develop his thesis, however, Tippett makes it clear that he allows for enough modification in the theory to permit the assimilation of word meanings, if not their function as truly poetic elements.

The stumbling block in all such theories is the insistence upon choosing between poetry and music. In actuality the song is neither one nor the other, but a true hybrid in which both art forms relinquish some, but not all, of their individual characteristics. The words of a poem work on several levels simultaneously. They are at once connotative and denotative; they function as symbols with assigned meanings, but also as vehicles for image, allusion, and metaphor. Even though the poem may lose its original poetic form when taken into a song, the words do not lose their function as language, their literal significance, in other words. They retain not only their meanings but their syntax as well; without such retention they would be mere gibberish.

At the same time, music cannot take over entirely without regard for the text that accompanies it. The expressive power of music is admittedly great, perhaps the more so because of its ability to arouse emotional responses of a general nature, which are neither bound to specific experiences nor related to specific objects. But in song, music must submit at least to some extent to the harness of the text. To use *Erlkönig* illustratively again, it would be unthinkable for the music to serve as a vehicle for a lullaby. The limitations imposed upon the music must be those of the text, if the result is to be artistically justifiable.

But beyond such obvious relationships, which must remain compatible, the most expressive element in both music and poetry, and the one that can make the greatest contribution to emotional response, is imagery. On the deepest level of meaning, this is the stuff of which both are made, although the vocabularies are different for each.

In poetry the chief vehicle of feeling is the image, in most cases borrowed from the poet's as well as the reader's memory of sense impressions. The poet's ability to arouse associations that reach beyond the poem's particular situation, and the reader's ability to unleash his thoughts and emotions and imagination—these abilities are indispensible for the experiencing of the poem at its expressive level. The literal sense of the words is necessary, not as a culmination of the experience, but as its inauguration.

13 Denis Stevens, *op. cit.*, p. 462.

In music the image results from the listener's sensitivity to the musical context, his ability to feel the movement, the tension and release, the vast variety of suggestions in the complex of sounds. As Ferguson puts it:

To each factor of the whole complex image, . . . not only an intellectual identification of the factor but an emotional response to it will be aroused. The sensuous glory of musical tone, the curve of a melodic phrase, the richness and the tension of an unexpected harmony will all possess emotional interest; . . . [14]

In an earlier section of his book, Ferguson draws upon Pratt for a wonderfully enlightening statement that is useful here. He quotes: "The music then sounds the way an emotion feels."[15] The only modification needed here is one I have already suggested—the realization that for expression to result, the sound must fall upon the sensibilities of a listener who is both aware and receptive. It is at this point that song functions most expressively. If the emotion aroused by the music is compatible with the emotion aroused by the poetry, the images have synthesized and the expressive experience is complete.

In this sense, then, the song must not be thought of as either music or poetry but rather as an amalgam that shares significantly in both arts and is equally dependent upon both. It is possible to discuss the poetry, in form and content, and it is possible to discuss the music, in form and content. But in a truly successful song they *function* concurrently.

For purposes of analysis, we can describe a deceptive cadence structurally by outlining the harmonic scheme as: I_4^6—V_7—VI, to use one possibility. We can also describe it as producing an image of frustration (or surprise or any of a number of other possibilities), which defines it at the expressive level. In song, when the poetic image is one of frustration particularized by the verbal content, and this is reinforced by a deceptive cadence or some other equally inhibitory device, then we can logically assign both structural and expressive significance to the passage, provided that in the process of description we have not re-created the expression itself but merely indicated the situation out of which it could arise. The *experience* must take place in the listener, emotionally and not analytically. And for the fullest realization, he must be musically as well as poetically sophisticated enough to absorb the total complex in a unified way.

Indeed, an awareness of the balance between musical and poetic imagery is one of the most valuable tools in the description of style. The baroque period, with its intense concentration upon musical device and architecture, tended to overburden the song with musical significance, both structurally and expressively. Paradoxically, the intention was to reproduce in musical terms the *Affekt* of the most significant expressive elements in the text. But in the process, insistence upon text repetition, extensive melismas,

14 Donald Ferguson, *op. cit.*, p. 47.
15 *Ibid.*, p. 27.

vocal display, and formal conventions, added to an infatuation with ornamentation, resulted in an imbalance between word and tone, so that the music in many cases did "swallow the words," to use Mrs. Langer's phrase. At the opposite extreme, Schubert's recourse to recitative passages in many of his early songs clearly indicates that he was unable at that stage to find a musical context commensurate with all the expressive demands of the poetry; its result is a poverty of musical imagery in relation to the suggestion of the text. But in the best songs of Schumann and Wolf the balance between poetic and musical expression produces an ideal synthesis that identifies the nineteenth century as the high point of lied composition.

The words of any song text normally function in two ways, denotatively and connotatively. From their literal meanings (denotation) and their syntax comes an awareness of the situation being presented. But the words also suggest an expressive situation beyond the particular situation, and in this connotative sense they reach expressive depths that transcend their literal meanings. In so doing, they represent the basic distinction between prose and poetry. Similarly, music can function in two ways, *although neither of them is denotative*. The first is as a complex of sounds that can be formally described. In this sense, music is loud or quiet, slow or fast, regularly or irregularly phrased, harmonically involved or simple. At the same time, the sounds can trigger emotional responses in the listener, who can feel relaxed, excited, sad or exhilarated, according to his capacity for involvement with the sounds and what they suggest expressively to him.

The key to expression in both poetry and music is the receptivity of the reader and/or listener. The emotional potential of a great poem may never be realized unless the reader is prepared by sensitivity and experience to respond to its imagery. Likewise, the emotional potential of great music may not be reached unless the listener is musically sophisticated enough to respond to its suggestion. The main point I have tried to make is that the form, the arrangement, and the structural components can be described and recognized by anyone possessing the requisite vocabulary. But for these factors to operate expressively, the potential must be present in both the music or the poetry *and* in the reader or the listener. In song, when the words evoke an emotionally oriented image and when the music evokes a compatible emotionally oriented image, the expressive potential has been fully realized.

Perhaps the most direct approach to the sort of image synthesis I have been discussing is the use of musico-poetic material that possesses strong emotional associations of a quite definite nature. One of the clearest illustrations of this sort of association (although certainly not one of the most subtle) is found in Schumann's setting of Heine's *Die beiden Grenadiere*. The actual situation described in the poem is that of two French soldiers returning home from the Russian campaign. They react differently when they learn that Napoleon has been captured and his armies conquered.

The first wishes to die but realizes that by doing so he would be forsaking his family. The other, placing his loyalty to his Emperor above his duty to his family, wishes only to be buried in his homeland, to await in the grave the return of his leader and the renewed outbreak of hostilities, and then to rise up and join in the glorious battle. Beyond the situation itself stretches the concept of patriotism, so dear to the nineteenth century, and a sense of nationalism, of personal sacrifice that insists that loyalty to country and Emperor is greater and more noble than personal ties and even life itself. These concepts, implied in the text, would assuredly have been met with emotional receptivity by any reader for whom patriotic sentiments were meaningful.

The music Schumann has provided employs a relatively straightforward rhythm, militarily marchlike and melodically direct and for the most part declamatory. The mode is minor, suggesting the then current feeling that such harmonic color befits sad or morbidly dramatic subject matter. As the more patriotic of the soldiers becomes involved in asking that he be returned to France for burial, the music takes on a more persuasive rhythmic character through the employment of triplets in the accompaniment, in addition to a performance direction for a quickening of tempo. Shortly thereafter, the rhythmic pattern changes once more, this time to an oom-pah figure, figuratively suitable to the excitement and the association of marching and soldiery. But when the grenadier imagines Napoleon and his forces riding over his grave, conjures up the roar of cannon and the clash of swords, and envisions himself called forth from the dead to rejoin his regiment in defense of the Emperor—then Schumann matches the patriotic fervor by employing that most patriotic of all symbols, the national anthem. In this case, of course, it is *La Marseillaise*—and in the major mode, too! Only a waving flag could be expected to arouse a more emotional response in the listener, and this sort of visualism is not possible in music. And so the grenadier sings Heine's words to the most nationalistically inspirational of all French tunes.

The device is obvious, of course, and it even seems a bit trite to us at this distance from the situation that inspired it. Nevertheless, the expressive intent is clear. It would be difficult to imagine another musical pattern that would put the poetic images of the soldier and his loyalties in such immediate synthesis with the emotional associations of the music. But the point that needs making most strongly is that unless the listener is aware of the significance of the tune of *La Marseillaise*, the musical imagery is crippled. And unless the poetic situation can arouse the fullest sense of patriotic fervor in the reader, the imagery of the poem is likewise weakened. In either case, although the music's formal characteristics may be described and the poem's literal significance articulated, little or no expression has taken place. Only when the experience goes beyond these surface factors and transcends them emotionally—only then has the song communicated expressively. For this to happen both poem and music must be functioning meaningfully on that particular level. It is possible to describe or to intellectualize form and content, but expression can take place only by feeling.

The fact that this sort of associative stimulus to emotional response was felt to be valid by many composers is demonstrated by the use of the same device by Wagner in setting Heine's French translation of the poem. Like Schumann, Wagner resorts to a quotation of *La Marseillaise* at the climactic point. In the same vein, Tchaikovsky uses the tune in his *1812 Overture*, though of course for a different purpose. Here, without words to enhance the imagery, he simply uses the national anthem to represent the French forces, pitting it musically against a familiar Cossack tune, which eventually "overcomes" it in the same sense as that in which the Russian forces overcame the invading French forces under Napoleon. The association of readily identifiable music with various dramatic situations was a common device in the nineteenth century and forms one of the basic rhetorical reservoirs for program music. The *Dies Irae* is quoted repeatedly in dramatic contexts where it could be expected to arouse a nonmusical associative response relevant to death or final judgment.

In America, Charles Ives was perhaps overly fond of quotations of this sort, although some of them operate magnificently. Besides using familiar tunes as basic thematic material, he sometimes makes extremely telling references that must be seen as predominantly expressive in character. One such is his use of both words and melody to the revivalistic song *Are You Washed in the Blood of the Lamb?*, which he refers to repeatedly in his *General William Booth Enters into Heaven*. By association, the quotation represents all the best and worst aspects of the evangelistic work of the Salvation Army, and no other device could get the point across quite so quickly and effectively.

One of Ives's subtlest references occurs in his hauntingly lovely setting of a portion of Whittier's poem *The Brewing of Soma*, which Ives entitles *Serenity*. At the final cadence of each of the two stanzas, the composer uses a direct melodic and harmonic quote taken from a hymn tune, *Serenity*, by William Wallace, which is associated with another Whittier hymn text, *Immortal Love, Forever Full*. This hymn, composed of excerpts from Whittier's poem *Our Master*, is in turn a development of the ideas expressed in Tennyson's great poem *In Memoriam*, the prologue of which begins with the words, "Strong Son of God, immortal Love."

The chain of associations is quite clear, but it can become expressively complete for the listener only if he is aware that the poetic insights of *all* the works center around the interpretation of Christ as Love Incarnate. All of them suggest that the conflicting theological ideologies that were reaching an almost hysterical climax during the span of years when the poems were written, and the song was composed by Ives, were tending to obscure the image of Jesus as the embodiment of faith and hope through love. The subject was dear to both Whittier and Tennyson, and if we follow Ives's reference to its conclusion here, we must assume that he shared the feelings of both poets. Unless the song is understood at this level a considerable portion of the expressive content has had no functional effect whatever.

It is not at all unusual to encounter musical configurations that suggest ethnic types, such as the rhythms of gypsy dances. One strong association of this sort is that of the Negro with syncopation. In his set of three songs, *Chansons de Négresse*, Darius Milhaud draws upon this association as an ethnic symbol, but the rhythms also provide an expressive paradox whose meaning extends beyond mere identification. Equating syncopation with the jazz idiom has given it an aura of gaiety and a strong suggestion of the dance, especially when it is presented as a persistent figure, as it is by Milhaud in these settings. The music, in this particular instance, belies the poetry, which is oriented around the hopeless despondency and the bitterness of the Negro social position. But it is this very paradox between the musical mood and the poetic mood that serves the expression so well. The music presents an image of the minstrel-show Negro—a concept still commonly held by the white community. In sharp contrast, the poetry presents the social and psychological deprivation felt by the Negro himself. The juxtaposition creates a powerful and penetrating expressive result.

Closely allied in concept to these illustrations is the use of musical material that is not actually quoted from pre-existing pieces or that bears no definite ethnic or other extramusical significance, but merely sounds familiar. The basis for association here is the use of some indefinable combination of idioms that is reminiscent of a type of musical expression. One illustration that comes easily to mind is the piano introduction to *La Grenouille Americaine*, the third of a set of five songs by Erik Satie entitled *Ludions*, based upon poems of Léon-Paul Fargue. The poem is sardonic and derides the ridiculous pomposity of the typical American tourist in France. Satie provides music that is delightfully and embarrassingly like the worst of the thousands of marches to be heard at sports events and militarily oriented parades in the United States. It makes possible immediate identification, given musical awareness and sophistication in the listener, and it adds a touch of musical burlesque to the poetic imagery.

A similar instance is the use by Hugo Wolf in his setting of Mörike's *Abschied*. The poem concerns a man who is disturbed by a visitor whose main purpose is apparently to criticize the former's overlarge nose. To express his annoyance, the possessor of the wondrous proboscis, when ushering the visitor out the door, nudges him from behind—causing him to tumble down the stairs. Wolf provides a piano postlude that marvelously suggests all the Strauss waltzes rolled into one. It is an apt accompaniment to the annoying visitor's exit and one cannot imagine a more fitting commentary on the scene and the mood of the person administering the kick!

Musical association is put to fine use by Samuel Barber in *The Crucifixion*, the fifth of his group of *Hermit Songs*. Based upon a twelfth-century text, the poem presents in starkly beautiful language the suffering of Christ and the Virgin Mother. To match the austerity of the text, Barber offers an accompaniment texture that exploits open fourths and fifths coupled occasionally with piercing pinpoints of dissonance, plus a motivic figure illustrative of the opening lines, "At the cry of the first bird." The cry is no romantic warble, however, but rather a dry, anguished shriek built on the interval of the diminished fifth. All this is effective musical imagery, used in meaningful relationship to the text. But beyond this, Barber structures his piece harmonically and melodically on the antique Phrygian mode, thereby adding a further expressive dimension that correlates in time to the events of the poetic situation. The song thus reaches us on the absolute as well as on the referential level—but only, of course, if we make the appropriate associations with the modal texture.

The point I have been trying to emphasize in these examples is that by means of reference points associated with musical quotations or styles it is possible to add a dimension to expression that is not embodied in the text alone. At the same time, however, the text is essential to full realization of the significance of the musical imagery—it explains it, in other words. This particular sort of imagery synthesis is possible only when direct and generally recognized extramusical associations are called upon. Musico-poetic expression cannot, of course, be limited to contexts of this type. In the history of song, in fact, this sort of manipulation, although convenient and effective, is relatively rare.

SUMMARY

On the level of expression in song, the greatest degree of correlation between word and tone results from a concordance of imagery. In most cases the musical imagery cannot be in terms as exact as those involved in the poetry. This accounts for the fact that many musical settings of the same poem can successfully approximate the poetic expression without utilizing identical or even similar musical realizations. At the same time it is possible for music to utilize references that are almost universally recognized and these associations can provide a means of precise correlation of imagery. Such instances include the quotation of folk, patriotic, or other familiar tunes, as well as the use of musical idioms that possess strong associations. When this is done skillfully and with taste, the expressive effect can be quite powerful.

Harmonic Imagery

IN TURNING away from the use of extramusical associations or of musical quotations with assigned "meanings" as aids to expression, it is hardly possible to assign to particular musical configurations an expressive import that will be universally acceptable. This fact, perhaps more than any other, accounts for the variety of responses among listeners, particularly as it is related to a fondness for or a prejudice against different musical styles. Why is one person strongly attracted to the music of the nineteenth century, for instance, while another, equally sensitive and responsive, finds the texture and artistic objectives of romantic music totally unrewarding? Even within the same general stylistic period, what besides individual response can account for a listener's love for Brahms and dislike for Wolf? Obviously the answer must be given in terms of the individuality of the reaction, rather than in terms of any absolute expressive characteristics within the music itself.

In view of this, the following discussion must be qualified by the admission that what I am doing is *suggesting* expressive possibilities, not assigning them definitively. Whenever possible, they will be related to the aesthetic concepts of the periods during which the songs were produced, and to the particular orientation of the composers as this is revealed in the music.

A great deal of attention has been given by both composers and commentators to the expressive properties of major and minor. This is closely tied to the development during the baroque period of a strong sense of tonality, along with the reduction of modes to two only. It was inevitable that particularized significances should be assigned to the key as well as the mode, the more so since such assignments already had a long history, dating back to the Greek doctrine of *ethos* and continuing in varying degrees of intensity throughout the Middle Ages and Renaissance. This interest reached a new crescendo in the baroque; from the wide range of comments that are available, only a few will be indicated in order to illustrate the thinking of the period. It should be borne in mind that the whole question of mode was closely associated throughout the era with the doctrine of *Affekt* and its ramifications for musical expression.

Discussing the musical representation of the temperaments, Einstein quotes from a 1650 publication by Kircher, *De musurgia Antiquo-Moderna in qua de varia utriusque Musicae ratione disputatur.*[1] The passage describes a Carissimi composition that makes deliberate use of major and minor to distinguish between laughing and crying. The composition itself is a duet for two sopranos and basso continuo, the singers representing the ancient philosophers Democritus and Heraclitus, one somber and the other gay.

A similar association is noted by Ivor Keys in his book *The Texture of Music.*[2] He refers to the thirteenth edition, published in 1697, of John Playford's *An Introduction to the Skill of Musick*, and quotes from it the following passage:

There are but two *Keys* in Musick, one *flat*, and the other *sharp*, which is sufficient to write down any *melancholy* or *cheerful* song whatever.[3]

In terms of the theoretical vocabulary of the time in England, the "flat" and "sharp" refer to intervals above the key tone (not the accidentals in the signature), and thus mean minor and major respectively.

Another Englishman, Roger North, in a passage which the editor dates as being written between 1715 and 1720, states:

As to the common passions of joy and sorrow, the two different keys, termed sharp and flatt [Ed. note: *i.e.,* major and minor] are a most apposite expression of them; for it is naturall and customary for men, without designe or affectation, to express themselves in the tone of those keys according as they are affected.[4]

North continues to develop his thesis and in so doing refers to the same Carissimi composition cited by Kircher.

Although references in German sources are numerous, the following is among the most interesting in this connection because of its point of view. George Buelow, in his study of Heinichen's treatises on accompaniment from a figured bass, quotes extensively from Heinichen's *Der General-Bass in der Composition* (1728) and includes the following statement:

Yet, to specify this or that key for the affect of love, sadness, joy, etc. is not good. . . . For we have heard famous composers write the saddest and tenderest music in D, A, and B♭ major, etc., as well as in A minor, E minor, C minor; and in similar scales [we have heard] the most powerful and brilliant music. It is

1 Alfred Einstein, *Essays On Music* (New York: W. W. Norton & Company, Inc., 1962).

2 Ivor Keys, *The Texture of Music* (London: Dennis Dobson, 1961).

3 *Ibid.,* p. 16.

4 John Wilson (ed.), *Roger North On Music* (London: Novello and Company, Ltd 1959), p. 111.

evident, therefore, that each key and all keys or musical modes without distinction are suited to expressing many and opposing affects.[5]

Buelow makes it clear that Heinichen is attacking a statement made by
Mattheson in the latter's *Das neu-eröffnete Orchestre* (1713), in which he
describes the properties of seventeen keys as they relate to arousing "affect".
The significant thing here is that Heinichen extends his criticism of
Mattheson to include the expressive character of modes as well as keys.
Heinichen apparently thought it was fruitless to make any generalizations
about either key or mode, although there was certainly a relatively strong
feeling among his contemporaries and predecessors that both had some
definite relation to "affect".

These and similar comments establish the fact that concern for the expressive possibilities of major and minor occupied the composers and the
public of the period in a vital way An actual examination of the music of the
time however, provides no really valid basis for generalization. In the end,
we should have to agree with Heinichen, whose position relatively late in
the period gives him a certain advantage in seeing the actual application of
the theories to the music itself.

A case in point is Henry Purcell, who might logically be expected to
come under the same general influence as Playford and North, but whose
songs show mixed tendencies. His *Strike the Viol*, for instance, clearly a song
of praise and good cheer, is in a solid C minor. In some songs, however,
he alters the mode in what seems a meaningful manner; one such is *I sigh'd
and own'd my Love*, in which one portion with the following text is set in G
major.

> I sigh'd and own'd my Love;
> Nor did the Fair my passion disapprove;
> A soft engaging Air not often apt to cause dispair,
> Declar'd she gave attention to my pray'r.
> She seem'd to pitty my distress,
> And I expected nothing less,
> Than what her ev'ry look did then confess.

The next section is given in G minor, and one would assume that the mode
alteration is text-oriented:

> But oh her Change destroys the charming prospect
> of my promis'd Joys, etc.

A return to G major accompanies the following:

> But while she strives to chill desire,
> Her brighter Eyes such warmth inspire,
> She checks the flame but cannot quench the fire.

5 George J. Buelow, *Thorough-Bass Accompaniment according to Johann David Heinichen*
(Berkeley: University of California Press, 1966), p. 271.

This sort of manipulation should be evidence that choice of mode is governed somewhat by textual mood. Again, in *Sweeter than Roses* the first section is set in C minor:

> Sweeter than Roses or cool Ev'ning Breeze,
> On a warm Flow'ry shore
> Was the dear kiss first trembling made me freeze,
> Then shot like Fire all o'er.

Appropriately, in terms of contemporary thought, the ensuing section is offered in C major:

> What Magick has Victorious Love,
> For all I touch or see;
> Since that dear Kiss I hourly prove,
> All, all is Love to me.

Unfortunately for those who make a case for the use of mode as more than a superficial device in expression, however, there are equally numerous instances where the connection is either nonexistent or so tenuous as to be difficult to justify. The beginning of *Love Arms Himself in Celia's Eyes* is set in C major with the following text:

> Love Arms himself in Celia's Eyes,
> Whene'er weak Reason would rebell;
> And ev'ry time I dare be Wise,
> Alas, a deeper wound I feel, etc.

For no readily fathomable reason, the mode is changed to minor for the next section of the song:

> Then cruel Reason give me rest;
> Quit in my Heart thy feeble hold,
> Go try thy Force in Celia's Breast,
> For that is disingag'd and cold, etc.

Although minor is appropriate enough here, it would have been equally so for the beginning of the song. It is not the mode itself that appears inconsistent, in other words, but the lack of textual motivation for the change.

In the 1965 reproduction of Purcell's *Orpheus Britannicus*,[6] a relatively long and involved song is reproduced under this heading: *The last Song the Author Sett, it being in his Sickness*.[7] The scheme of modes bears little relationship to the text. Beginning in C minor the text reads, in part:

> From Rosie Bow'rs where Sleep's the God of Love,
> Hither ye little waiting Cupids fly,
> Teach me in soft Melodious Songs, to move
> With tender Passion, my Heart's darling Joy, etc.

6 Henry Purcell, *Orpheus Britannicus* (Ridgewood, N. J.: Gregg Press Inc., 1965).
7 *Ibid.*, Vol. I, p. 63.

A change of meter but not of mode accompanies the following:

> Or if more influencing is to be brisk and Airy,
> With a Step and a Bound,
> And a Frisk from the Ground,
> I will Trip like any Fairy.

The cadence here is on $E^\flat$ major, but the chances are slim that this is anything other than a perfectly normal movement to the relative major, since the return to C minor is completed under the following:

> As once on Ida Dancing,
> Were three Celestial Bodies,
> With an Air, and a Face,
> And a Shape, and a Grace,
> Let me Charm like Beauty's Goddess.

Confusion is confounded when the mode changes to C major, and after several excursions in intermediate key centers, culminates in $E^\flat$ major during the following portion of the poem:

> Ah! 'tis all in vain
> Death and Despair must end the Fatal pain;
> Cold Despair disguis'd like Snow and Rain,
> Falls on my Breast.

The piece continues without exhibiting a recognizable relationship between mode and poetic content.

Inconsistencies between theory and practice are not limited to Purcell and England. Among the Italian pieces in minor that are based upon gay or amorous texts are Durante's *Danza, danza, fanciulla*, and Mancini's *Dir ch'io t'ami*. On the other hand, major is used for Torelli's *Tu lo sai*, Marcello's *Lontananza e gelosia*, and Caldara's *Si t'intendo*, all of which are expressions of the sorrows of love in one vein or another. The conclusion to be drawn is not that the composers of the middle and late baroque were insensitive to the demands of the text, which they most certainly were not, but rather that they did not always equate mode with mood, despite much of the contemporary theorizing.

During the latter half of the eighteenth century, however, a more consistent pattern seems to evolve, although even here there are enough exceptions to make a definitive generalization hazardous. In one of Mozart's most beloved and widely performed songs, for instance, the following text is given in F major:

Wie unglücklich bin ich nit,	How unhappy I am,
Wie schmachtend sind meine Tritt',	How my footsteps languish
Wenn ich mich nach dir lenke!	When I turn toward you.

Nur die Seufzer trösten mich,	Sighs are my only solace,
Alle Schmerzen häufen sich,	All my sorrows increase
Wenn ich auf dich gedenke.	When I think of you.

The principal expressive device harmonically is the intensive use of diminished-seventh chords for the second stanza and a brief insertion of F minor at *alle Schmerzen häufen sich*. Such harmonic coloration is certainly appropriate, but it is specific to the passage rather than being a reflection of the total poetic mood.

During much of the late eighteenth century, in fact, composers seem to have relied increasingly upon alternation between major and minor for expressive purposes rather than making a definite choice of mode for an entire composition. Mozart frequently resorts to such alternation, as in the piece just cited and many others, including the often quoted *Das Veilchen*. Beethoven continues the tradition, and in many of his songs (*Freudvoll und leidvoll*, the *Sechs geistliche Lieder von Gellert*, and numerous others) makes frequent minor-major gestures that correlate vividly with the text. At the same time, however, such mournful texts as those in *Neue Liebe, neues Leben* and *Der Abschied* and the almost morbid *In questa tomba oscura* are given a basically major setting, although they make telling use of harmonic coloration including chromatic movement as expressive illustration.

One rather cautious and tentative generalization might be drawn. Toward the close of the eighteenth century there does seem to have developed a general feeling that minor, as a modal color, was appropriate (but not exclusively so) for expressions of sorrow, longing, poignancy, stress, and so on. Although there are exceptions, some of which have been noted here, most of the songs and arias presented in this mode do reflect a text that is related in some way to these emotional states. It is less likely, however, that the use of major is as consistently or exclusively associated with poems expressing joy, triumph, or general gaiety. Apparently composers felt that such factors as tempo, expressive harmonic excursions (in particular chromaticism), and a gently lyric and pensive melodic line could be used successfully in the service of a sorrowful text even within a basically major tonality. To this extent, then, minor was generally meaningful in its "affective" significance, but major seems to have been less so.

It remained for Schubert to put mode to its most telling and consistent use as a factor in song composition. In view of the voluminous comments that have been made by other writers about this aspect of his approach, it seems unnecessary to cite more than a few typical examples here. They clearly reveal that the use of minor and major, either as a basic color or as an expressive variant, is almost always meaningful in terms of the poetic mood.

The Rückert poem used for *Lachen und Weinen* provides an irresistible opportunity for modal illustration.

Lachen und Weinen	Laughter and tears
Zu jeglicher Stunde	At all hours
Ruht bei der Lieb	Can have so many causes
Auf so mancherlei Grunde	When one is in love.
Morgens lacht' ich vor Lust	In the morning I laughed with pleasure,
Und warum ich nun weine	And why I now weep
Bei des Abendes Scheine,	In the evening light
Ist mir selb' nicht bewusst.	I myself do not know.

Translation from International Music Company edition.

Schubert takes full advantage of the text by setting practically all the references to laughter in major and the references to tears in minor.

Sometimes the composer uses minor to express moods other than sadness, of course. One such example is in his setting of Goethe's lyric from *Wilhelm Meister*, which Schubert titles *Mignons Gesang*. The initial two stanzas, in which Mignon recalls the country of her birth and her childhood home, are given in major, suggesting the fondness of her memories of those happy scenes. But when she recalls her journey across the threatening Alps in the company of her abductors, the mode is changed abruptly to minor:

Kennst du den Berg und seinen Wolkensteg?	Knowest thou the mountain and its cloudy path?
Das Maultier sucht im Nebel seinen Weg;	The mule seeks in the fog its road;
In Höhlen wohnt der Drachen alte Brut,	In caverns sleeps the dragon's ancient brood,
Es stürzt der Fels und über ihn die Flut.	The rock is falling, and over it the torrent.

Translation from International Music Company edition.

Throughout the cycle *Die schöne Müllerin*, fluctuating nuances of mood and situation find their reflection in many ways; perhaps the most consistent of them is an alteration of the established mode. In *Danksangung an den Bach*, where the basic mode is major, at the tentative, wishful question, "Did she direct you? Or have you bewitched me?"[8] minor is used. In *Tränenregen*, for the sudden poetic mood of poignancy in the last stanza, the presentiment of impending sorrow is given in minor: "Then tears welled in my eyes, and the mirror became all ruffled." After eight songs in major, songs that establish the depth of love and the hope of fulfillment, the appearance of the rival, *Der Jäger*, is announced in minor. And in the next song, *Eifersucht und Stolz*, when the miller confesses his annoyance to the brook, the minor mode persists until he sends his message to the maiden: "Say to her: 'He has cut a pipe of reeds from my banks, and

8 This and succeeding quotes from the cycle are based upon translations from the International Music Company edition of Schubert songs.

plays pretty songs and dances for the children,"' which is in major. The use of minor for *Die liebe Farbe*, the constant interplay of major and minor in *Die böse Farbe*—both are involved with textual mood. And again in *Trockne Blumen*, having projected himself into the grave to the accompaniment of the minor mode, the miller imagines his faithless sweetheart wandering past his burial place and, in remorse, recalling the goodness of her departed lover:

Und wenn sie wandelt am Hügel vorbei	And when she passes along the hillside
Und denkt im Herzen: der meint' es treu!	And thinks in her heart: "That was a true lover!"
Dann Blümlein alle, heraus, heraus,	Then, all you flowers, come forth, come forth!
Der Mai ist kommen, der Winter ist aus.	May will have come and the winter be over.

Translation from International Music Company edition.

In Schubert's terms, the expressive direction of this final stanza could be given musical completeness only in a change to major. And how restful is the major mode for the requiem-like final poem of the cycle, *Des Baches Wiegenlied*, where the torments of the rejected suitor are soothed in the cradle of his beloved brook.

In this cycle, as elsewhere, Schubert is also fond of altering modes during the course of dialogues. Thus, in *Der Müller und der Bach,* the saddened miller speaks his lines in minor while the comforting brook is in major.

One of Schubert's earliest and greatest songs, *Erlkönig,* already shows his fondness for major-minor contrast. The fear of the child is heightened by the use of minor (as well as by sharp harmonic dissonances), and the seductive promises of the Erlking are always in major until, significantly, he threatens to take the child by force. Interestingly, the double mood of the father, torn between fear for the infant's safety and a desire to quiet his terror, is reflected in an uneasy alteration between modes. Similarly, in *Der Tod und das Mädchen* the hysteria of the maiden is presented in minor but the soothing promises of Death move smoothly into major.

In general, the use of major and minor persisted throughout the nineteenth century until the breakdown of tonality carried with it the relative loss of meaning for modal color so far as expression was concerned. In Brahms's *Wie bist du, meine Königin,* for instance, when the third stanza refers to the barrenness and sultriness of the desert, the mode moves abruptly from major to minor, retaining this color throughout the stanza except for modulatory movements in preparation for the return of major for the final strophe.

On a larger scale, the same composer's *Vier ernste Gesänge* make striking use of mode to mirror the underlying moods of the texts. The first two songs are bitter in their viewpoint toward both life and death. In death man can hope for no better fate than the animals, and in life suffering and pain are so inevitable that those who have never been born are better off than either the dead or the living. The first stanza of the third song is equally bitter in its denunciation of death as the agent that robs the happy man of his wealth, abundance and satisfactions. Only in the second stanza of this song does the previously prevailing mode of minor change to major in order to strengthen the poetic imagery of solace, which is brought by death to the weary and disheartened. Significantly, the final song, with its glorification of love, remains consistently in major.

The use of mode for musical reflection of text is not confined to nineteenth-century Germany. In France, Reynaldo Hahn found it an attractive device on a number of occasions in his songs. One of the most striking is in his setting of Daudet's *Trois Jours de Vendange.* The first stanza is in E♭ major:

Je l'ai rencontrée un jour de vendange,	I met her on a vine harvesting day,
La jupe troussée et le pied mignon,	Her skirt tucked up, showing dainty feet,
Point de grimpe jaune et point de chignon, etc.	Without her yellow chemisette and without chignon, etc.

But for the second stanza, darker in mood, the setting utilizes the tonic minor:

Je l'ai rencontrée un jour de vendange,	I met her on a vine harvesting day,
La plaine était morne et le ciel brûlant,	The plain was gloomy, and the air was torrid,
Elle marchait seule et d'un pas tremblant, etc.	She walked alone with unsteady steps, etc.

To underline the even heavier third stanza, the mode remains but the key lowers to B minor darkening the color even more severely:

Je l'ai rencontrée un jour de vendange,	I met her on a vine harvesting day,
Et j'en rêve presque tous les jours:	And I dream of it almost daily;
Le cercueil était couvert en velours, etc.	The coffin was covered with velvet, etc.

Translations from International Music Company edition.

The key relationship is an interesting one, being simply the enharmonic spelling of the submediant (C♭) in E♭ minor. However, the use of the minor form of the submediant rather than the major form destroys the original tonic note (the E♭ becomes a D) and thus does away with the feeling of the initial tonal center. This could be interpreted symbolically as bearing a relationship to the loss of life of the woman in the poem, although such esoteric interpretations strike me as being too extreme, perennially popular though they may be.

This particular key relationship is merely an extension of a favorite derivative of minor-major fluctuation—the use of key centers in a primarily major context that belong more properly to minor, and vice versa. In many cases such "borrowed" tonalities simply represent an expanding concept of the general harmonic vocabulary, where the nomenclature of a major tonality is felt to be readily exchangeable with that of its parallel minor. The use of such relationships is not at all uncommon in the work of Mozart and Beethoven, to suggest only two composers of an earlier period. One instance is Beethoven's use in *Die Ehre Gottes aus der Natur* of E♭ major in a harmonic fabric that is otherwise very solidly in C major. On the other hand, as a purely expressive device, use may be made of a single chord borrowed from the variant mode, and in such a manner as to suggest pure text illustration. Example 6.1, from Schumann's *Dein Angesicht*, is most readily seen in such terms:

EXAMPLE 6.1

The use of the supertonic of the variant mode is most effective in under-lining the poignancy of the text: "It is so mild, so angel-like, and yet so pale, so full of pain."

In much the same way, Ernest Chausson in *Le Charme* makes use of the minor subdominant as the song draws to its final cadence, Example 6.2, and it is evident that the motivation is found in the poem's reference to the "first tear."

EXAMPLE 6.2

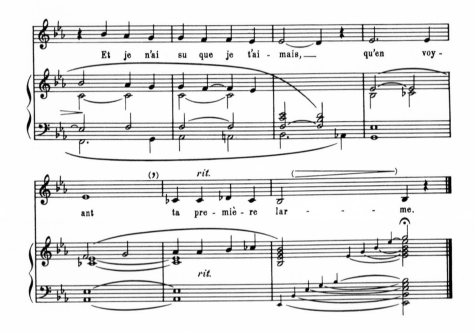

Although the device of lowering the third of the subdominant chord in the course of a plagal cadence has become something of a harmonic cliché, this was not the case when Chausson composed his song. In any case, the utter simplicity of the musical statement is entirely in keeping with the ingenuous quality of the line: "And I only realized I loved you when I saw you shed your first tear."

The sudden insertion of similar "borrowed" tonalities that serve as new key centers (as opposed to modulations to them) can be equally effective in reflecting sudden changes of poetic mood. Schumann's *Widmung* is a case in point. The first exuberant stanza is given in A♭ major with a rhythmically exciting accompaniment figure over which the voice soars ecstatically in a melodic style characterized by relatively large intervals.

Du meine Seele, du mein Herz,	You are my soul, my heart,
Du meine Wonn', o du mein Schmerz,	My delight, my sorrow,
Du meine Welt, in der ich lebe,	My world in which I live,
Mein Himmel du, darein ich schwebe, etc.	My heaven to which I soar, etc.

But the second stanza presents a sharp contrast:

Du bist die Ruh', du bist der Frieden; etc.
You are rest, you are peace, etc.

For this strophe Schumann moves without preparation of any kind into the key of E major, the enharmonic form of the submediant in A♭ minor. Not only does the abrupt key change correspond structurally to the beginning of a new strophe, but it matches equally well the sudden new poetic thought.

Schumann, like Schubert before him, is fond of this particular key relationship and uses it frequently in similar situations. The same device announces the entrance of the witch, Lorelei, in *Waldesgespräch*, the third song of the cycle *Liederkreis*. And again in the fifth song of the *Frauenliebe und Leben* cycle, the ecstatic *Helft mir, ihr Schwestern*, an identical harmonic movement accompanies the mood change from the excitement and happiness of the opening lines to the sudden realization that marriage also means a sundering of family ties: "But you I greet with sorrow, sisters."

Recent investigations in the psychology of music have thrown considerable doubt on the assumption that minor really carries with it a sense of sadness, doubt, or threat, and that major is to be equated with joy, triumph, peace, etc. In spite of this, however, there seems to be considerable evidence to support the contention that such modal color has been used in exactly those contexts, if only because of the conditioning of composers and consumers of music. Such conditioning was an ever increasing factor in song expression throughout the seventeenth, eighteenth, and nineteenth centuries. Much of the manipulation of mode during these periods can be understood only in the light of that ideological background.

More difficult to generalize than the expressive potential of minor and major is the use of particular keys to reflect particular moods. A considerable body of commentary has been devoted to the subject. One of the most exhaustive studies is by R. Hennig, who makes a strong case for a positive expressive relationship between key and absolute characterization of mood.[9] Révész devotes an entire chapter to the problem, but reaches no conclusions that can be generally applied.[10] A number of composers have advanced the proposition that transposition of their works has a destructive effect upon the expressive characteristics. Among this group Beethoven is typical in his

9 R. Hennig, *Die Charakteristik der Tonarten* (Berlin: F. Dümmler 1897).
10 G. Révész, *op. cit.*

opposition to altering the keys of his songs, since such alteration disrupted what he felt to be the absolute character of the pieces.

Besides the psychologists and the composers, musical analysts and commentators have addressed themselves to this subject. Among those directly concerned with song are Eric Sams[11] and Ernest Porter[12]. The former attempts to generalize on Hugo Wolf's approach, indicating that composer's preference for A major in spring songs, D major for contentment or elation, D minor for discontent or anger, and numerous other key-mood affinities. In the end, however, he admits to exceptions and in fact there are so many that no defensible conclusions are possible. Porter, discussing Schubert and his approach to song composition, finds no signs of partiality on the composer's part nor any evidence of an aversion to transposition.

In all likelihood the association of key and expressive content has been more traditional than inherent, and it seems to be even less exploited than the association of minor and major with their assigned characters. The roots of the tradition are to be found, like the major-minor theories, in the Greek doctrine of *ethos*, in terms of which the Dorian mode was used to express solemnity, the Phrygian to convey military inspiration, and so forth. The eighteenth-century preference for F major to project a mood of pastoral simplicity and peace is merely an extension of this same concept. In the course of the nineteenth century keys that utilized an increasing number of accidentals grew steadily in popularity. Lip service was given to the belief that such tonal centers heightened the expression, but it is more likely that their use was motivated simply by a search for remoteness and strangeness as an end in itself. Also involved was the desire to utilize the full possibilities of all instruments, including the piano. In song, where the accompaniment is assigned to a tempered instrument, the coloristic difference between C♯ and D♭ as tonalities becomes totally academic, regardless of what distinctions there may be for an untempered instrument such as the violin. There may be something to be said for the range in which a song is conceived, however. The somber character of Brahms's *Vier ernste Gesänge*, for instance, seems to find a better reflection in the lower vocal registers for which he designed them. But my impression is that, given the immense body of song to which the modern performer is heir, such distinctions demand relatively infrequent application.[13]

Much more in evidence as an expressive device is the obscuring of tonality itself through the delayed entrance of the tonic—a procedure that

11 Eric Sams, *The Songs of Hugo Wolf* (London: Methuen & Co., Ltd., 1961).

12 Ernest G. Porter, *Schubert's Song Technique* (London: Dennis Dobson, 1961).

13 The reader will have noticed, I feel sure, that many of the musical examples cited in this book are given in transposed keys. This is largely due to my own conviction that in songs accompanied at the tempered keyboard there is little argument for insisting upon the presentation of original keys only. The performing repertoire would be severely restricted if singers were confined by academically-imposed limitations to the literature originally conceived for their particular ranges.

is continually exploited in the nineteenth century. Porter cites a number of excellent examples from Schubert, one of which is *Nähe des Geliebten*. In this case, although the key signature suggests G♭, the opening bars of the accompaniment begin in B♭ major and proceed chromatically to a first inversion of the tonic at the voice entrance. A strong establishment of the G♭ tonality is avoided until the initial vocal cadence. As Porter suggests, this places great strength upon the opening poetic statement. The device is appropriate to each stanza of the poem (the composition is strophic) in helping to emphasize the growing intensity of the poetic thought as the singer, in imagination, draws nearer and nearer his beloved.

> I think of you when . . .
> I see you when . . .
> I hear you when . . .
> I am with you, though you are yet so far away . . .

The tonal insecurity here does more than merely spotlight the vocal statement, however. It also sets the mood of longing and lack of fulfillment that is so typical of the poetic imagery. The searching of the opening chromaticism matches with musical imagery the searching of the poet for the presence of his *Geliebten*.

As the harmonic manipulation of the nineteenth century reached a crescendo, this sort of tonal evasion often permeated an entire composition, if the text suggested an appropriate image. Strauss, in his *Ruhe, meine Seele*, provides a harmonic background as chromatically restless as the poet's search for peace. This total fusion of musical and poetic imagery is one of the expressive strengths of the German *lied*, rarely matched outside this medium.

Such tonal vagaries have other implications, of course, sometimes serving principally to give the piano a share in the structural cohesiveness of the song. Schumann opens the first piece of the *Dichterliebe* with a chromatic passage that does not reach the song's tonal center until the voice completes its first phrase. The result here is simply to emphasize the unity of the prelude and vocal line, neither being entirely independent of the other but rather a part of the entire musical fabric. This is one of Schumann's favorite devices; another instance from the same cycle is in *Das ist ein Flöten und Geigen*. In this instance, the promise of the key signature is never fully satisfied in voice and piano simultaneously, sometimes being evaded by pedal points (some on the dominant) and sometimes by cadential deceptions of various types. The evasions do not seem strongly related to poetic imagery, however, although the accompaniment patterns are suited to the dance and the vocal patterns to the trumpet calls. But the harmonic vagaries are more structural than expressive, helping to mask the "cracks" between phrases and sections.

Schumann's use of tonal ambiguity or delay was not always in the service of binding the form, however. His setting of Goethe's *Kennst du das Land* illustrates the use of such harmonic devices in relation to the content of the poem. Few poetic heroines have been as involved as Mignon in the quest for identity. Not only is she unaware of her parentage and her place of birth, but she is totally confused psychologically and emotionally because of the obscurity of her past. Schumann provides a harmonic fabric that reflects this confusion perfectly. Nowhere in his basically strophic format is there a sense of "home," and even the few tentative arrivals at a key definition are immediately frustrated by chromatically deceptive movements. All of this is highly suggestive of the frustrations of Mignon herself.

Ambiguity or delay of tonal definition has a close relative in ambiguity or delay of mode. The line between modal vacillation and modal ambiguity or delay is in fact a very thin one, and not always easy to determine. However, the key signature provided by the composer can often be taken as an indication of his feeling in the matter. In Schubert's *Auf dem Wasser zu singen* the signature suggests A♭ major. Despite this, however, the piano introduction and the first period of the vocal line are in the tonic *minor*. The next phrase is in the submediant of the minor tonality, returning during the succeeding phrase to the tonic, again in minor. Only with the repetition of the last poetic line of each stanza does A♭ *major* emerge. The effect is electric. One might argue here that the final statement of each strophe is simply an extension of the Picardy-third principle. But this does not seem logical in view of the key signature that Schubert provided. It is more likely that he conceived the piece in the major mode but was holding that color for the climactic portion of each stanza in spite of the excessively chromatic notation that this necessitated.

Another instance by the same composer, *Der Wanderer*, seems to show musico-poetic relationships of a more subtle nature than mere climactic punctuation. The key signature suggests C# minor or E major. Nevertheless, the extremely chromatic opening is in C# *major*. Succeeding sections of the song vacillate between the two key signature tonalities or closely related ones, but there are numerous and persistent chromatic passages that tend to confuse the key *and* the mode. The final cadence confirms E major. Both tonal and modal restlessness may be interpreted as a reflection of the imagery of the text, matching musically the poetic expression of homelessness, instability, and longing for security.

Harmonic commentary of all sorts became the stock-in-trade of song composers in the romantic century. The justification for reliance upon harmony as a vital tool for expression lies chiefly in its capacity to project mood. The addition of unexpected harmonic background to even the tritest melody can add an expressive dimension that rescues it from cheapness. Romantic thought was preoccupied with mood for its own sake and harmony is the moodiest of all the materials of music. The intent of the romantic poets was toward the ultimate in pure feeling: emotional states that go beyond the capacity of words to express. They were involved with the mysteries of nature, with the unreachable stars and the silent, brooding night, with death, and with ecstatic and inarticulate love and pain and loss. All of these states of being can best be reflected, in musical terms, through harmonic coloration. Thus the intensely personal expression of the lyric poets found a ready response in the equally intense and personal harmonic excursions of the composers. Because of the sheer wealth of expressive harmonic devices, a complete discussion would demand a full consideration of the style of each individual composer, a procedure patently beyond the range of this study. However, a few typical illustrations can be given.

Reynaldo Hahn catches the poetic implications of Gautier's *Infidelité* in terms of an almost hynotically static harmonic background reinforced with a pedal point that relents only occasionally. The significance is apparent only at the close of the poem.

Voici l'orme qui balance	Here is the elm tree that rocks
Son ombre sur le sentier;	Its shadow on the path;
Voici le jeune églantier,	Here is the young wild rosebush,
Le bois où dort le silence,	The forest, where silence slumbers,
Le banc de pierre où, le soir,	The stone bench, where at eventide
Nous aimions à nous asseoir.	We loved to sit.
Voici la voûte embaumée	Here is the fragrant canopy
D' ébéniers et de lilas	Of ebony trees and lilacs,
Où, lorsque nous étions las,	Where, when we became tired,
Ensemble, ma bien-aimée,	Together, my beloved,
Sous des guirlandes de fleurs,	Under garlands of flowers
Nous laissions fuir les chaleurs.	We evaded the heat of day.
L'air est pur, le gazon doux . . .	The air is pure, the grass is fragrant . . .
Rien, rien n'a donc changé . . .	Nothing, nothing at all has changed . . .
que vous!	but you!

Translation from International Music Company edition.

The last line clearly explains the lack of harmonic movement, as well as the use of pedal points.

Harmonic suggestion may appear as an intensification or even an alteration of poetic emphasis, by giving an expressive direction that might not be readily apparent in a reading of the poem. Such is the case in Fauré's *Fleur jétée*:

Emporte ma folie	Carry away my passion
Au gré du vent,	At the will of the wind,
Fleur en chantant cueillie	Flower, gathered with a song
Et jetée en rêvant,	And thrown away in a dream.
Emporte ma folie	Carry away my passion
Au gré du vent,	At the will of the wind,
Comme la fleur faucheé	Like a cut flower
Périt l'amour.	Perishes love.
La main qui t'a touchée	The hand that has touched you

Fuit ma main sans retour,	Shuns my hand forever;
Que le vent qui te sèche,	Let the wind that withers you
O pauvre fleur,	Oh, poor flower,
Tout à l'heure si fraiche,	A while ago so fresh,
Et demain sans couleur,	And tomorrow colorless,
Que le vent qui te sèche,	Let the wind that withers you,
O pauvre fleur,	Oh, poor flower,
Que le vent qui te sèche	Let the wind that withers you,
Sèche mon coeur.	Wither my heart.

Translation from International Music Company edition.

The language here suggests no dramatic outburst; one feels rather, because of the emphasis upon *wither, perish, dream,* and *colorless,* an almost morbid sense of lifeless abandonment of passion and feeling. Fauré's reaction to the poem was entirely different, however. He apparently saw the poetry as a reflection of bitter and thrusting rejection. Not only does he permeate the musical texture with a driving rhythm and an exciting and dramatic melodic line, but he adds the force of harmony—chromaticism, successive dissonances, restlessness created by ever fluctuating key centers. Thus a new dimension has been added by the music, a dimension that speaks to the *result* of the poetic content rather than to the content itself. This music feels the way the poet must feel because of the poetic situation. It reflects the bitterness that follows loss. The reaction in the music is to the resentment and frustration that accompanies the loss of love rather than to the decay of the emotion itself.

The power of harmonic movement is perhaps strongest when deception is involved. As a structural device, the deceptive or interrupted cadence has served to decompartmentalize the musical fabric, to encourage the flow of musical movement from beginning to end of a composition rather than from phrase to phrase or part to part. The application of deception creates an increasing unity in songs from Schumann onward, but apart from its mechanical utility, it assumes an expressive responsibility in the work of some composers.

Schubert makes extensive use of it for indicating a change of scene or poetic direction. In *Kriegers Ahnung* the shifting tonal centers serve constantly to delineate stanza separations, but at no point is the key expectancy more meaningfully evaded than between the first and second strophes. The text of the initial stanza, given in C minor, is heavy with foreboding:

In tiefer Ruh liegt um mich her	In deep sleep lies around me
Der Waffenbrüder Kreis;	The circle of my brothers-in-arms;
Mir ist das Herz so bang und schwer,	My heart is so anxious and heavy,
Von Sehnsucht mir so heiss.	So passionate in longing.

Translation from International Music Company edition.

A brief piano interlude alternating between tonic and dominant anticipates the return of the tonic for the opening of the second stanza. But, reflecting the change of poetic mood, the second stanza begins with a deceptive movement to the submediant. The text:

Wie hab ich oft so süss geträumt	How often have I sweetly dreamed
An ihrem Busen warm!	Close to her warm bosom!
Wie freundlich schien des Herdes Glut,	How warmly gleamed the glowing hearth
Lag sie in meinem Arm!	As she lay in my arms!

Translation from International Music Company edition.

The song continues to exploit stanza, mood, and key relationships, although much of the treatment is repetitive enough to overburden the poetic substance with what might be considered an excess of musical rhetoric.

Schumann is particularly adept at focusing on the most striking imagery in the poem and using an equally striking musical device to dramatize it. In his *Tief im Herzen trag' ich Pein*, for instance, the richest image is in the lines:

Wie der Funke, frei und licht,	Like the spark, that free and shining,
Sich verbirgt im Kieselstein,	Hides inside the pebble's core,
Trag'ich innen tief die Pein.	Deep inside I bear my sorrow.

Translation from International Music Company edition.

To introduce the second line Schumann uses an accompaniment motive that has already been utilized and has been regularly harmonized with a dominant-to-tonic cadence in G minor. At this point, however, while the motive is identical, the harmonic movement is from dominant to submediant. The element of surprise is important in bringing the full attention of the listener to bear on the words.

Deception came also to symbolize the romantically unrealized desire for the resolution of the dissonances of pain and sorrow. In this sense, a delay of the promised harmonic fulfillment can create an atmosphere of continual frustration, of hope never completed by achievement, or desire never satisfied. It is partially in this expressive context that the harmonic evasiveness of Wagner and his followers must be understood. Mahler, in his *Kindertotenlieder*, creates a harmonic texture that is permeated with deception, symbolic of the longing of the father for the impossible return of his departed children as well as of the impossibility of fully understanding the meaning of death. Thus the musical materials are put to use as imagery, not to illustrate individual words or phrases, but rather to imbue the entire fabric of sound with musical connotations that match those of the poetry. The same cycle makes extensive use of appoggiaturas in the same expressive format of yearning for completeness. They are usually specific to the word or phrase in which they appear, but they are at the same time such an insistent element as to become almost an expressive cliché, although they certainly bear musico-poetic justification.

On the negative side, infatuation with harmony for harmony's sake is often all too apparent in the nineteenth century. Many songs, even by composers as skillful and dedicated as Wolf, are so meandering as to be almost incoherent. That composer's *Auf eine Christblume*, for instance, drifts about endlessly, changing accompaniment styles almost as often as it exchanges tonal centers. The motivation may well be present in the poem —the search for harmonic stability can be seen as illustrating the search for the flower itself. But from the standpoint of relative expressive weight, it seems to me that the musical symbolism outweighs the poetic imagery. Cooper recognizes some of the dangers as well as the underlying reasons for such overemphasis when he comments on Schumann's settings of the *Wilhelm Meister* songs:

Painfully oppressed by the philosophic significance of Mignon and the old harp-player, he rambles on in a portentous, pseudo-symphonic style, with frequent modulations and unnatural vocal phrases, losing the thread of the poem and of his own musical design.[14]

Schumann and Wolf were not alone in having this problem; it resulted from the aspirations of the romantic century. The attempt to reach the heights of musical expression quite naturally led to excesses of all sorts. The use of over-ripe harmonic illustration was no exception.

SUMMARY

Of all the elements of music, harmony probably has the greatest strength as an expressive force. Unaided, it can create a climate of expectation, frustration, surprise, and even encourage a mood of foreboding, brightness, longing, or any of the myriad other emotional states that poetry might evoke. It is in these contexts that harmonic color and manipulation has most consistently served the musico-poetic enterprise. As a factor in the definition of stylistic variations among periods and composers it is an invaluable tool.

---

14 Gerald Abraham (ed.), *Schumann, A Symposium* (New York: Oxford University Press, 1952), p. 110.

7

Melodic and Rhythmic Imagery

Powerful though it may be, harmonic color is not the only agent of expressive possibilities in music. Melody and rhythm, sometimes in close alliance, have long been recognized for their effectiveness. Some of the most interesting and exhaustive comments on these two musical factors as they function in arousing a meaningful response are to be found in the discussions of the baroque period, in particular those which deal with the doctrine of *Affekt*. The excerpts quoted at the beginning of Part II were concerned primarily with the minor-major dichotomy, but numerous others are directed toward melodic and rhythmic devices.

The interest in such devices was fostered by the assumption, allied with the then-new recitative style, that speech and melody can complement one another in a rhetorical fashion—or, to be more exact, that the musical figurations chosen by the composer can be so organized and presented that they correlate effectively with the figures of speech that are indispensable to the rhetoric of language in its role of expressive projection. Treatises on the art of composition and musical theory traced such procedures in detail, suggesting guidelines to the proper use of musical materials so that they would match the "affect" of the text. Manfred Bukofzer summarizes both the philosophy and its application, as well as indicating helpful original sources, in his chapter on "Musical Thought in the Baroque" from his study, *Music in the Baroque Era.*[1] His work should be consulted for a deeper understanding of the subject than could result from the brief synopsis given here.

One original source, a 1638 publication by Monteverdi, *Madrigali*

---

1 Manfred F. Bukofzer, *Music in the Baroque Era* (W. W. Norton & Company, Inc., 1947). See especially pp. 388–390. A more detailed exposition is given in Chapter 8 of Beekman C. Cannon, Alvin H. Johnson and William G. Waite, *The Art of Music* (New York: Thomas Y. Crowell Company, 1960). For those readers familiar with German, the readily available sources are, among others: Johann Mattheson, *Der volkommene Capellmeister* (1739) (Bärenreiter-Verlag, Kassel und Basel, 1954). Joseph Müller-Blattau, *Die Kompositionslehre Heinrich Schützens in der Fassung seines Schülers Christoph Bernhard* (New York: Bärenreiter, 1963).

guerrieri ed amorosi, articulates in the Foreword the close connection between
rhetoric and melodic rhythm.

> I have reflected that the principal passions or affections of our mind are three,
> namely, anger, moderation, and humility or supplication; so the best philosophers
> declare, and the very nature of our voice indicates this in having high, low,
> and middle registers. The art of music also points clearly to these three in its
> terms "agitated," "soft," and "moderate." In all the works of former composers
> I have indeed found examples of the "soft" and the "moderate," but never of the
> "agitated," a genus nevertheless described by Plato in the third book of his
> *Rhetoric* in these words: "Take that harmony that would fittingly imitate the
> utterances and the accents of a brave man who is engaged in warfare."[2]

Monteverdi goes on to explain that he has devised a system of rapid
sixteenth notes that satisfy the "affect" of anger, and he expresses the
conviction that with this innovation music has become perfect, having
added anger to its other two characteristics, softness and moderation. In
support of his thesis he offers a book of madrigals of war and love.

By the middle of the period attempts were being made to express one
single affection that would remain constant throughout an entire composition, unifying the expression. In this connection, Mattheson cautions that
care should be taken to avoid tone painting of individual words or phrases
which, by their too specific character, are apt to disrupt the unity of
expression[3].

Bukofzer emphasizes the fact that the same musical figures may serve
different purposes in differing contexts and that their definite significance or
meaning is dependent upon a text or title.

> Since they did not "express" but merely "presented" or "signified" the affections,
> musically identical figures lent themselves to numerous and often highly diver-
> gent meanings. It is therefore misleading to isolate certain figures and classify
> them in a system of absolute meanings as motives of joy, steps, beatitude, and so
> forth. Nor should these procedures be misrepresented as emotional program
> music or as the psychological expression of feelings. The affections were non-
> psychological, static attitudes and were therefore peculiarly fitted for musical
> representation.[4]

This would seem to imply that the author considers music somehow in-
capable of projecting psychological attitudes. His statement is difficult to
reconcile with the practice of the period. It is not clear from the statement
exactly how a musical figure can "signify" something without thereby
being meant to carry a certain expression, especially if we are dealing with
emotional states, such as joy or sorrow. However, it is not necessary to

2 Oliver Strunk (ed.), *Source Readings in Music History* (New York: W. W. Norton
& Company, Inc., 1950), p. 413.

3 Mattheson, *op. cit.*

4 Bukofzer, *op. cit.*, p. 389.

quibble about semantics at this point. What is most important is the fact that the composers, performers, and listeners of the day apparently felt strongly that certain musical complexes possessed the ability to represent their counterparts in affective language. Schweitzer does, in fact, develop an extensive rhetoric of expressive motives in his study of J. S. Bach.[5] He catalogues the musical material of the chorales specifically by their motivic representation of peace, grief, joy, tumult, etc. As Bukofzer suggests, this may be carrying the matter too far and it could possibly account in part for the fashionable pastime of deriding Schweitzer's scholarship. In any event, it dramatically illustrates the close connection that can be made between music and word, in Bach's work as well as that of his high baroque contemporaries.

For purposes of discussion it might be admitted that it is at least theoretically possible to distinguish between a musical configuration that "expresses" and one that "signifies." A basis for such a distinction might be between the use of musical material that creates a mood on the one hand, and that merely illustrates or tone paints on the other. In actual practice, however, the two functions sometimes overlap.

Italian song from the seventeenth and eighteenth centuries is quite revealing. An example in point is Alessandro Scarlatti's *Va per lo mare*.

Va per lo mare, che la circonda,	The little boat, over wave after wave,
onda per onda la navicella,	Sails on the sea which surrounds it.
Così il mio core nel mar d'amore	In like fashion, my heart, in the sea of love,
Or scende or s'alza	Now descends, now rises,
Come la sbalza la tua procella.	As it is thrust about by the storm you create.

> Translation from International Music Company edition.

The basic imagery here is the relationship between the boat tossed by the sea and the heart tossed by love, both in waves of some violence. The general "affect," then, would be one of turbulence. Scarlatti responds to this suggestion with a musical realization befitting the scene in its use of a triplet figure in undulating motion. Although it is introduced in the accompaniment during the four measures preceding the entrance of the voice, it does not occur in the vocal line until the word *onda* (wave) and is restricted to that word alone. The only other vocal illustration of importance occurs in a descending pattern at *now descends* and ascending at *now rises*, both of which are quite specifically representative. Neither figure is derived from the accompaniment pattern or the wave motive. It is certainly an academic question whether any of these melismatic passages are intended to convey a general sense of "affect" or are meant to be definitely illustrative at isolated points in the text. It seems to me that both functions are at work simultaneously. Just how much the undulations of the melody and accompaniment serve to arouse a feeling of unrest in the

5 Albert Schweitzer, *J. S. Bach* (New York: The Macmillan Company, 1949).

listener, an "affect" commensurate with the expressive core of the poem, is largely a matter of individual reaction, of course. There is a strong suggestion that the relationship existed in the composer's mind and there is every likelihood that the musical patterns carry two different but related responsibilities, one representative and the other expressive. A good deal of the music of the period relies on just this sort of duality and it is fruitless to attempt to separate representation from expression.

When the poem is not so obviously pictorial there is greater opportunity to respond musically to the mood itself rather than to visual suggestion. Legrenzi's *Che fiero costume* is less oriented toward tone pictures than is Scarlatti's. The text in part:

Che fiero costume	What ruthless ways
D'aligero nume,	Has the winged god!
Che a forza di pene	By wounding us
Si faccia adorar!	He makes us fall in love!

Translation from International Music Company edition.

The poem continues in the same vein, rather bitterly denouncing the fate of the poor soul who is tricked by a pretty face. Uppermost here is the vehemence of the poet, the sense of angry frustration at being duped by Cupid, and the turbulence of renunciation. The short lines of the Italian and the relentless feeling of the meter[6] combine to give a sharpness and curtness to the sentiment. Legrenzi captures the mood in musical terms with his syllabic treatment of the words and his driving melodic line. The musical imagery is consistent enough to justify the supposition that this is not mere illustration but more a direct reflection of the "affect." The music, by its vigorous forward thrust, arouses the sensations of vehemence and curtness that form the expressive core of the poem. One would assume, then, that this is a successful realization of the principles Mattheson projects.

The most influential and widespread formal arrangement of baroque vocal music was the *da capo* aria, and it was particularly well suited to the musical delineation of text. It provided for a change of musical material for the *b* section and this was designed usually to reflect the change of text that accompanied it. In the following portion of a solo cantata by Benedetto Marcello, the poetic and musical images are altered in just this manner. The text:

Lontananza e gelosia son le pene,	Separation and jealousy are the punishments
Che mi tolgono ogni bene,	Which make me unhappy
Che m'affliggono così	And afflict me so.

6 This is brought on in part by the use of *scenario* verse, which tends to regularize the accent. In this case the meter transcends its mechanical function by adding an expressive dimension with quite definite musico-poetic overtones.

Non ha pace l'alma mia,	My soul has no peace,
E infelice abbandonata pensa sempre	Unhappy, abandoned, it thinks always
A quell'ingrata che partendo la tradì.	Of the ungrateful one who, in leaving me, betrayed it.

The affective sentiments here are the bitterness and sense of being chastised that the poet is complaining about. But the last three lines, which are set as the *b* section of the aria, project an image that is doleful and melancholy rather than resentful, and the language itself is less vigorous than in the opening lines. In Marcello's realization some slight but noticeable homage is paid to the differences.

The sharply dotted, ragged rhythms of the first section, in combination with the often disjunct nature of the melodic line create an impression of sturdy complaint and considerable angry resentment (Example 7.1).

EXAMPLE 7.1

The center section retains enough of the original musical character to insure a feeling of continuity, but offers a more lyric melody, Example 7.2, which is appropriate to the change of poetic language.

EXAMPLE 7.2

Of importance, too, is the sparser use of dotted rhythms in this section, an expressive contrast to the *da capo* portion.

The poetic and/or musical affect of the sections is not always differentiated in this manner, however. The main departure is often in key rather than in melodic or rhythmic character. The following text from a piece by Giovanni Bononcini is representative:

Se ti piace di farmi morire	If it pleases you to let me die,
Vo' morir, ma lontano da te,	I will die, but far from you,
Che di morte è più crudo il martìre	For my anguish is more cruel than death
Quando penso che manchi di fe'.	When I think of your unfaithfulness.

Translation from International Music
Company edition.

The opening section uses a gently flowing melody (Example 7.3) in keeping with the sentiments expressed in the poem.

EXAMPLE 7.3

Se ti pia-ce di far-mi mo-ri-re   Vo' mo-rir, ma lon-ta-no da te,

Copyright by International Music
Company.

The center section, Example 7.4, is obviously a closely related derivative, altered by a key change and very slight melodic modification.

EXAMPLE 7.4

Che di mor-te è più cru-do il mar - tì - re   Quan-do

Copyright by International Music
Company.

The only significant departure from this sort of musical fabric in either section is the presence of a sixteenth note roulade on one of the many repetitions of *lontano* in the *da capo* portion and a similar treatment of the word *penso* in the *b* section. Such devices often serve merely to bring into prominence what the composer feels are words deserving of special attention—they serve as spotlights, that is, as opposed to being associated with any deep expressive significance. The implications of harmony should not be overlooked. One of the very important expressive devices in both sections is the use of harmonic color on the emotion-bearing words *morire* and *martire*. This type of illustration has had a long and fruitful history in song composition, as has been indicated in Chapter VI.

Not all baroque solo vocal music was cast in the *da capo* mold, of course. There was a considerable body of song that was strophic. In such pieces, if the affective figures were too specific in nature, they sometimes ran into conflict from stanza to stanza. One such is found in Falconieri's *Occhietti amati*, where the very expressive melisma on *fiamme* (flaming) in the first stanza is meaningless in the second and third stanzas where the words are *io* (I) and *tua* (your), respectively. As a general rule, the strophic compositions from the mid-seventeenth century onward were more successful in expression to the extent that they avoided specifics of affective illustration.

The search for affecting musical figures led to the exploitation of melody simply as melody. Some of the most glorious tunes, fully expressive in their own right, are found in the vocal music of the high baroque period. But invitations and opportunities for virtuosic display are everywhere apparent. Add to this the contemporary demand for extemporaneous ornamentation and wide-ranging roulades and it becomes clear that the overwhelming emphasis was not upon depth of musico-poetic synthesis but rather upon musical opulence, principally vocal—which means melodic.

At the same time, however, growing interest in harmonic clarity based strongly in common-chord techniques led away from the highly descriptive melodic types that are characteristic of baroque style. In place of motivic organization, apparent in all music of the early eighteenth century but particularly well suited to vocal works where the motives are "explained" in the text, the tendency became ever stronger, as the century advanced, to seek out melodies that were clearly and regularly phrased, based upon tonic, dominant, and subdominant harmonies, and even relatively restricted in range. A growing interest in folk song was one of the important shaping factors, and it encouraged a type of nonillustrative tunefulness, idiomatic to that style. A great many songs of the last half of the century tend to be melodically pleasing with a certain general appropriateness to the text of the poem but little more than a superficial expressive relationship. The rhythms of the poem are followed in a metrical sense rather than in a way that would bring out the subtleties of poetic movement; concentration is upon musically oriented declamation rather than careful poetic delivery. Much of this is caused by the general insistence upon regularity and clarity of the musical substance itself.

Concurrently, some of the more musically sophisticated composers who gave some attention to song, notably Mozart and Haydn, often carried into their compositions the excessively decorative and descriptive melodies of the Italian opera. In such cases, the poetic expression more often than not was lost in the musical detail. Many of the Haydn songs were originally designated as "Pianoforte Songs," in fact, and were published in such a way that they could be performed as solo compositions for piano just as readily as by voice and accompanying piano. The obvious conclusion is that the words must have been of little more than subsidiary concern, and the songs themselves often bear this out. Melodic ornaments of all sorts fall on words like *the* or *and* as well as on unaccented syllables. This cannot be excused as a translation problem because the original texts in many cases were English, and those in German show no more word-tone awareness.

From the standpoint of depth of expression, then, the period is not a rich one for song. The simpler types tend to be too spare and general in musical substance and the more elaborate types tend to overwhelm the poem with musical superfluities. This is not meant to imply that the melody of the period is inexpressive; it is, in fact, among the most beautiful to be found at any stage in the development of Western music. What is missing for the most part is a desirable synthesis of musico-poetic relationship. An additional hampering factor is the fact that, with a few important exceptions, the songs are cast in the strophic format even though the poems themselves are seldom of such a generalized nature as to make this entirely satisfactory. Haydn himself complained about the poets' failure to establish a uniform mood. And, in addition, the music is so satisfying *as music*, apart from the words, that the great bulk of the song literature of the time can be readily transcribed into music for instrumental solo or ensemble with little or no loss of expression or appeal.

Toward the end of the century, an additional factor was introduced that inhibited the development of a melodic concept that might have resulted in a more meaningful synthesis of tune and word. Stendhal writes in 1817:

Melody reached its zenith about 1780; [and he is talking here about melody *as* melody, for its own sake] after this date, music changed its nature, harmony won the upper hand, and the singing line declined.[7]

Along with the decreasing attention paid to sheer opulence of vocal tune came an increase in the importance of motivic exploitation in the accompaniment as an expressive factor. This is a characteristic of Schubert's songs that has gained him great respect. The "water" motives in his accompaniments to *Die schöne Müllerin* are not merely descriptive (although they are certainly that), but expressive as well. The character of the accompaniment in *Danksagung an den Bach*, for instance, tells us a great deal about how the singer feels about the brook. At first it is a happy, singing stream. But it can both comfort and share the unhappy lover's pain in *Der Müller und der Bach*, and it not only sings a lullaby but becomes a rocking cradle in *Des*

7 Quoted in Bence Szabolcsi, *A History of Melody* (New York: St. Martin's Press, 1965), p. 159. This is a well documented work that should be consulted for elaboration of the generalizations I have drawn in this discussion.

Baches Wiegenlied. These are more than just accompaniments, even though they are deceptively simple; they are characterizations.

Nor is it uncommon for the commenting motives to appear in sections where the voice is not active and then recede in favor of the vocal melody, as in *Lob der Tränen.* Although the key of this song is D major, the introductory piano material (which appears consistently as interlude and postlude) suggests D minor through its use of the minor subdominant and the poignant melodic augmented second. Obviously this is a commentary on the symbolism of the text and is meant to duplicate it in musical imagery of wistful melancholy.

This mood of melancholy and wistfulness seems to have become crystallized in the melodic figure of the sixth, major and minor, ascending and descending. It is the significant interval in the introductory material of *Lob der Tränen*, and occurs repeatedly in other works throughout the romantic century. A similar instance is in the first song of Schumann's *Dichterliebe*, where it occurs in the piano prelude as an ascending interval and in the vocal line as a descending skip.

The whole business of assigning meanings to particular melodic figures is a hazardous one, but tempting. If we are to acknowledge, with Deryck Cooke, that the figure 5–6–5 in a minor key is a musical symbol for grief[8], there could be no better evidence than in the third song of Berlioz's *Les Nuits d'Été—Sur les Lagunes*. This doleful lament, beginning with the words, *Ma belle amie est morte, je pleurerai toujours* (My fair friend is dead, I will mourn forever), is permeated with the melodic figure that Cooke has identified. Introduced initially in the accompaniment, where it recurs with almost maddening frequency, it appears repeatedly in the vocal line as well. At the climax of the piece, an outburst of passionate sorrow, Example 7.5 occurs:

EXAMPLE 7.5

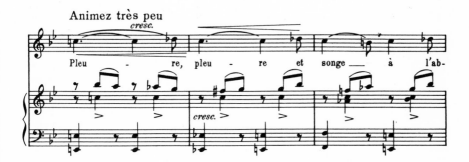

8 Cooke, *op. cit.*, p. 146.

Here both the piano and voice insist on the figure. The dying strains of the
song, both vocal and pianistic, are reiterations of the motive. There can be
little doubt that, for Berlioz at least, the figure carried all the expressive
significance assigned to it by Cooke.

Unfortunately for anyone trying to build a case for a consistent use of this
particular melodic formula in identical contexts, however, the figure has
been used for other expressive purposes. Wolf, in his *Und willst du deinen
Liebsten,* exploits what is only a slight variation of it in entirely dissimilar
circumstances (Example 7.6).

EXAMPLE 7.6

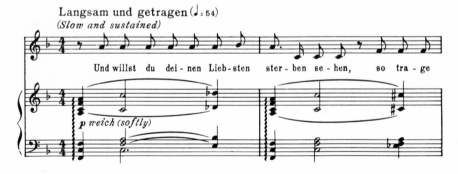

The fact that the minor sixth degree appears in a major context has little
bearing on its melodic significance. The same thematic material recurs
throughout the song, varied rhythmically and carried into first one tonal
center and then another. The poem itself is not a sorrowful one in spite
of the opening words: *Und willst du deinen Liebsten sterben sehen* (And if you
wish to see your lover die). On the contrary, the piece is extremely sensuous

in every way and the undulating melodic contour of the motive, together with the richly insinuating harmonic excursions, create an atmosphere as voluptuous as any found in the *lieder* repertoire.

It would seem, then, that melodic motives work expressively in relation to the context in which they appear rather than in any absolute sense from composition to composition. Without perceptibly relying upon any stereotyped motivic "meanings," Debussy fully exploited the expressive possibilities of motivic-harmonic insinuation in his mature songs. Nowhere in the literature, probably, is there a set of pieces as sensuous as his *Chansons de Bilitis*. Not only is the harmonic vocabulary of impressionism a complex of sounds deliberately designed to arouse what certainly corresponds to a sexual response, but the almost sly insertion of brief, tantalizing melodic motives into the accompaniment texture serves to suggest rather than to develop or extend the musical ideas. Climactic points are seldom in the same directly dramatic vein as in *lieder*, although they are certainly capable of stirring the imagination. Example 7.7, from *La Chevelure*, has nothing if not passion—but it belongs properly to the boudoir, more than to the recital hall.

EXAMPLE 7.7

As far as the motivic structure itself is concerned in this particular song, the basic material is sparse and simple—a chromatically descending line that is initiated in the accompaniment in the first measure, picked up by the voice on its entrance, and carried through numerous transformations in the course of the composition. The nature of chromaticism as it appears in such contexts seems peculiarly well suited to suggestion rather than statement, in fact, and when combined as it is here with such an openly suggestive text, the texture is one of purple seduction. The "midnight" mood of Debussy's

tantalizingly dissonant harmonic vocabulary is appropriate in every way as
a coloristic background to the melodic motives as well as to the imagery of
the poem. The erotic symbolism of the hair is a much exploited one in the
drama and poetry of the period, possibly because of the association with
going to bed, which must surely have involved loosening the tresses from
the elaborate coiffures of the day. Thus freed from its restrictions, the hair
became an object for boudoir-oriented attention, and hence a symbol of the
ultimate in intimacy.

The use of motives for concurrently structural and expressive purposes
is also apparent in Samuel Barber's *Dover Beach*. Reference was made earlier
to the tone-painting characteristics of the leading motive that pervades this
extended song. But aside from its pictorial effectiveness, it also relates to the
deeper symbolism of the poem. The poet is drawing an analogy between the
ebb and flow of the sea's tides and the ebb and flow of religious faith. The
"wave" figure with which Barber infuses the musical texture both looks and
sounds like the undulating motion of the sea. In addition, as Barber puts it
to use, the figure rises to climactic points and falls away from them, much
as in a symbolic sense faith itself tends to climax and subside. At no point
is this put to more dramatically impressive use than in the measures quoted
in Example 7.8:

EXAMPLE 7.8

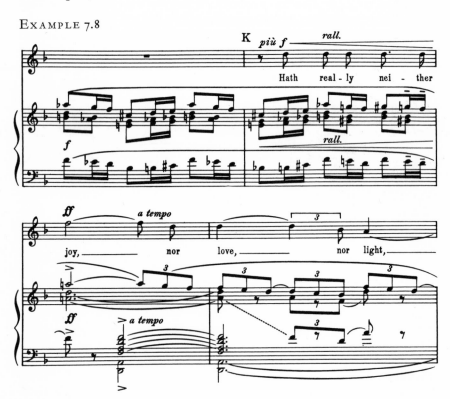

Nor cer-ti-tude,— nor peace, nor help for pain;—

Here the mutation of the original motive into a relentlessly descending pattern matches the musical imagery precisely to the poetic imagery—the rushing out of faith, the ebb of the tide, the total denunciation of the text. This is physical description as well as psychological mirroring.

In a format more given to symphonic techniques than Barber's, Brahms unifies the *Vier ernste Gesänge* through the use of motivic material that suits the varying emotional suggestions of the texts and yet has definite structural significance. The *ostinato* pattern of the initial song, as relentless (and empty) as death itself, tends to bind the musical material as well as to project the symbolism of despair found in the Biblical quotations. Introduced first in the accompaniment, it invades the vocal line and continues to operate through much of the song. The departures from it are based largely upon passages derived from a broken outline of the diminished seventh chord, a motive that carries over in varying permutations into the next two songs. As an ascending pattern it is wonderfully suited to the dramatic outcries of the first piece and as a descending figure it serves to symbolize the oppression and wailing of the second song as well as the heaviness and dissonance of death in the third.

The *ostinato* principle has been a useful device in song, often involving harmony and rhythm as well as melody. Wolf uses it with great expressive power in a number of his pieces, one of the most effective of which is *In der Frühe*.

Kein Schlaf noch kühlt das Auge mir,	No sleep has yet refreshed my eyes,
Dort gehet schon der Tag herfür	But the daylight is already seen
An meinem Kammerfenster.	Through the window of my room.
Es wühlet mein verstörter Sinn	My distracted mind is seized
Noch zwischen Zweifeln her und hin	By all sorts of fears
Und schaffet Nachtgespenster.	And produces nightmares.

—Ängste, quäle	Do not fear,
Dich nicht länger, meine Seele!	Do not torture yourself any longer, my soul!
Freu dich! schon sind da und dorten	Rejoice! Already here and there
Morgenglocken wach geworden.	Morning bells have awakened.

Translation from International Music Company edition.

The principal musical responsibilities are invested in the accompaniment *ostinato*, which persists throughout the song. The first and darker portion of the poem is given in a series of four different key centers, all but one in minor. The thematic material is reiterated in each. The final four lines, more hopeful in character, are given similarly in four tonal areas but all in major, while the *ostinato* continues unabated. The result is not only structural unity but expressive depth as well. The harmonic excursions correlate with the poetic implications of passing time and changing moods. The rhythmic persistence relates both to the heaviness of the opening lines and to enduring faith of the final statement. The melodic figure serves to bind the whole fabric into a unified musical texture. Meanwhile, the voice is given a typical Wolfian line, which combines elements of lyricism and recitative, allowing for clear articulation of the text, which is so important to the understanding of all elements of the composition.

Other instances of the exploitation of expressive commenting motives in the work of the same composer are found in *Auf einer Wanderung, Agnes, Im Frühling, Der Musikant,* and innumerable others. The principle of motivic insistence is Wagnerian, closely related to the *leitmotiv* concept, and it is as well suited to the short song form as to the more fully developed music-drama. Much of the heightened expressiveness of the late romantics is a result of this kind of motivic independence in the piano. Where the accompaniment is freed from its role as a mere support for the vocal line, it can develop its own commentary, offer its own interpretation of the textual imagery, and thereby assume much of the expressive responsibility. At the same time, the voice is able to take on a corresponding freedom of declamation. These factors in combination constitute the basis of lyric-recitative, which became such a meaningful tool in the hands of all composers who came under Wagner's influence, directly or indirectly.

Those composers of our own century who have not simply echoed the stylistic mannerisms of late- and post-romanticism have shown even greater resource in the use of motivic manipulation, but often this has been primarily formalistic. Linear byplay within the accompaniment as well as between accompaniment and voice is typical of the work of Barber (*Mélodies passagères, Hermit Songs*), Britten (*A Charm of Lullabies, Seven Sonnets of Michelangelo*), Rorem (*Rain in Spring, As Adam Early in the Morning*), and many others. Those who have been drawn to the school of dodecaphony and its derivatives, of course, find the use of melodic-rhythmic mutations an inevitable tool of the trade, usually (but not exclusively) in the service of construction. In a practical sense, the fluctuating and often experimental nature of recent harmonic theory and practice has left the song composer with melodic-rhythmic manipulation as his most consistently reliable inheritance from the past. The return to contrapuntal principles has tended to minimize the effectiveness of harmony as a coloristic device, so that motivic interplay has become increasingly important.

SUMMARY

Like harmony, the forces of melody and rhythm have been utilized for expressive purposes in song. They have served as the principal motivation not only in creating the sense of forward motion and slackening of pace, but also in articulating emotional climaxes or in painting musical figures that echo the imagery of the text. Changes and developments in melodic style are often directly related to the type of poetry available to song composers, but they are also connected to the general musical aesthetic of the time or the individual. In many cases the melodic interplay between voice and accompaniment has been of great significance in the relation between poetic and musical imagery.

III

The Flux of Style—
A Chronological Survey

Introduction

B<small>ECAUSE</small> I have been most concerned in this study with variations in style rather than the total output of song, there has been a deliberate attempt to limit illustrative material. Typical examples only, rather than all possible ones, have been suggested in connection with each subject. In the same sense, the survey that follows is conducted under certain restrictions.

The limits I have set are in terms of the importance of varying *types* of song and the influences that bear upon them. For this reason, many fine and beloved songs and composers will not be mentioned, not because they are insignificant in terms of available performing repertoire but because they suggest neither a meaningful departure from the prevailing norms nor an unusually important stylistic contribution to those norms. As has been acknowledged in the introductory remarks to Part I, relatively detailed accounts of song composition and composers are available and serve the purpose of surveying the field in a quantitative sense. There is no point in duplicating this material. I am concerned more with the fluctuating ideals that have guided and controlled the differing emphases given to song composition from the seventeenth century to the present day.

Solo vocal music of the late sixteenth and early seventeenth centuries throughout Europe was characterized by a disenchantment with polyphony as a satisfactory context within which the text might be projected. This disenchantment was almost universal, although its manifestations varied from place to place.

The most dramatic rejection of the polyphonic style occurred in Italy, where the experiments of Caccini, Rinuccini, Peri, and others led to the establishment of what was to become the standard vocal utterance of opera and the solo cantata. The new style allowed the voice a remarkable range of expressive freedom, providing at the same time an opportunity for all sorts of virtuosic display.

A parallel in France was the change in style of the sixteenth-century *air de cour*, a change characterized by a movement away from rhythmic regularity and melodic "folkiness" toward a more highly ornamented type of composition. Although sometimes published in part-song arrangements, the airs were most frequently performed to the accompaniment of a lute, and are thus monodic in conception. Their popularity on the continent led, according to Bukofzer, to their counterpart in England, the lute song.[1]

Like the *air de cour*, the lute song was conceived in its earliest form as a composition appropriate for either solo or ensemble performance. The first collection appeared in 1597—John Dowland's *First Booke of Songs or Ayres*—and the title page bears the following inscription: "SO MADE, THAT ALL THE / parts together, or either of them / severally, may be sung to the Lute, / Orpherian, or Viol de gambo."

In Germany, the trend toward vocal monody was quite gradual. The transition from the polyphonic canzonets, the *Tenorlieder*, the villanelle, and similar concerted types reached a midpoint with Hans Leo Hassler's *Neüe teütsche Gesäng* in 1590 but did not come to fruition until the appearance in 1623 of Johann Nauwach's collection of *Arie passegiate*, unashamedly based upon Italian sources. More characteristically German is the same composer's *Teutsche Villanellen* (1627).

From the outset of the interest in solo song, two general tendencies are apparent. On the one hand is the emphasis upon vocalization, embellishment, expressive illustration of text both melodic and harmonic, and similar theatrical elements. On the other hand is an awareness of the demands of poetic structure and, together with this, a curtailment of the more flamboyant musical devices in favor of a format with greater harmonic and melodic clarity and a more generalized, less illustrative reflection of the text. In a general sense, the lute song and the German *continuo lied* represent the latter type, while the more florid and colorful Italian songs and the *airs de cour* are typical of the former.

Throughout the succeeding three centuries the operatic and song styles stand in some dichotomy to one another, although influences of one upon the other are never entirely absent. At all stages, although with varying degrees of intensity depending upon time and place, the two streams of solo vocal expression can be found—one almost folklike, the other involved with artifices and theatricalisms of all sorts. Not until very late in the nineteenth century were the characteristically operatic and song idioms brought to bear concurrently in a truly sensitive way in the service of both music and poetry. Any adequate study of the shifting patterns of song composition and musico-poetic expression must recognize that the intimate character of the true song has continually fought for survival alongside the vocally dramatic influence of the opera. Sometimes the fight has been successful, sometimes not.

Within this context, it is the purpose of this section of the book to discuss the music and poetry of the songs that have persisted in the performing repertoire since the appearance of Dowland's first collection of airs in

[1] Bukofzer, *op. cit.*

England and the *Nuove Musiche* of Caccini in Italy. As has been indicated, it will be necessary to restrict the discussion severely to those examples that best illustrate various concepts and stylistic characteristics. Nor will there be extended consideration of song literature that has not survived in readily available performing editions, although such literature has often great historical importance. Reference will be made to these relatively neglected song types, however, when it can be demonstrated that they were influential on the main stream of song composition.

The Baroque

THE LUTE SONG

O F A L L the song types that have flourished since the beginnings of the seventeenth century, none had a shorter life span than the English lute song. Initiated by John Dowland in 1597, the greatest activity continued only until about 1617, the date of the fourth book of songs by Thomas Campian, although a collection by John Attey did appear in 1622 as the final example of the type. Although performance was possible in an ensemble situation, the more popular style was as solo with lute accompaniment and it is in this format that the songs have survived and become part of the current repertoire. Thanks to the pioneering work of Edmund Fellowes, the pieces are available in transcriptions for the keyboard and voice as well.[1] Performance can be satisfactory in such an arrangement, but much of the peculiar appeal of the songs is lost without the intimate character of the lute accompaniment. In the absence of a qualified lutenist, the best compromise is probably either a guitar or a harpsichord.

The most representative composers of the school are John Dowland, Thomas Campian, and Robert Jones, who issued the greatest number of collections. Dowland's four volumes appeared in 1597, 1600, 1603, and 1612. Campian published five, the first of which he shared with Philip Rosseter in 1601, followed by two of his own about 1613 and two more about 1617. Jones brought out five groups, the first in 1600 and the fifth in 1610. While numerous other composers, including Thomas Morley and Thomas Ford, contributed one or more collections of considerable musical value, their work tends to reiterate the stylistic patterns established by Dowland and Campian.

It is possible to make a few generalizations about the songs themselves, although there are many significant exceptions. They are for the most part cast in the strophic format and tend to phrase in musical units that correspond to the poetic line. There is frequently a disregard for run-on lines,

---

1 Edmund Horace Fellowes (ed.), *The English School of Lutenist Song Writers* (London: Stainer & Bell, 1920 *et seq.*).

even in the work of the poetically sensitive Campian, who provided his own verses. The general practice is to provide no introductory material for the lute except occasionally a beginning chord—this is particularly true in the earlier songs—and little interlude music, although this varies from composer to composer. In most of the settings there is provision for the repetition of the last section of the song, normally comprising the final two poetic lines. In some cases, as in a six-line stanza, this provides a means of musical balance, the result falling into a pattern of two double periods musically. In other cases no such symmetry occurs and the effect is merely an emphasis of the final poetic statement of each strophe.

Harmonically the pieces follow the general patterns of the period. The feeling for key is unsettled, compared to later baroque music, with a great deal of vacillation between major and minor feeling. This is primarily a result of the contemporary convention that insisted upon the use of a major chord at all medial and final cadences. Chromaticism is not unusual and is most often associated with somber, soulful, or extremely passionate passages in the text. Except for the chord relationships which result from the still-embryonic sense of tonality, the use of minor and major as a primary mode (apart from the cadence convention just mentioned) is related to poetic mood. The favorite keys are G, D, C, and F, although others do occur.

Melodically the songs tend to a tonal rather than a modal character, although a carryover from the modality of the previous century is sometimes found. The greatest influence here is probably the madrigal tradition, out of which the lute song most certainly evolved. In general the treatment is syllabic and rather direct rhythmically, but here again there is variation among composers, Dowland being perhaps the most imaginative. In spite of the avowed dedication to treating the words carefully from the standpoint of accentuation, barbarisms occur with some frequency. This factor is difficult to tie down, of course, since the barring is quite irregular, in keeping with the contemporary notational practices. Nevertheless, syncopes are used in numerous contexts where they cannot be disguised and in many cases the effect is more defensible musically than poetically. The vocal ranges are limited, normally involving no more than an octave, there are seldom any extensive roulades or illustrative passages, nor is there widespread exploitation of dramatic melodic intervals that would call attention to the voice in an instrumental sense.

The general texture of the songs retains much of the polyphonic, imitative character of the preceding period. This is, of course, in sharp distinction to Italian practice of the same years. In this sense, the lute song must be seen as an adaptation of already established musical practices rather than as a rejection of tradition. Still, there is considerable variation among the approaches of the composers. Dowland is inclined to involve the lute much more intricately than is Campian, especially in his later songs. Thomas Morley is even more elaborate, frequently employing extensive introductions and interludes.

The statement by Philip Rosseter in his 1601 *Book of Airs* (of which half were Campian's) is helpful in delineating the general objectives of the lutenist song writers. Addressed "To the Reader," it projects the following principles (I have modernized the spelling):

What Epigrams are in Poetry, the same are Airs in music, then in their chief perfection when they are short and well seasoned. But to clog a light song with a long Præludium, is to corrupt the nature of it. Many rests in Music were invented either for necessity of the fugue, or granted as a harmonic license in songs of many parts: but in Airs I find no use they have, unless it be to make a vulgar and trivial modulation seem to the ignorant strange, and to the judicial tedious. . . . The lyric Poets among the Greeks and Latins were first inventors of Airs, tying themselves strictly to the number and value of their syllables, of which sort you shall find here only one song in Sapphic verse, the rest are after the fashion of the time, ear-pleasing rhymes without Art. The subject of them is for the most part amorous, and why not amorous songs. . . ? But there are some, who to appear the more deep and singular in their judgement, will admit no Music but that which is long, intricate, bated with fugue, chained with syncopation, and where the nature of every word is precisely expressed in the Note, . . . But such childish observing of words is altogether ridiculous, and we ought to maintain as well in Notes, as in action a manly carriage, gracing no word, but that which is eminent, and emphatic. . . .[2]

The plea for simplicity of execution is clearly put, and most of the songs do substantiate it.

Campian, of all the lutenists, provides the most direct and uncomplicated approach to the text, both musically and in his treatment of the poetic rhythms. This is undoubtedly because he is a poet first and a musician only incidentally. In 1602 he published his *Observations in the Art of English Poesie*, a brief but concise exposition of his poetic theories. In it he gives a good deal of attention to the various poetic meters, the weight and length of the varying syllabic schemes, and the like. It is not surprising, then, to find him carrying over, especially in his earlier songs, a fairly literal transfer of poetic rhythms into musical rhythms. Songs like *I Care not for these ladies, Follow thy fair sun, When to her lute Corinna sings, Follow your saint*, and most of the others from the first collection, make appropriate rhythmic shifts of gear to match the fluctuating rhythmic patterns of the poetry. The problems he does encounter are most frequently the result of reluctance to use a pickup musical attack even when the verse form would seem to suggest one (as in *Though you are young*, or *My sweetest Lesbia*) and an uncomfortable habit of sometimes sustaining an insignificant syllable (as in *Though you are young*, where he gives a great deal of musical importance to such words as *am, is,* and *do*) in order to continue a musical rhythm that apparently attracts him.

Campian's poetic rhythms are remarkably fluid and when he is able to devise a musical scheme that successfully reflects them, the result can be

2 Quoted in Fellowes, *op. cit.*, Vol. IV.

favorably compared with the best work of the great song composers of any age. The following is typical of some of his finest work:

> Follow your Saint, follow with accents sweet;
> Haste you, sad notes, fall at her flying feet.
> There wrapped in cloud of sorrow, pity move,
> And tell the ravisher of my soul I perish for her love.
> But if she scorns my never-ceasing pain,
> Then burst with sighing in her sight and ne'er return again.

Relying upon a strictly chordal type of accompaniment and a gently undulating melody without rhythmic complexities of any kind, the musical setting of the irregular fourth and sixth lines comes off perfectly naturally. Campian is equally successful with the mixture of iambs and trochees that give such striking interest to the first two lines of the poem. He employs an identical sort of mixture in one of the songs from his *Fourth Book of Airs*, which Fellowes dates as *circa* 1617. The poem:

> Love me or not, love her I must or die.
> Leave me or not, follow her needs must I.
> O that her grace would my wished comforts give!
> How rich in her, how happy should I live.

Interestingly enough, in setting this text (there are two additional stanzas), Campian borrows from his earlier song and uses the identical tune and rhythm as in the first two lines of *Follow your Saint*, with slight harmonic modifications. Having stolen that much of his former inspiration, however, he fashions an entirely different period for the closing two lines, in keeping with the metric patterns of this later poem.

Perhaps because he was not himself as accomplished a lutenist as Dowland, Campian's accompaniments do not show a wealth of musical imagination. The lute rhythms very frequently double the melodic rhythms, and almost as often consist of merely supporting chords. The result is a texture quite like a hymn or even a folk song. His tunes are typically made up of a first section consisting of a period repeated literally or with only minor modifications, followed by a second section of different material that is formally somewhat freer. Sustained notes are most apt to occur primarily at cadence points, which, in turn, emphasize the rhyme scheme. There is rarely a temptation to illustrate the text, although such passages do occasionally occur. One particularly effective one is in *Beauty is but a painted hell* from the *Fourth Book of Airs*, where there is quite meaningful major-minor fluctuation in direct relationship to the text.

Another even more pictorially oriented section is in *Mistress, since you so much desire*, from Campian's group of songs in Rosseter's 1601 *Book of Airs*. A harmonic sequence is provided that exactly mirrors the following text

by moving from A minor to B major to C major to D major, and the melody
line ascends sequentially at each repetition:

> But a little higher; but a little higher,
> But a little higher; but a little higher, etc.

The song itself is an interesting commentary on Campian's developing
control of his musical materials as well as his sometimes bawdy poetic
taste. Published first as a very sedate endeavor, not notable for melodic or
rhythmic imagination, it appears in his *Fourth Book* in 1617 in a much more
facile musical realization and considerably revised textually in the direction
of lewdness. The sequences described above are retained in the second
version, although much of the balance of the composition is greatly varied.
Since the tendency in some quarters is to regard the lute song generically
as an almost effeminate type, it might be well to give the texts of both
versions as testimony that the poetic content was not always as delicate as
the sound of the accompanying instrument.

MISTRESS, SINCE YOU SO MUCH DESIRE
(1601)

> Mistress, since you so much desire
> To know the place of Cupid's fire,
> In your fair shrine that flame doth rest,
> Yet never harboured in your breast.
> It bides not in your lips so sweet,
> Nor where the rose and lilies meet,
> But a little higher,
> There, O there, lies Cupid's fire.
>
> Even in those starry piercing eyes,
> There Cupid's sacred fire lies,
> Those eyes I strive not to enjoy,
> For they have power to destroy.
> Nor woo I for a smile or kiss,
> So meanly triumphs not my bliss.
> But a little higher
> I climb to crown my chaste desire.

The change of orientation revealed by the 1617 version of the poem is a
commentary on the lustiness of this invigorating period in England's
history:

> Beauty, since you so much desire
> To know the place of Cupid's fire,
> About you somewhere doth it rest,
> Yet never harboured in your breast,
> Nor gout-like in your heel or toe,
> What fool would seek Love's flame so low?

But a little higher
There, O there lies Cupid's fire.

Think not, when Cupid most you scorn,
Men judge that you of ice were born.
For though you cast Love at your heel,
His fury yet sometime you feel.
And where-abouts, if you would know,
I tell you still, not in your toe,
But a little higher,
There, O there lies Cupid's fire.

A similar strain of sensuality runs through many of the poems, although the great majority treat the tender sorrows or joys of love and courtship more delicately. The principal departure from a concentration upon the problems of amorous adventures is found in the 1613 *First Book of Airs*, which contains a group of eighteen songs that are religious in nature. Campian's own address to the reader in this latter publication gives some indication of his objectives in song writing:

In these English Ayres I have chiefly aimed to couple my Words and Notes lovingly together, which will be much for him to do that hath not power over both. The light of this will best appear to him who hath pays'd [*i.e.*, paced] our Monasyllables and Syllables combined, both which are so loaded with Consonants as that they will hardly keep company with swift Notes, or give the Vowel convenient liberty.

A comparison of his early songs with those in his later collections reveals that he did gain more "power" over the musical problems of text setting. The awkward declamation of such songs as *Your fair looks, Hark, all you ladies,* and *Come, let us sound with melody* from his 1601 group is not in evidence in 1617. The poetry itself in the later books tends to be more regular metrically, so that musical rhythms are not required to fluctuate awkwardly. At the same time, Campian becomes less reluctant to repeat poetic phrases when repetition can serve text and music in a complementary fashion. As a result, the texture of the last songs is more supple, more relaxed musically, and much less forced in every way. This undoubtedly accounts for the fact that Campian is best remembered for songs like *There is a garden in her face, Love me or not,* and *I must complain* from his last book.

By contrast to Campian's, the songs of John Dowland bear evidence of his complete mastery of musical materials. Dowland was not only an accomplished performer who traveled widely on the European continent and was showered with recognition everywhere; he was a tremendously skillful composer. His command of the lute, and the musical sophistication that resulted from his contacts with music and musicians in all the major European cultural centers are reflected in his settings. As the first of the

lutenists to turn his attention to song, and because of his consummate skill
in the use of musical materials, it was he who established most of the
stylistic characteristics of the genre, characteristics that were modified only
slightly by those who followed him in the field. Campian is the most
significant exception to this generalization, possibly because of the imbalance between his powers as a poet and his skill as a musician.

Only in his late songs does Dowland provide introductory material for
the lute. The one exception is the first song of the second collection (1600),
I saw my lady weep, and this introduction is extremely brief. In general the
fourth book, entitled *A Pilgrimes Solace*, contains the most elaborate pieces.
Among the contents are three songs for voice, lute, treble viol, and bass
viol. All are extended compositions in a full-blown chamber ensemble
idiom, employing extensive text repetition, adventurous harmonic devices,
introductory and interlude material of considerable length and musical
importance—in short, the most colorful features of the Italian school.
One of the songs is, in fact, set to an Italian text, *Lasso vita mia*; the other
two are *Go, nightly cares* and *From silent night*. Several of the succeeding
songs in the book are equally ripe musically, although not scored specifically for an ensemble, among them *In this trembling shadow cast* and *If that a
sinner's sighs*. These are not really typical of Dowland's usual style. It should
be mentioned, however, that a 1610 collection entitled *A Musicall Banquet*
contains several pieces in this vein, most notably the hauntingly beautiful
In darkness let me dwell, which makes extensive use of text reiterations,
colorful dissonances, chromatic passages, and dramatic declamation as
well as having a long introductory passage and many accompaniment
interludes.

Dowland established a principle of text setting that became typical of all
the lutenist song writers, with the exception of Campian. He tends to provide a separate musical idea for each poetic line rather than building his
melodies largely on repeated phrases or sequential patterns. There are
exceptions, of course, but for the most part repetitions and sequences
are reserved for repetitions of textual words or phrases where they share
both a poetic and a musical importance. In the later songs this becomes
less true, primarily because repetitions become more numerous and reliance
upon identical or similar musical patterns could easily lead to dullness.
In any case, the tendency to associate distinctive musical material with
individual poetic lines lends a sort of rhapsodic character to many of the
songs, a character that becomes more and more pronounced in the course
of lute song-development. Among the many advantages this effects are the
strikingly pure declamation and the careful attention to verbal import,
particularly evident in Dowland's work, but which also appear in that of
other composers, depending upon their degree of sensitivity. An additional
factor is the irregularity of the barring, which frees the poetry from the grip
of a metrically repetitious accent.

Dowland shows considerable skill in setting his poetry without falling into formal traps. In *It was a time when silly bees* from the *Third Book of Airs* (1603), for instance, he has the following run-on line to deal with:

> And in that Time I was a silly bee
> Who fed on Thyme until my heart 'gan break,

Although there is a perfectly acceptable cadence on the word *bee*, the next phrase is marked by a rest after the word *Thyme*. It is quite natural and easy to sing across the cadence, making the line connection entirely satisfactory, and the articulation created by the rest that follows *Thyme* brings the pun into nice focus.

An even more troublesome passage is found in *To ask for all thy love* from the 1612 *A Pilgrimes Solace*, where the poem reads, in part:

> I do not sue
> Nor can admit,
> Fairest, from you
> To have all; yet
> Who giveth all hath nothing to impart
> But sadness.

The difficulty is the word *yet*, acceptable as a rhyme for *admit* in terms of the period, but not easy to fit into the phrasing. Dowland solves the problem by means of partial disguise, avoiding a strong cadence at *To have all*, but nevertheless beginning the next measure with yet, which ties it in musically and syntactically to the following line. While the device is successful for the first stanza, in which the problem occurs, it creates problems of its own in the succeeding two, where there is no run-on at the same place. This is the perennial problem of strophic composition, of course, and it furnishes yet another piece of evidence, if one is needed, that composers traditionally treat the first strophe and let the rest come along as best they can. However, these and similar compensatory gestures on Dowland's part do tend to distinguish his work from that of Campian and other sometimes less adept composers of lute songs.

A revealing comparison can be made between Campian's setting of his own poem, *I must complain,* and Dowland's. The poem is extremely hard to treat in both stanzas, but particularly in the first.

> I must complain, yet do enjoy my love;
> She is too fair, too rich in beauty's parts.
> Thence is my grief: for Nature, while she strove
> With all her graces and divinest arts
> To form her too too beautiful of hue,
> She had no leisure left to make her true.
>
> Should I aggrieved then wish she were less fair?
> That were repugnant to my own desires.
> She is admired; new suitors still repair

> That kindles daily love's forgetful fires.
> Rest, jealous thoughts, and thus resolve at last:
> She hath more beauty than becomes the chaste.

The problem begins in the third line and continues through the fifth, and only the most irregular musical realization could do justice to the syntax. Neither Campian nor Dowland come off with complete success, but the latter certainly is more imaginative.

Campian sets the first two lines with a six-measure period, which he repeats literally for the next two lines. The final two lines use new musical material and are, as is usual, repeated. Not only does the repetition of the last two lines pick up a dependent portion of the poetic text, but the run-on nature of the poem itself is totally uncompensated for in Campian's musical realization. Although the music itself is quite regular and even attractive, almost no musico-poetic synthesis is brought to the sense of the poem.

Typically, Dowland provides a setting that is much freer musically, as well as slightly repetitive textually. The first two lines present no problem and he treats them rather simply except for emphasizing the first three words by giving them sustained notes in a slow rhythm and underlining them with solid chords. Rather than trying to disguise the *caesura* in the third line, he sets *Thence is my grief* as the most dramatic portion of the song —held notes in the voice, high in register, and highlighted by a melodically interesting and chromatic accompaniment. Having gotten that portion of the line out of the way, he moves along in fairly straightforward fashion musically until the end of the fifth line. There are cadences and there are rests (singers need to breathe), but the music itself moves in a fairly regular flow. The one "bridge" that is not handled with complete adequacy is the movement from the fourth to the fifth poetic line. The traditional repeated portion with which most lute songs close is given by Dowland to the final poetic line, rather than to the last two lines as in Campian's setting. And he emphasizes the text through two repetitions of *She had no leisure*, thus extracting enough words to satisfy his musical needs. The result is a much more pliant and graceful song than Campian's and one that contrives to salvage a considerable portion of the syntax without entirely disrupting the musical logic.

One of the formal distinctions that can be made in Dowland's development as a song composer is concerned with the traditional repetition of the final section of his songs. All but two of the pieces in his first collection indicate the repeat. In the second group, published in 1600, only three years later, there are eleven songs that do not involve repetition. The third and fourth collections include five and ten songs respectively in which no final repeat is suggested. The reasons are not clear, but the effect is certainly more poetically satisfying.

Dowland shows considerable imagination in the area of formal organization. In the famous *Lacrimae* (*Flow my tears*) from the *Second Book of Airs,* in which the poetic stanzas are relatively short and there are five to deal with, he sets the first two stanzas to the same music. The third and fourth employ different material, and the final strophe yet another musical realization. The effect is something between strophic modification and through composition. The same device is used in the third book for *O what hath overwrought?*, a three-stanza poem in which Dowland sets the first two stanzas identically and departs for the third. Because of the frequently free rhapsody that characterizes the composer's approach, the one-stanza poems practically always emerge as through composed, of course. Such cases are *If that a sinner's sighs, Lady, if you so spite me*, and *In darkness let me dwell*, among others.

The harmonic style of Dowland and his fellow lute-song composers is typical of the practices of the period. Many of the songs are perfectly tonal, in the modern sense of the word, often even projecting a feeling of strongly related key centers and applied dominants. Others retain a feeling of modal progressions, placing, for instance, E♭ major alongside an established context of F major, or juxtaposing F major on G major without benefit of what present-day ears would accept as a modulatory gesture. The establishment of consistent key relationships and tonally oriented modulations is only intermittently apparent. Much of the chromaticism still results from melody lines within the accompaniment rather than from decisive harmonic progressions, as in the later years of the seventeenth century.

Typical of the vacillatory sense of key is the renowned *Weep you no more, sad fountains*, in which the strongest feeling is G minor, but which employs tonal centers of F major and D minor in a modal style. Another of the unusually archaic characteristics of this piece is the final cadence on what strikes modern ears as being the dominant (D major). The last section of the piece does suggest some hesitancy between D minor and G minor. The final appearance of D major is simply in compliance with the conventional use of major chords for cadences, and it accounts for the uncomfortable sense of being suspended on a dominant chord that does not resolve. Also involved in the frequent use of nondiatonic key relationships is the tendency to compose phrases of different material for each poetic line. This often produces not only a series of melodically independent segments but (within certain limits) ones that are harmonically independent as well.

Dowland is sparing in his use of purely illustrative passages of a tone-painting nature, relying more upon general musical mood. He resorts to them occasionally, however, and one very effective and extended section is in *Sorrow, stay,* from the *Second Book of Airs*. Probably the temptation was too great to resist at the words:

> But down, down, down, down I fall
> And arise I never shall.

Amid much repetition of the text, he illustrates *down* with repeated descending scale passages and *arise* with ascending scales. The piece is otherwise quite elaborate, extremely rhapsodic in style, often with sharply different musical textures used for adjoining phrases or sections, and includes numerous interludes.

It was not unusual for the lutenists to score their songs for duets or dialogues for two voices, sometimes even adding a concluding section for chorus and soloists together. Dowland provides a number of these concerted types of composition in several of his collections and they give the impression of being small chamber cantatas. This is perfectly in line with the announced possibilities of most of the songs—ensemble performance—but on a more organized scale.

Nor is Dowland reluctant to use musical quotations. The popular *Now, O now I needs must part,* from the *First Book of Airs,* is based entirely on a borrowed tune. In the same group of songs is *Can she excuse my wrongs?,* where the final section is devoted to a chantlike melody in the voice. The lute is given a popular song, identified by Fellowes as *Shall I go walk the woods so wild?,* the words of which are appropriate to the sentiment of Dowland's song text.

A word should be said about the general character of the poems that attracted this foremost of the lute-song composers. Although there are exceptions, the poetry tends to project a mood of melancholy and the poignancy of lost or betrayed love. Like Campian, he bases some of his songs upon religious themes (primarily in *A Pilgrimes Solace*). There is no sign of the bawdiness in which Campian sometimes indulges himself. Nor do many of the poems concern themselves with rollicking or spritely themes, with the significant exception of the charming *Fine knacks for ladies.*

The work of Robert Jones must be at least briefly recognized, if for no other reason than that he was so prolific. Fellowes admits in the prefaces to Jones's collections that the editor's task is a hazardous one because of what appear to be numerous printer's errors in the original printings. Regardless of the reasons, the music itself does reveal a strangely undeveloped sense of harmony in comparison to other lutenist composers. The occurrence of cross-relationships, as Fellowes points out, is much more pronounced than in the songs of Campian and Dowland. There are numerous instances of the use of an F$\sharp$ in the accompaniment against an F$\natural$ in the vocal line, or vice versa. Another of his harmonic peculiarities is the frequent use of parallelisms, one of his favorites being D minor to E minor to F major or the reverse. Even more shocking (and related to cross-relationships) is his use of F minor to E minor to D major. On innumerable occasions he begins a phrase in G minor and cadences in B$\flat$ major, jumping back immediately to G minor for the opening of the succeeding phrase. Likewise, he does not hesitate to state a phrase quite firmly in G minor, cadencing on the dominant but moving without warning to B$\flat$ major for the opening of the succeeding phrase. The result is not quite modal, not quite tonal, and extremely unsettled.

Aside from these rather annoying habits, undoubtedly rooted in the ill-defined harmonic practices of the period as well as in a certain lack of imagination, Jones uses a relatively uncomplex musical texture. Like Campian he prefers block chords with very little interweaving of the accompaniment voices, sparse interludes, few imitative passages, and uncomplicated rhythms. His use of text repetition is even more pronounced than Dowland's, and he almost invariably sets the reiterations to either the same musical notes or a sequence of them. Also like Dowland he offers a goodly number of duets in the course of his five groups of songs, most of which are of greater musical interest than his solo pieces. They employ quite skillful imitative passages between the voices, often involving the lute as well, and often use a considerable amount of melismatic material. His taste in texts is cosmopolitan, running the course from melancholy to flippant, conversational to pensive. Even more than Campian, he is attracted to the earthy, and some of his songs are frankly lewd.

Taken as a group, the lute songs represent a strong surge in the development of interest in the solo song with accompanying instrument. They were never really designed for public performance, although many of the composers themselves, Dowland in particular, are known to have presented them to small gatherings. Intimate and quite personal in style and design, they are an altogether satisfying expressive medium within the limits of their musical and poetic range. Although they lay unnoticed in library archives until Fellowes issued them in suitable editions over a period of years from 1920 onward, the songs have since enjoyed considerable popularity and have been widely recorded and performed. The slightly archaic harmonic style has a particular appeal to historians, but the songs are accessible to any type of audience since they represent in every way the beginnings of more modern musical practice. Although they are almost exactly contemporaneous with the outbreak of Italian monody, there are relatively few points of comparison between the two types, either in content or intent.

ITALIAN MONODY

One feature shared by Italian monody and the English lute song is the fact that both developed from the practice of adapting ensemble music to use in solo performance with an accompanying instrument or instruments. At first such pieces retained much of their polyphonic character, but there is evidence to suggest that a polyphonic texture was felt to be unsuited to the expression of the text, whether used by a group or a soloist. In a letter to Caccini written about 1580 by Giovanni de' Bardi, the latter decries the use of contrapuntal techniques that obscure the words and confound the ears. He cautions Caccini:

In composing, then, you will make it your chief aim to arrange the verse well and to declaim the words as intelligibly as you can, not letting yourself be led astray by the counterpoint like a bad swimmer. . . .[3]

3 Oliver Strunk, *op. cit.*, p. 295.

Although the reference was to music for ensemble singing as well as for solo performance, Caccini must have put the suggestion to use. In the Dedication to *Euridice* (1600), he refers to compositions that he had written "many years ago" (*i.e.*, about the time of Bardi's letter), which he was to publish in his *Le nuove musiche* in 1602. In the latter work, he identifies these same compositions as madrigals for a single voice and expresses the belief that "they had more power to delight and move than the greatest number of voices singing together."[4] The pieces in *Le nuove musiche* are true solo songs, with the most meager accompaniment suggested over a *basso continuo*, an accompaniment that allows for no distraction from the vocal expression. Thus, while the desire to provide music suitable for accompanied solo singing was the same in Italy and England, the motivating factors and the results were sharply differentiated. The lute song was destined to exert no really lasting influence upon the development of song as a genre, either in England or elsewhere. But the work of Caccini, carried into the field of early opera, set a pattern for solo vocal performance that was to serve throughout Europe for nearly two centuries until the emergence, with Schubert and his immediate predecessors, of the true *lied* style.

There seem to have been two distinct types of early Italian monodic song. One, usually referred to as the madrigal (but not to be confused with the five-voiced ensemble pieces that continued to flourish both in England and Italy during a part of the seventeenth century), was a piece that allowed for the greatest vocal liberties, including suitable changes of tempo and dynamics, and that encouraged the insertion of embellishments of all sorts. The accompaniments to madrigals were chordal for the most part, with sustained bass notes (usually performed on a string instrument) beneath a harmonic texture that normally changed with relative infrequency. The keyboard players were urged not to devise figurations that might detract from the interest of the voice (the bearer of the all-important text), although they were at the same time encouraged to add musical interest at cadences or at such places as might be acceptable without disrupting the vocal expression. The singer, in turn, was cautioned against indulging in purely decorative flourishes, reserving his technique for only those expressive devices that would most enhance the text. Uppermost in the minds of all involved performers was supposed to be the projection of the deepest passions of the words, along with a rejection of any artifices that would interfere or call attention to themselves.

The other style of monodic song was the aria (not to be confused with the later piece called by the same name, which was extracted from the opera, cantata, or oratorio), generally patterned after dances and employing dance rhythms. Here the bass moved more regularly and at a quicker tempo, and although the accompaniment was often just as chordal as in the madrigal, it was also more apt to double the rhythms of the voice rather than moving only when a harmonic change was demanded. In essence, the madrigal was

4 *Ibid.*, p. 379.

a type of recitative—painstakingly declaimed, richly expressed, sparsely accompanied, and performed with considerable freedom. The aria, on the other hand, was more tuneful in conception, rhythmically regular, allowing little time or opportunity for embellishment, and relatively well regulated in performance. In addition, it was most likely to be strophic in composition whereas the madrigal was more rhapsodic in conception.

Because of the very nature of the madrigal, it was an invitation to text illustration of all sorts—pictorial as well as emotional—despite the abhorrence with which such procedures were viewed by some commentators and theorists. As early as 1581, a treatise was published entitled *Dialogo della musica antica e della moderna*. Its author, Vincenzo Galilei, was one of a group known as the *Camerata*, of which Bardi and Caccini were fellow members, from whose discussions and experiments Italian monody, in fact, evolved, and he treated the practice of text illustration in no uncertain terms. Incensed at the tendency to imitate by musical means such words as *fly, weep, laugh, harsh chains, shriek*, and numerous other examples, he denounced such imitation out of hand. Nonetheless it crept into even the earliest efforts of the seventeenth-century composers, and turned up fully developed in Da Gagliano's *Valli profonde* in 1615.

Likewise, the emphasis on vocal expression that the madrigal encouraged could have had no other result than the complete domination of the music by the virtuosity of the singer. This was the tool by which the performer could assert his command of the craft of singing, and it was not long before the operatic *castrati* had assumed tyrannical control over public performance throughout Europe, a control that extended to musician and librettist alike. In many ways, it was this very tyranny over both compositional style and performance practice that impeded the development of real song on any large scale. For song remained a private or small-group occupation; it simply could not compete with the vocal pyrotechnics and theatrical demands of the opera and its derivative types of expression.

Any discussion of the differences inherent in Italian monody and English song of the early baroque must take into account the basic dichotomy not only in compositional motivations and performance practices, but also in the music itself. The lute song was a finished product for the most part. All the accompanying parts as well as the vocal melody were given on the page. Not only the harmonies but the movements of individual voices in the lute were indicated in the tablature—with no suggestion of improvisation or on-the-spot "realizations" on the part of the performers. Presumably the singer and the lutenist (if they were not the same person) had only to follow the notation and add whatever expressive involvement they were capable of. This was never the case with the Italian monodic song. The accompaniment directions consisted of the barest figurings above a single bass line, figurings that indicated most but by no means all the harmony. That the realization of these scanty directions was neither obvious nor easy is evidenced by the number of baroque treatises devoted to instructions for playing from a figured bass. At the same time, the singer was expected to add in no inconsiderable measure to the melody on the page, from the standpoint of suitable ornamentation and embellishment. In addition he was expected to heighten the expression to a large degree by the very way he used his vocalization abilities. This is made clear by Caccini in *Le nuove musiche*, where he gives detailed instructions on what we would now consider vocal production, including evaluations of the use of falsetto and other singing devices.

The result is that the re-creation of this music presents innumerable obstacles for the present-day performer. The meaningful description of stylistic characteristics is likewise full of pitfalls simply because the musical characteristics are not as clear-cut and open to analytical appraisal as is the music of later periods. One can recognize certain melodic and harmonic tendencies in the lute song. But in Italian monody, what is on the page is actually only part of the story, so that the nonspecialist is largely at the mercy either of the editor or of his own imagination.

The problem may be illustrated quite succinctly by reference to a single factor of some harmonic importance: the use of major and/or minor chords at cadence points.[5] In discussing the lute song, I pointed out the almost universal custom of employing major chords for all cadences, medial and final. An examination of the music is enough to verify this, since the harmony is fully spelled out in the lute tablature and the keyboard transcriptions of it given by Fellowes in his editions. Thus there seems to be no good reason to question the existence of the tradition. But that was in England.

In Italy, Agostino Agazzari, in a 1607 treatise entitled *Del sonare sopra il basso*, states unequivocally:

Since all cadences, whether medial or final, require the major third, some musicians do not indicate it; to be on the safe side, however, I advise writing the accidental, especially in medial cadences.[6]

This would seem to indicate that the convention was current not only in England, but in Italy as well. Despite this, however, there is no consistency among the editions of early Italian song that have been made available to the performer. One would assume that Agazzari's statement is based upon actual practice rather than upon his own theories, since he is concerned in his article with instructions for playing from a figured bass rather than with the theory of the figured bass itself. In other words, he is giving directions for realization, not merely suggesting compositional safeguards.

5 Robert Donington addresses himself to this problem in his *The Interpretation of Early Music* (New York: St. Martin's Press, Inc., 1963, pp. 80–84) as it relates to the use of the leading tone. I go into the matter in some detail because of its application to performing editions, upon which most singers must inevitably rely and concerning the idiosyncrasies of which they are often completely unaware.

6 Oliver Strunk, *op. cit.*, p. 426.

And we might logically deduce that the statement would apply to music of at least the immediately preceding years as well as of the years that would immediately follow his instructions of 1607.

Two songs will illustrate the problems that such harmonic conventions present to the editor, the performer, and the commentator attempting a definitive account of style. Among the most widely circulated pieces from the earliest years of Italian monody are the *Lamento* from Monteverdi's opera *Arianna* (1608) and the solo madrigal *Amarilli* from Caccini's *Le nuove musiche* (1602).

Although the complete score of *Arianna* has not been preserved, the *Lamento* (*Lasciatemi morire*) was published in several forms by Monteverdi. It appeared first as a solo song, later as a five-part madrigal, and still later as a sacred monody entitled *Pianto della Madonna* in an extensive collection, *Selva Morale et Spirituale*. All three versions are reproduced in the set of Monteverdi complete works edited by Malipiero. Only one of the versions, the five-part madrigal, indicates the composer's complete harmonic realization, however, and here all the cadences are given as major. The other two versions involve the realization of a figured bass, which is all that Monteverdi supplied, of course. In both instances, the editor has used three minor cadences, including even the immensely important final one.

It is impossible at this distance in time to clearly define Monteverdi's intentions or to state authoritatively what would have been the practice in contemporary performance. It is entirely possible that the harmonic conventions governing a five-part madrigal were not the same as those governing a monodic song. The whole question is complicated by Monteverdi's sparing use of figuration, never very complete. That this frugality was not peculiar to one composer is confirmed by Agazzari's statement quoted earlier.

Other realizations of the piece are available in what would be considered editions more readily accessible to performers. One such is a three-volume collection of Italian songs and arias that surveys the music of the *bel canto* period from about 1600 to 1750. The set is entitled *La Flora* and is edited by Knud Jeppesen; it includes many works not published in other editions and is therefore a valuable source for the performer. In this version, all the cadences are given in major. The same situation prevails in Schering's *Geschichte der Musik in Beispielen*, a well-respected historical anthology with great scholarship status. The two most widely circulated performing editions are by Parisotti and Floridia. Both realizations include the same minor cadences as in the complete works. Other inconsistencies occur among the various versions, most notably the addition of appoggiaturas and the underlay of words, which results in some rhythmic differences.

The point is: what should this piece really sound like in the context of stylistic performance practices of the period when it was written? It seems to me that the convention indicated by Agazzari, the harmonization given by Monteverdi himself in the five-part madrigal, and the contemporary tradition reflected in the English lute song combine to suggest that major cadences are more authentic. Further evidence is the fact that in the monodic music of the time, whenever the vocal melody cadences on the third of the indicated chord, it is clearly major, even if this involves the addition of an accidental by the composer. The ambiguity always results when the melodic line ends on the root or fifth of the chord. None of these factors is completely convincing in isolation, but considered in combination they do carry some weight.

A case cannot be made upon the basis of a single song, despite the implication of universality in Agazzari's remarks. Adding to the confusion are the inconsistencies within the work of the same editor. Although Jeppesen applies the convention of major cadences to Monteverdi's *Lamento*, in his realization of Caccini's bass for *Amarilli* he utilizes a number of minor chords at cadence points, but makes the final one major. Schering also vacillates between major and minor, but uses major more often than does Jeppesen. Parisotti's realization is different again, but makes a concession in favor of major for the final cadence. Parrish and Ohl, in their *Masterpieces of Music before 1750*, do not include *Amarilli*, but they do reproduce a version of another solo madrigal from *Le nuove musiche* entitled *Dovrò dunque morire*. All the cadences turn out to be altered to major. Unfortunately for anyone trying to make a case for an Italian convention here, the introductory notes to the song indicate that the editors have taken their realization from the version published by John Dowland in his *A Musicall Banquet* (1610), in which he provided a lute accompaniment. Obviously he was simply following the tradition of the lute songs, in which major cadences were customary. On the basis of this one piece, then, transplanted to a foreign tradition, it is impossible to draw any conclusive generalizations.

The inescapable fact is that, although much of the evidence seems to indicate that there are arguments favoring the use of major chords at all medial and final cadence points, one cannot afford to be adamant about this point as an irrevocable principle of style. At the same time, it can most assuredly be suggested that more use of major is indicated than is evident in the work of most editors of widely circulated performing editions. One of the negative side-effects of ignoring what may have been a significant element of harmonic practice in early Italian monody is the resulting implication that both key feeling and the consistent use of major or minor as a harmonic color for expressive purposes was more prevalent in Italy than in England. It is unlikely that this is true and it is even more unlikely that such a deduction ought to be based on evidence found in the more readily accessible performing editions.

The recent interest in recording historically accurate performances provides some strange sidelights. In connection with *Amarilli* and the whole business of major and minor cadences, the waters are as muddy as in the printed editions. The set of records issued by RCA Italiana under the title *Storia della musica Italiano* and performed largely by Italian musicians includes this song. The performance follows Jeppesen's edition, so that there is a mixture of major and minor cadences. The unusually scholarly set recorded for Archive Productions' research period on seventeenth-century monody also includes the song, and here again the cadences show no consistency. However, the Vanguard disc featuring Italian songs of the Italian baroque, recorded by the esteemed English counter-tenor Alfred Deller and his consort, also features the song, and in this performance all cadences have been altered to major. Is Deller performing from the Dowland arrangement or is he applying what he feels to be a convention of the period? Even more to the point, which historically accurate performance is historically accurate? Quite possibly the answer cannot be given in exact terms. As in so much baroque music, it's a performers' world and the choices fall legitimately to them, just as they did at the time the music first appeared.

Setting aside cadence conventions and editorial problems, the songs of the early Italian baroque tend to furnish each poetic line with different music without at the same time destroying the continuity as much as this might suggest. Because of this, however, the pieces have the same sectionalized harmonic feel that was noted in the lute songs. Particularly in the earlier ones, it is the usual practice to handle one phrase in G minor, for instance, with a cadence on the dominant, and to follow it immediately with a phrase in B♭ major without any modulatory bridge. Even within the phrase there is a still underdeveloped sense of tonality in the modern meaning of the term. Caccini is fond of the progression G minor, D major, G minor, F major—a series of chords that retains more modal than tonal flavor. Really chromatic movements, harmonically and melodically, are almost always associated with textual emphasis. Andrea Falconieri's *Bella Fanciulla* (1616) is typical of the general approach to this sort of illustration.

Because of the initial infatuation with expressive projection of text and because this naturally suggests that each poetic phrase has a certain musical feeling that is autonomous to it, there is in the earlier songs little attempt to develop a musical fabric based on sequential patterns. The exception to this generalization involves repeated words and phrases from the poem, as in the lute song. Practically all musical sequences (harmonic and melodic), repetitions, or modified repetitions are associated with a poetic phrase that is repeated. There is a real relationship, then, between the text and the musical embodiment of it. In general the practice was to repeat the final poetic line in this manner, but there are numerous examples of repeated words or phrases within the body of the songs as well, a practice most prevalent in the madrigals. Caccini's *Amarilli* is a typical piece in which all the musical reiterations match those of the words. The same sort of rhapsodic construction is found in Da Gagliano's *Valli profonde*, where musical sequences and/or repetitions growing out of repeated portions of the text are numerous. Jacopo Peri's *O miei giorni fugaci* is yet another example, although here the repetitions are reserved for the final line of the poem. The arias, more direct and metrically organized because of their debt to dance rhythms, are less apt to indulge in either musical or textual reiterations or sequences, except for the last phrase.

The movement away from this relatively free style of composition had several motivations. The first was the gradual takeover by music of what were originally the prerogatives of the poem. The most natural way to extend and at the same time to unify the musical fabric is by motivic manipulation, and perhaps the most obvious manipulation, aside from exact repetition, is the use of sequences. Throughout the seventeenth century there is an ever increasing reliance upon just this type of construction, not only in vocal but in instrumental music as well. Because of the strong association between words and motives that was built up in the earliest stages of Italian monody, it was inevitable that musical sequential patterns would carry identical portions of the poem. The inference, of course, is that the musical demands supersede the poetic requirements, because extensive repetitions tend to dull the poetic imagery rather than to strengthen it. Thus the movement away from a free melodic style toward a musical style based primarily on sequential progressions can be exactly equated with the movement away from an emphasis upon the declamatory and expressive demands of the text and toward an emphasis upon the exigencies of musical structure. These factors, more than any others, created the expressive paradox of the *Affektenlehre*, a doctrine that has received a vast amount of commentary. The text came to serve only one purpose. It was sufficient if it furnished a basic and readily discernible expressive suggestion that could be realized in musical terms, preferably brief and amenable to sequential extension. At no time in the history of song has the poem suffered the disruption to which it was subjected in the baroque. Such compositions as Carissimi's *Ma no, non fuggir* and Stradella's *Ombre, voi che celate* make no attempt to retain even a vestige of the poetic syntax. Instead, the words are given to the music with complete abandon and the text becomes so repetitious as to be practically meaningless as literature.

A second factor that motivated the movement away from concern for the declamatory demands of the text was the growth of vocalization as a factor in performance. Although even the early monodists were concerned that the voice should be handled in such a way as to bring out the fullest expressive content of the poetry, they took considerable pains to warn performers away from excessive vocal display as an end in itself. However, as more and more skilled singers (in particular the *castrati*) were drawn into participation in opera and cantata performances, the composers, on demands made by singers, supplied a type of music that was suitable for the virtuosic nature of the performers. The usual pattern was to select several significant or illustrative words from the poem, illuminate them by assigning flamboyant melismas to them, and rely upon the result to carry the burden of musical structure and expression. Again the sequence was the handiest tool, because it allowed for almost unlimited extension of a motivic idea. Not only were such roulades a more than acceptable instrument for purely vocal pyrotechnics but they served the music itself equally as well by providing the basic material of the form. Carissimi's *Vittoria, vittoria* is typical of this sort of melismatic construct that relies heavily upon sequential progressions for its unification.

At mid-seventeenth century, in fact, the most influential composer, in terms of setting a musical standard that had moved decisively away from the free melodic style of the earlier years, was Giacomo Carissimi. Although he is best remembered for his sacred compositions, he was also active in the field of the secular cantata and it was in this area that he was most influential on Francesco Cavalli and Marc Antonio Cesti. Carissimi's vocal pieces are typically musical rather than freely declamatory. The sense of tonality is sufficiently well defined to make such devices as deceptive cadences meaningful, and he employs a number of purely musical tools, such as rhythmic *ostinatos*, extensive sequential passages, and rhythmically oriented melodies. In the cantatas (sacred and secular) as in the oratorios, he makes a clear distinction between recitative sections and arias. The recitatives are more speechlike in rhythm and melodic line than the madrigals of the early part of the century, and the arias take on a musical rhythm founded in a regularly recurring metric accent. They are generous with coloratura passages and set the pattern in every way for the exploitation of gymnastics that was to characterize later baroque vocal style. His immediate contemporaries, Cavalli and Cesti among others, show the same general tendencies.

Alessandro Scarlatti is conceded to be the most typical as well as one of the most prolific exponents of high baroque aria style. In his works are found all the repetitive texts, the motivic development, the challenge to vocalization, the formal insistence upon *da capo* construction, and the tonal solidarity of the beginning of the eighteenth century in Italy. To this he added considerably more harmonic imagination than many of his contemporaries, as well as a fluidity of melody that sets him apart. Other notable composers in the same medium were Alessandro Stradella, Giacomo Perti, Benedetto Marcello, and Antonio Caldara, to indicate but a few of the host of contributors to the vocal literature of the period. The compositions of these men, together with the vast repertoire drawn from Handel and Bach, form the bulk of Italian baroque solo vocal music before the public today, at least on the concert and recital stage.

One of the most important developments, primarily musical in nature, that inhibited retention of the original concern for the text was the gradually increasing reliance upon the *da capo* format as the standard for cantata and opera arias. The necessity of repeating the *a* section, purely a matter of musical formalism, creates an embarrassing situation so far as the poem is concerned, since there is little or no artistic purpose served by the reiteration of the words. The justification is almost completely in terms of creating

an artistic balance musically between unity and variety, a sense of fulfillment that results from the return of familiar musical material following a
digression. The form is not totally disassociated from the text, of course,
since the *a* section is always based upon a text that differs from that used
in the *b* section. The earliest examples of real *da capo* construction (of which
Francesco Cavalli's *Vaghe stelle* from a 1655 opera, *Erismena*, is typical) show
neither the distinct change of melodic material nor the clearly defined key
contrasts that mark the fully developed types later associated with Neapolitan composers, in particular Alessandro Scarlatti. But they do betray
their preoccupation with music over text in their insistence upon word
repetitions, and they are already laced with extensive florid passages.

The typical *da capo* aria is based upon a four-line poem of which the *a*
section treats the first two lines and the *b* section the last two. While both
sections are extremely repetitive textually, the *b* section tends to be less so
and not as long. In performance the singer was expected to add suitable
extemporaneous ornamentation and *fioritura* when returning to the *da capo*
portion, and his fame could hinge upon his skill and imagination at this
point. Because of the overwhelming emphasis on virtuosity the musico-
poetic relationship is at the barest minimum, the poem ceasing to function
as literature except in the most superficial way. It is little wonder, then, that
the texts are uninspiring as poetry and that practically all the expressive
content is found in the music. R. H. Thomas sums it up:

A paradox of the Da capo aria is that, while it provides more extensive resources
of musical expression, the composer is best served by a text that says little
rather than much and in a way sufficiently commonplace not to attract or demand
too much attention in its own right. . . . One cannot therefore safely say that
Erlebach was handicapped by his poor texts. . . . The contrary is more likely
to be the case. The more an aria strained to unfold all its musical possibilities,
the more convenient it was if the text did no more than provide an *Affekt*,
and there were even those who inclined to the view that a simple and uncomplicated *Affekt* was the ideal.[7]

In the process of developing the musical resources and possibilities to
which Thomas refers, it was inevitable that virtually all the poetic factors
should be sacrificed. The establishment of the bar line as a relentless organizing principle of the musical rhythm results in the imposition of a metric
accent that is frequently at odds with the spirit of Italian verse rhythms.
In the context of the *da capo* aria, however, this is of little significance
since the repetition of words and phrases in itself destroys the poetic line
entirely. The rhyme scheme is annihilated along with the rhythm. In many
cases, it is all but impossible to ferret out the basic poetic line and this dimension of the poetic form is lost in performance. What does come through
consistently is the word or words which carry the *Affekt*, since reiteration

7 R. H. Thomas, *Poetry and Song in the German Baroque* (Oxford: Clarendon Press,
1963), pp. 88–89.

makes them unavoidable. Again, this is all that was felt necessary in terms of the aesthetic emphases of the period. Despite all the superficialities, however, the *da capo* aria and its related types from the mid- and late-baroque have persisted and flourished in the repertoire, a tribute to the attraction performers and public alike have felt for the musical properties alone. But it must be admitted that because of the musico-poetic imbalance, this body of song, more than any other, can successfully communicate even when the specifics of the text are unintelligible. Translation of a few key words is sufficient for performer and listener; the weight of the expression belongs to the music.

From its inception, Italian monody was pointed in a different direction than its contemporary counterpart in England, the lute song. The latter remained an intimate type of song, designed and for the most part utilized in very small gatherings and often in private. It was never oriented to the demands of the theater nor was it ever envisioned as a dramatic projection of the text, although its objectives always centered around a concern for the proper expression of the words. It grew out of the practice of small social ensemble groups singing for mutual pleasure, but adapted as easily to the needs of a single soloist performing for himself alone.

On the other hand, the Italians put their experiments into the service of the theater at an early stage. In his *Nuove musiche* preface, Caccini makes it clear that the vocal style used by him in his contributions to the operatic productions of the *Camerata* was a direct outgrowth of his previous solo madrigal style.

.... having in those times [i.e., about 1585] made a beginning of such songs for a single voice and believing that they had more power to delight and move than the greatest number of voices singing together, I composed in those times the madrigals ... in that very style which later served me for the fables which were represented in song at Florence.[8]

Thus, in the initial stages at least, there was no difference between the madrigals and airs, which were truly chamber music, and the solo excerpts from the earliest operas. In the course of the century the arias were to be enlarged enough to reflect their importance in the dramatic works for which their style was utilized. In the process the strong metric feeling first associated with the airs because of their basis in dance rhythms assumed more and more importance in all the song types. At the same time the melodic contours broadened enough to accommodate the virtuoso demands of the professional vocalists who used them primarily for purposes of display. The rhythmic freedom that characterized the earliest solo madrigals was applied to recitative but with growing concentration on speech accents and pace at the expense of the expressive elements so dear to Caccini and his contemporaries. Song, as a type of composition independent of a dramatic context, was largely neglected, not to be revived

8 Strunk, *op. cit.*, p. 379.

in Italy to any significant degree until the very late nineteenth century. Opera and opera-related idioms (oratorio and cantata) claimed the attention of all the leading composers for the voice, and the Italianate style as well as the Italian singers themselves dominated the vocal music of all Europe.

THE *CONTINUO LIED*

There were reactions, however, and although the types of song they represent have not survived in the performing repertoire except for groups principally interested in the revival of neglected music of the past, they are important to the development of song. They constitute historically important evidence that, along with a desire to provide material for the theatrical tastes of the public and performers, there was a continuing concern that poetry should enter meaningfully into vocal expression.

Representative of this stream of composition was the German *continuo lied*. Thomas has covered the type so well in his study[9] that there seems no need to repeat or enlarge upon his material here except to draw a few pertinent conclusions about the relationship of the *continuo lied* to the general development of song expression.

Relying for its texts upon a generalized lyric poetic expression, the *lied* was distinguished from most other song types of the period by its insistence upon nonoperatic devices. The typical format was strophic and there was an avoidance of melismatic illustration of individual words and phrases, a concentration upon simple harmonic background and unspecific melodic figurations—in other words, an attempt to carry over into art song the most characteristic features of the folk idiom. This sort of aesthetic objective did not deny the principles of *Affekt* nor was it an attempt to obviate the expressive role of music. What it did aspire to was the creation or retention of a balance between poetic and musical utterance. The more dramatically inclined composers felt no compunction about text repetition, in fact utilized it insistently in the interest of musical extension. But the leading *continuo lied* composers (Heinrich Albert, Adam Krieger, and Johann Rist) adhered quite strictly to the poetic form, correlating lines of the poem with musical phrases, cadences with rhyme, and poetic meter with musical meter. The poetry itself was lyric, avoiding dramatic suggestion for the most part and making no unusual declamatory demands. As a result, the songs are markedly general in nature and one set of words can often be exchanged for another bearing the same metric scheme and line length without doing perceptible damage to the expressive effect.

The danger inherent in such attempts as the *continuo lied* to generalize the music is that the very avoidance of musical excesses can, and often does, result in an impoverishment of expression. The musico-poetic balance that is so ardently sought can actually curtail the role of music to such an extent that the poetry exerts a restrictive control rather than a cooperative one.

9 Thomas, *op. cit.*

The *continuo lied* displays exactly such weaknesses and it is probably for this reason that it has remained of historical interest only.

Although not fully established as a song type until the 1640's, it was already losing its distinctive features by the last decades of the century. Predictably, the factor that led to its disintegration was the encroachment of operatic style with its highly dramatic illustrative musical configurations.

Even in Hamburg, where extreme simplicity had been a feature of the *lied* and where also the recently founded opera had a relatively popular basis, the *lied*, in so far as it still existed, was becoming more elaborate and ornate.[10]

By the early part of the eighteenth century, operatic musical devices had infiltrated the *lied* to such an extent that it had virtually lost its individual character, although much of the poetry itself retained its principally lyric quality.

Even as late as the 1740's, important composers were still trying to resist the vocal influences of the musical stage in their songs, but without much success. Georg Philipp Telemann, for instance, in the foreword to a collection of *24 Oden* which he published in 1741, struck out against the excesses of *fioriture* and the overmeagerness of the characteristic *continuo lied*. He insisted on simplicity but not primitivity, and on the maintenance of a *tessitura* that would discourage virtuosic display. His ideal was a song which would be "comfortable for all throats," and which would "neither call for the voice of a wren in the high register nor that of a bittern in the low, but should remain in the middle of the road."[11]

As a matter of fact, Telemann's odes are not overly complicated pieces nor are they as musically sterile as many of his predecessors'. The melodies are more shapely and the harmonies more adventurous. But at the same time, the metric-rhythmic schemes are often extremely repetitive and refuse to move away from a rigidly applied poetic meter. His usual formal approach is to set the first two poetic lines to a musical period, then repeat the music exactly for the succeeding two lines. The balance of the strophe is given enough new music to carry the text, usually a period or a double period, depending upon the length of the poetic stanza. This is then repeated exactly, words and music. The musico-poetic difficulties are almost as apparent here as in the *da capo* aria. Musically the form is entirely satisfactory and the repetitions offer a means of extending basically brief material. But the reiteration of the last three or four lines of a poem's stanzas is certainly no service to the poet.

Telemann's contemporary, Johann Görner, is less bound to the typical form of the *lied*, and at the same time provides a melodic line more given to melismas (often on unimportant words or unaccented syllables) and ornamental devices. Although he pays lip service to simplicity, he nevertheless

10 *Ibid.*, p. 79.
11 I am indebted to Dr. Gordon Kinney for this translation.

represents the late baroque tendency to yield to the temptations of operatic style.

It seems heretical to avoid a lengthy discussion of the two greatest masters of the baroque, Bach and Handel. However, they represent a culmination of style rather than a significant stage in its development, insofar as their contributions to solo vocal music are concerned. Both are almost unremittingly oriented in the cantata-oratorio-opera tradition of the time, bringing to it the factors that distinguish them as musical geniuses but not innovators. Only in one area did Bach approach real song—in his *Geistliche Lieder und Arien*—and in these the debt to the *continuo lied* is undeniable. A secondary, but not unimportant, source for the style was the chorale; these two types, in combination, sum up his approach in these songs. What he added was his particular affinity for melodic-harmonic integration and while this is not inconsiderable, it cannot be interpreted as furnishing an impetus toward the development of song either in Germany or elsewhere. In the larger solo forms, he makes extensive musical and vocal demands much in the manner of the theater. What does distinguish him from most of his contemporaries in these media is his unrelenting ensemble demands upon both singer and instrumentalist. The interplay between voice and accompaniment seldom allows for purely vocal display; the voice is an instrument that contributes to the total musical texture and there is little or no opportunity for virtuosity for its own sake —although the demands made upon the voice are certainly in the realm of the true virtuoso.

Handel, whose contributions to vocal literature were exclusively large-scale, is considerably kinder to the voice. The phrasings in the melodic line are designed for the singer rather than the instrumentalist. Only rarely does he indulge in the contrapuntal vocal-accompaniment textures that are characteristic of Bach, contenting himself with furnishing a harmonic support (most characteristically homophonic) that focuses attention on the voice in true operatic style. Often the accompaniment takes on a completely static quality, sometimes even dropping out altogether, in order to invite the freest delivery of the voice line. All the encouragement to indulge in *fioriture*, so typical of the last great age of extemporaneous performance, is found in excerpts from his solo cantatas, oratorios, and operas. The wealth of material he left for the singer belongs truly to the singer, not to the ensemble as in Bach's work. Only sporadically did Handel turn his attention to real song, an area that obviously held little attraction for him, and these songs are not included even in the historical collections (although they are projected) and are extremely difficult to locate in editions of any sort. Predictably, they tend toward text repetitions and in general betray his primarily dramatic interests.

The cross-fertilization of operatic and *lied* styles was of tremendous significance to the future course of song, particularly in Germany. Without a continuing history of deliberate attempts to work out a proper balance between music and poetry it is doubtful that the synthesis evident in the nineteenth-century art song could have come about so readily. Not the least important factor was the establishment of a tradition of songlike poetry, preparing the way for the outburst of romantic lyricism during the final years of the eighteenth century.

Whereas during the seventeenth century verse had been shaped to rather mechanical rhythms and to effects gained from the play of words, the flux of feeling itself could now begin to be thought of as musical. Thus, in the time of Mozart, in the youth of Goethe, Klopstock could say that the perfection of lyrical poetry resided "in the melodious course of passion or feeling."[12]

The dichotomy between extensive musical illustration of text and a more controlled, sometimes too-meager musical texture did not end with the baroque operatic style and the *continuo lied*. It was to continue with little basic change of ideologies into the last half of the eighteenth century and beyond. Before giving attention to this, however, it is necessary to turn again to England.

HENRY PURCELL

Most of the solo vocal music composed during the period between the decline of the lutenist school and the appearance of Henry Purcell's works is available only in historical editions. In spite of the lack of attention given this material by publishers, however, it would be a mistake to assume that nothing was happening in the area of song composition. Henry Lawes and John Wilson, among others, were actively engaged in setting contemporary poetry in the 1650's and 1660's. Their songs were designed for singing to the accompaniment of a theorbo-lute or bass-viol and are generally quite simple in approach. There is almost no repetition of text, little attempt at illustration or embellishment, and they rarely depart from a purely syllabic style. Almost all are strophic in form and include no introductory material.

On the other hand, Matthew Locke was drawn to the more dramatic style of the recitative and furnished a substantial amount of music for the Restoration theater. More exactly contemporary with Purcell, John Blow represents the full-blown transfer of the Italian approach to song. His pieces were written for performance with a keyboard or theorbo-lute and were published with figured bass. They are almost excessively repetitious textually, include numerous tempo changes and extensive tone painting, and most often provide an instrumental introduction. What they lack is the imagination and control that Purcell brought to his compositions, and it is probably for this reason that they have been neglected by publishers and performers alike.

Thus the tradition of composing for solo voice and accompanying instrument persisted through the turmoil of the Cromwellian period and into the

12 Thomas, *op. cit.*, p. 111.

Restoration. The gradual infiltration of the Italian monodic style added elements of theatricalism that were adaptable to the reawakened interest in the stage, and Purcell appeared at the most advantageous time for his immense talent to make itself felt most effectively.

Purcell was involved with creating music for such a wide variety of media that it is almost impossible to generalize about his style. The source material itself is not always reliable as an indication of the type of composition. The *Orpheus Britannicus*, published posthumously and including many of his best-known songs and arias as well as numerous part songs, identifies *Ah Belinda, I am prest* as being a "Single song" although it is an excerpt from his opera *Dido and Aeneas*. The mere formality of dating his compositions has been troublesome for historians, although recent scholarship by Franklin Zimmerman has helped clarify the situation.[13]

The earliest songs, as distinguished from pieces written for stage works or particular public festivals, tend to be relatively simple in concept, syllabic and without musically illustrative material. Typical of this type are *Sweet, be no longer sad* and *More Love or more Disdain*, both from 1678. This is followed by a period in which the songs are more markedly theatrical and, in fact, barely distinguishable from the solos included in works for the theater. It is this style that has been most closely associated with Purcell and it is at this point that it is most futile to attempt sharp distinctions between his songs and his arias or excerpted pieces. Typical of this class are *Corinna is Divinely Fair* and *Fly Swift ye Hours,* both from 1692, but already anticipated earlier, as in the popular "mad song," *Bess of Bedlam,* 1682. Late in his life, Purcell turned briefly to a type of song that Zimmerman identifies as a counterpart of the German *volkstümliches-lied* in which a folkish type of poetry was reflected in a comparable musical setting.[14] The *Knotting Song* (1695) is included among these. At the same time, however, Purcell was still providing elaborate musical settings of numerous poems that were in themselves elaborate enough to encourage such treatment, one such being *If Musick be the Food of Love* in 1695. He had set the text in a much simpler style in 1692 and again in 1693, and a comparison of these earlier settings with the final one reveals his continuing and even growing desire to illustrate the text more fully at each succeeding attempt. The 1695 setting is barely distinguishable in style from the colorful *Sweeter than Roses* of 1690 or the 1695 piece, *From Rosy Bowers*, another of the "mad songs," both of which are from stage works.

For the most part, the Purcell who is most familiar to public and performer alike is the man of the theater. In this idiom and in those "Single songs" that borrow heavily from it, the construction is most apt to be sectional, with recitative or recitative-like passages alternating with more lyric ones.

13 Franklin B. Zimmerman, *Henry Purcell. An analytical catalogue* (London: Macmillan & Co., Ltd., 1963).

14 Vincent Duckles and Franklin B. Zimmerman, *Words to Music* (Los Angeles: University of California, 1967). Papers on English 17th Century Song.

In most cases, the more tuneful sections are complemented by a skillful, moving bass line, one of Purcell's strengths as a composer and one that is frequently an important factor in the formal organization. One of his favorite devices was the ground bass and he uses it in both dramatic works and in solo songs. In the former category, one thinks first of the two most persistently performed arias from *Dido and Aeneas*: *When I am laid in earth* and *Ah, Belinda, I am prest*, but there are innumerable other instances. Closely allied to the ground is the *ostinato* figure, rhythmic and/or melodic, which Purcell also resorts to with some frequency, as in the 1692 setting of *If Musick be the Food of Love*.

There is in general a strong reliance upon bass and melody interplay, often even a real dialogue. In many cases this is based on illustrative or affective figures and involves the use of extensive melismas. Frequently, the motives are introduced first in the accompaniment, picked up by the voice, and then serve as a structural basis for the entire song or passage. Typical of this organization are *Fly swift ye Hours, I see she fly's me,* and *I sigh'd and own'd my Love*. The Italian influence is perhaps strongest at this point, but to it Purcell added his peculiar genius for logical and consistent control of form, so that the elements of construction and expression work together more meaningfully than in the compositions of many of his contemporaries in England and abroad. The type of interaction among the musical and poetic materials that is typical of Purcell at his best is the fullest realization of the principles of *Affekt*. The "passions" of the text are projected but without interference to the demands of musical continuity. At the same time, the figures chosen by Purcell are always appropriate ones in terms of the highly stylized poetic and musical vocabulary of the time.

His use of text illustration is not confined, of course, to material shared by the voice and bass. Often he gives the representative figure to the voice alone, sometimes in a pictorial sense (*flies, sing, roaring*), sometimes more as a reflection of the mood suggested by the word (*languish, cheerful, victorious*), and again as a happy combination of both (*sighs*). This sort of pictorialization is not restricted to the music for the theater but occurs often in the solo songs, as in the *Knotting Song* and *Fly swift ye Hours*.

Along with melodic illustration, Purcell utilizes a wide range of rhythmic figures, including rests, for both representative and affective purposes. The so-called Scotch snap (♪♩.) appears frequently as a means of expression and as an aid to declamation, as in *I looked and saw within the Book of Fate* on the often repeated *never*. Another favorite device is the insertion of rests between reiterated words, where they help in articulation but also illustrate the sense and sound, as in *Music for awhile* where the word *drop* is effectively set in this manner, and in *Ah, how Sweet it is to Love* where the repetitions of *all* are so treated.

By Purcell's time, the bar line had become solidly established as a factor in metrical control and this is always evident in his musical organization, sometimes at the expense of the poetic scheme. He is especially fond of changing meters as a means of changing mood and also of defining more clearly some sections in his more elaborate pieces. In the process, however, and particularly when the poetic meter does not itself change, barbarisms result. One such instance among many others is in *We sing to Him* from the *Harmonia Sacra* where the change to $\frac{3}{4}$ for the final two lines of the poem places the word *and* on a strong beat at each of its appearances. In a less elaborate context the same problem occurs in *More Love or more Disdain*. On the other hand, in the Conjurer's Song (*Ye twice ten hundred Deities*) from *The Indian Queen*, a highly illustrative recitative and aria, the change to $\frac{3}{4}$ for the lullaby in the final two poetic lines is highly effective.

Purcell was composing at a time when the feeling for tonality was well established and his key relationships are generally the common ones of dominant, subdominant, or relative major and minor. Within these he uses dissonance and chromaticism very often as illustration, particularly in the longer and more dramatic songs. Diminished-seventh chords, appoggiaturas (often approached by a dissonant melodic interval), restless but usually well controlled modulatory passages, and all the other harmonic and harmonically-related vocabulary that was to become the composer's stock-in-trade can be found in abundance in Purcell's vocal music. It is there, in fact, in such abundance as to discourage illustration. Despite the contemporary commentary that centered around the affective use of major and minor, however, there is no real consistency in his employment of mode for text illustration. Such pieces as *From Rosy Bowers, More Love or more Disdain,* and the 1692 version of *If Musick be the Food of Love* fail to establish an understandable relationship in this regard, and many other instances might be cited. Only in the most general sense do the gayer texts gravitate toward major; the incidence of minor in relation to a somber or reflective mood is much less in evidence.

From the performer's standpoint, the same annoying editorial problems exist for Purcell as for other composers of the baroque. The primary one is, as always, the realization of the figured bass. Often the bass line itself is not reproduced accurately but includes melodic and rhythmic distortions that hamper rather than enhance the musical intent. Even the vocal melody is sometimes altered, presumably in the interest of declamation. It is true that declamation cannot be considered Purcell's greatest strength as a song composer, but correction of this fault is not really within the realm of editorial responsibility. In the true spirit of the age in which he lived, Purcell was often prepared to sacrifice the accentuation (but never the sense) of the word in order to carry out his musical scheme as satisfactorily as possible. In a similar sense, the bass line is always of great importance to the musical movement as well as to the harmonic implications. Casual alterations in either of the parts supplied by the composer can only frustrate the musical expression without adding anything desirable.

Purcell's position as one of the gods of British music has been widely recognized. Although his immediate predecessors as well as his contemporaries adopted the theatrical devices of the Italians, he was able to put them to more telling use and in a wider range of expression than any English composer before or after him. And despite the fact that there remained a considerable interest in song throughout the succeeding two centuries in England, both the poetry and the music are undistinguished. Not until late in the nineteenth century did composers of the first rank turn their attention once again to the short lyric vocal piece.

It is worth noting, I think, that only in England did the song persist as a widely performed medium of expression throughout the seventeenth century. Although by Purcell's time it had taken on most of the coloration of opera, including indiscriminate text repetition, harmonic and melodic illustration, extreme vocal demands, extensive musical manipulation, and all the other paraphernalia of fully developed baroque Italianisms, it was still current as a type of vocal expression divorced from its use as part of a larger form. The change of intent from the lute song to the Purcell and Blow type of song is a change from private to public use. Purcell's songs from the 1680's and 1690's are barely distinguishable from his solo pieces from the stage and church works. All are cut from the same theatrical cloth; they are no longer for individual enjoyment but demand an audience. At the same time, they are *songs*, and they form the most significant and most frequently performed representatives of that medium from the later baroque period—and are also the most easily accessible in performing editions. To this extent, they have no counterpart in Italian, German, or French vocal music.

FRENCH BAROQUE MONODY

In France the break from polyphony followed much the same general pattern as in the other countries we are considering. During the latter half of the sixteenth century it became customary to use polyphonic vocal works as solo pieces by arranging the supporting voices for lute accompaniment. In the early seventeenth century, the most popular solo forms were the *air de cour* and the *récit*, and both eventually found their way into the very widely performed *ballet de cour* later in the century. The *airs de cour* included a number of types named for their subject matter. Among the most important of these were the *bergerettes* and *pastourelles* (shepherd and shepherdess pieces), the *chansons à boire* and *chansons à danser* (drinking and dance songs), and the *romances* (a continuation of the medieval troubadour lyrics). All were brief songs, usually strophic in construction and providing for some repetition of the various sections much in the style of the *continuo lied*, the lute song, and the early Italian solo aria or air. As in these sister forms, the texture was primarily homophonic and the conception quite simple, without illustrative or decorative gestures in the music.

The *récit* was a counterpart of the Italian solo madrigal, markedly freer and more rhapsodic than the *air de cour* and with more musical illustration of text as well as more richly ornamented passages, both written by the composer and invited from the performer.

From the beginnings of monodic song in France, the tendency was to exercise more care in declamation than in Italy, where the emphasis was upon melody for its own sake. As the songs were taken into the *ballets de cour* and later, with Lully, into French opera, this concern for treatment of the word underlay the controversies that arose concerning the merits of French as opposed to Italian style. Centering first around the operas of Lully, the discussions during the first decade of the eighteenth century were led by François Raguenet (pro-Italian) and Le Cerf de La Viéville (pro-French). Later in the century it was to break out anew in the "Querelle des Bouffons" and the arguments over the relative values of the Italian style of Piccini and the French style of Gluck. Although there is plenty of disagreement to be found, much of it expressed in vitriolic terms, there is one point on which all sides could agree; the French style of lyric declamation did more to articulate the text in a meaningful way, dramatically as well as linguistically, than did the Italian style. Even the early recitatives of French opera, derived directly from the seventeenth century *récit* as it was used in the *ballet de cour*, tend to be a combination of recitative and aria style, less abrupt and patter-like than their counterparts in Italian opera. At the same time, the arias themselves are more songlike, briefer and less decorative or virtuosic than those of the Italians. There is so much less distinction, in fact, between the various components of opera that Hasse's wife could complainingly ask while attending a French opera: "When are we to hear an *aria*?"[15]

All this has been so widely discussed in other contexts that it is needless to labor the subject here. What should be borne in mind, however, is that even at this stage of French vocal music when, as in Italy, the song was being adapted to larger and more dramatic forms of expression, the French were paying a good deal of attention to the demands of the words. So far as song itself was concerned, the overwhelming interest in opera tended to obscure or stifle interest in it as a short lyric piece that could command an audience of importance. But the interest in declamation was to continue and when, in the nineteenth century, composers once again turned their attention to song as a significant part of their composition, that very interest was to help define the characteristics of the French *mélodie* style, particularly that of Debussy and his followers. In the seventeenth as in later centuries, the niceties of speech and poetic rhythms are always more carefully reflected by the French. Correspondingly, there is much less interest in text repetition, usually so destructive to the sense of the words as well as to the poetic form. Typical of the style are the *récits* found in Lully's *Ballet Royal D'Alcidiane*

15 Cuthbert Girdlestone, *Jean-Philippe Rameau* (London: Cassell & Company, Ltd., 1957), p. 113.

(1658) and others of his ballets, an approach that carried over with little real alteration into the operas.

Although large numbers of song collections were published during the early years of the seventeenth century, most of the material is at present very difficult to obtain, particularly in performing editions. Among the representative composers are Pierre Guédron, Gabriel Bataille, Antoine Boesset, and Michel Lambert, none of whom are apt to stir much interest except among music historians. Evidence of the decline of interest in independent song following the adoption of the *ballet de cour* and the opera during the second half of the century is found in the lack of attention given the form by the most important composers of the period. Except for the excerpts from his ballets, Lully is not represented. The extremely prolific François Couperin left only three *airs* for voice and continuo, one of which is in the form of a rather elaborate set of variations (or *doubles*) in which the first couplet is set to the basic melody and the succeeding four couplets are ornamented versions, each different. This is a continuation of practices that were established in France before the seventeenth century began. Jean-Philippe Rameau, too, ignored the song as a type, although he did compose a number of chamber cantatas for solo voice, continuo, and often another stringed instrument. Some of the pieces are unashamedly Italianate in character but others display a typically French restraint.

The Classic Era

O F T H E countries whose songs constitute the basic performing repertoire, only Germany persisted throughout the eighteenth century in an attempt to develop a meaningful musico-poetic partnership. In France the most significant and popular type of song was the *romance*, sometimes simple and strophic in character, sometimes more Italianate and illustrative. However, the composers who were attracted to it are now as forgotten as their compositions. What importance they have in the continuing development of a true song style lies in the fact that they kept alive at least a minimal interest in setting short, lyric texts to music, an interest that was to lead in the nineteenth century to the contributions of Halévy, Berlioz, and their successors.

In Italy all was opera and thus it remained until the twentieth century, when Respighi and Casella initiated a revival of interest in song. Although a number of nineteenth-century composers of stature, Rossini and Verdi among them, did write a few songs, they are more like miniature operatic arias and scenes than anything else and are barely distinguishable from the sort of vocal composition associated with their stage works.

In England an astounding amount of effort was expended on song composition but most of it was wasted on poems that were little more than ditties. The subject matter was either sentimentally patriotic, often upon themes of the sea and sailors, or else involved toasts and other accouterments of drinking. Another favorite subject, of course, was love, but never put forth with the subtlety or depth of feeling found in the French and German poetry of the period. Despite the fact that composers such as Thomas Arne, James Hook, and Charles Dibdin are represented, there is little beyond historical and sociological interest in the songs themselves. Titles such as *Let's Drink and Sing, My Brother Soldiers Bold, My Betsy is the Blithest Maid,* and *Bold Jack the Sailor* are typical. One is hard put to find a piece not in major, a sample of harmonic adventurousness beyond the tonic/dominant/subdominant tyranny, or a melody of distinction. Most were written for and performed in the music halls of the day (Vauxhall was the best-known) and many were included in the type of ballad opera that had been inaugurated with the *Beggar's Opera* in 1728. The compositions that have survived at all, in fact, are mostly from such stage works, an outstanding example being *Preach not me your musty rules* from Arne's *Comus*.

In Germany the story is very different. A seemingly endless succession of *Oden und Lieder* poured forth during the last half of the eighteenth century, many of them from the pens of the greatest composers of the day—C. P. E. Bach, Gluck, Haydn, Mozart, and Beethoven. In addition there were collections by composers who were leading figures of the period but whose works failed to win fame outside Germany—men like André, Kunzen, Zumsteeg, Reichardt, Zelter, and a host of others. Drawing upon the poetry of Klopstock, Goethe, and other poets of real merit, they initiated a type of song that was to culminate in the establishment of the *lieder* of Schubert as the prototype for lyric expression throughout the nineteenth century. Although a large portion of the late eighteenth-century song output is worthwhile in itself, and still very much a part of the performing literature throughout the Western world, the real contribution these pieces have made from the historical standpoint is in providing a heritage and a tradition that lay ready for Schubert to draw upon. The refinements he brought to song composition cannot be underestimated. But neither should the influence of his inheritance, which reaches back into the baroque *continuo lied* (and farther) but which is most highly concentrated in the last half of the eighteenth century.

The movement toward a true lyric *lied* was inaugurated by Krause and Marpurg in Berlin with their publication of *Oden mit Melodien* in 1753.[1] In the foreword of this and succeeding publications (1756 and 1761) they articulated their objectives in song, which drew aesthetically upon the *continuo lied* of the preceding century as well as upon the French *chanson*. Uppermost was the fashioning of a melody that was self-sufficient even without accompaniment and readily accessible even to the untrained musician, one that rejected theatrically oriented *fioriture* as well as illustrative devices of any kind. Under their influence a number of collected works appeared, the composers of which were known as members of the Berlin School. Also involved were the advent of the Singspiel, a counterpart of the English ballad opera and the Italian *opera buffa*, and the wealth of German folk song. A number of composers commented upon their philosophies and methods in prefaces to their collections, so that there is firsthand information available in this respect.

Among the earliest members of the Berlin School was C. P. E. Bach, and

---

1 For much of the material dealing with the Berlin School, I am indebted to Max Friedlaender's remarkable two-volume study, *Das Deutsche Lied im 18. Jahrhundert* (Stuttgart und Berlin, 1902). This work, which is in three parts, includes a wealth of musical examples, valuable biographical comment upon song composers of the eighteenth century, and a prodigious quantity of information characterizing the types of song composition, their formal properties, and their principal representatives.

in the preface to his settings of Gellert's *Geistliche Oden* (1758) the composer sets forth his approach.

In fashioning the melody, I have, as much as possible, looked at the entire song. I say "as much as possible" because no one who understands melody can be unaware that one must not ask too much of a melody to which more than one strophe is sung, since the variation of the accent of the multi-syllable words, even often the substance, etc., makes a great difference in the musical expression. It will be seen in my work that I have sought to avoid by various methods, many of that sort of variation.

Perhaps because of the melodic restrictions under which Bach felt he had to work, the real interest in his songs is harmonic. And in spite of his adherence to the principles of Krause and Marpurg, there is considerable harmonic (and melodic) illustration, even in the Gellert songs, which are his first attempts in this genre. His treatment of *Bitten*, for instance, which Beethoven set later (1803), already suggests a sort of majesty of declamatory style that Beethoven was to at least partially echo in his song. The similarity between the two settings is most evident at the words:

Herr, meine Burg, mein Fels, mein Hort;	Lord, my fortress, my rock, my refuge;
Vernimm mein Fleh'n, merk' auf mein Wort.	Hear my supplication, heed my words.

In later songs he departs even further from the oversimplification of the Berlin School objectives. In *Die Trennung* there is strong reliance upon the bass repetition of diminished fifths to suggest the tolling of bells as well as upon the use of diminished-seventh chords and even a melodic interval of the diminished seventh. Nor does he restrict himself entirely to the strophic format. *Nonnelied* is a true strophic variation, and the variations include harmonic and melodic manipulation to emphasize textual changes of mood.

Christoph Gluck is best known for his operatic efforts, in particular the reforms against Italian style which he inaugurated. However, he gave some attention to song, his most popular collection being a group of settings of odes by Klopstock, which were published about 1770. They are simple, tuneful pieces for the most part, but not completely without musical dramatization in their resort to mode change at appropriate places in the text. As in most of these earlier songs the format is primarily strophic, but Gluck has several examples of ternary structure in the *da capo* tradition. His Klopstock odes were first issued in North Germany but later published in Vienna, a significant factor in the transplanting of interest in German song to the city that was to produce the most outstanding examples from the eighteenth century.

The song type most typical of the pre-Schubert era in Germany, the *volkstümliches lied*, was established during the last quarter of the century. The first composer of stature to give a great deal of effort to it was Johann Reichardt. His 1779 *Oden und Lieder von Klopstock, Stolberg, Claudius und Hölty*, is prefaced with such a clear statement of aims, methods, and performance advice that it is worth reproducing here in some detail.

My melodies originate every time from repeated reading of the poem for itself, without trying [for a melody], and all that I do further is this: I repeat it so long with small modifications, not writing it down until I feel that the grammatical, logical, expressive, and musical accents are so well united with one another that the melody speaks correctly and sings agreeably—and not for one strophe alone, but for all.

Should one feel and understand that, then so much better for the performance. If not, then the singer must read the words in their entirety beforehand, and read them until he feels that he reads them with genuine expression, and not until then, sing them. Indeed because of the strength and weakness [of accent] which the singer must place differently in the many strophes, at different places, it is necessary that he has read with deliberation the whole song before he sings it. . . . I would further add that the singer who is not in a position to read verse quite well could correct his declamation afterwards through the accent of such music, and could thus learn to read correctly and significantly by means of correct, significant singing.

In a later publication, *Frohen Liedern für Deutsche Männer* (1781), the composer further emphasizes his ideals:

Song melodies, which everyone who has merely ears and throat should equally agree, must be able to stand by themselves without any accompaniment, must in the simplest succession of tones, in the most distinct, firmest movement, in the most precise conformity of segment and division, etc., must so encompass the correct style that one cannot think of the song without the words, nor the words without the melody—so that the melody will seem completely for the words, nothing for itself alone.

He goes on to assert that in a conflict of words and music, the latter must give way. It is at this point that he takes issue with Haydn and Mozart, complaining that they have given him no models to follow in the area of what he considers to be the true song. His disgruntlement is undoubtedly based on his distaste for the operatic elements that invade the *lieder* of these two greater composers.

It is obvious that Reichardt was willing, even eager, to give priority to the poem, allowing it to dictate musical meter and rhythms as well as to carry the burden of the expression. His *Frohen Liedern* was, in fact, published in melodic form only, without benefit of accompaniment, although this is not Reichardt's usual practice. He set a great number of Goethe texts that were later used by Schubert, and the best way to understand the relative simplicity and directness of his style is to compare them to Schubert's treatment. Among the most profitable for use as a basis for such comparison are *Freudvoll und leidvoll, Erlkönig,* and *Jägers Abendlied.* In general Reichardt's songs are attractive and without illustration of a drastic nature, although he is not completely averse to using changes of accompaniment style in order to depict phrases that deal with the breeze, for instance, nor to the use of mild harmonic dissonance when it seems appropriate, in spite of his avowed intent to avoid such devices. In *An Lida* he even resorted to sections of recitative and arioso, a format that was to appeal strongly to the young Schubert. Reichardt indicated this style as a *Deklamation* and followed *An Lida* with others of the same type, thus acknowledging the inadequacy of a sharply restricted musical format in dealing with more dramatic or less regular poetry.

Among the North Germans who continued the principles of Reichardt were Johann A. P. Schulz, Christian Friedrich Schubart, and Friederich Kunzen. The latter was among the first to openly admit that one format would not handle all contingencies. In the foreword to his 1788 publication of *Weisen und lyrische Gesänge* he wrote:

This collection was entitled *"Weisen und lyrische Gesänge"* in order to indicate that two types of song should be anticipated. By "Weisen" the composer means those which are fostered by Mother Nature, which without displaying it have adapted a certain charm which must stir everyone, whether he loves music or not . . . in a word, such songs as we have to exhibit under the title "folksongs."

He soon found, however, that he would have little success with a great part of the public which has become too much accustomed to the often all-too-luxuriant Italian song; he chose, therefore, a type which comes somewhat closer to those for which the poetry, which here takes a higher play of imagination, presented the opportunity at hand to him—and called them lyric songs.

The concession to public taste is clear, but Kunzen was nevertheless at some pains to make as little use as possible of decorative embroidery in his music and to insist that performers must avoid adding ornaments that are not expressly given in the score.

At the turn of the century, Carl Friedrich Zelter was still clinging to the aesthetic objectives of the Berlin School but at the same time indulging in brief flights of Italianate coloratura, as in his *Theilung der Erde.* He was particularly drawn to narrative poems and drinking songs, although many of his texts are rather stickily sentimental. His importance as a song composer springs from his close association with the favorite poet of the period, Goethe. The latter was firm in his belief that musicians had no right to tamper with the poetic form in any way and in particular should avoid text repetitions and disruption of the strophic concept—and, of course, no aria-like devices, such as musical illustration of text or florid vocal passages. Zelter, especially when setting Goethe's texts, does show a musical restraint that is often regrettable.

Of the South Germans who concentrated on the *volkstümliches lied,* Johann Zumsteeg was the most influential on the young Schubert. His style falls somewhere between the relative simplicity of Reichardt and the some-times excessive laciness of Haydn. Among his most popular songs were ballads, many of them quite dramatically set, to which Schubert was par-ticularly attracted. One of the latter's earliest efforts, *Hagars Klage*, is in fact an almost exact copy of Zumsteeg's piece. Even when not setting ballads, Zumsteeg was apt to get quite dramatic. Friedlaender refers to a setting of Schiller's *Die Entzückung. An Laura* in which there are many tempo changes, long piano interludes, recitatives, and even a closing allegro for the piano. In concept this is strongly related to Reichardt's *Deklamation* style as well as to many of Schubert's first song attempts. A further influence on Schubert was Zumsteeg's inclination to present a theme in contrasting modes for textual purposes and to provide an accompaniment that is often independent of the voice and assigned an important representative role. In almost all these respects, the composer illustrates a movement away from the excessive restraint of the true *volkstümliches lied* toward, under Italian influences, a more musically expressive song style.

It was in Vienna that song production flourished most strikingly during the two decades immediately preceding Schubert's first efforts. By all odds, the best study on the subject is by Editha Alberti-Radanowicz, and the bulk of what follows here is based upon this research.[2] The author makes it clear that in Vienna the influences of both the German *volkstümliches lied* and the Italian aria style were felt with almost equal strength. The work of Reichardt, which represents to some extent an amalgamation of the two styles, was widely circulated in the city, as was that of Mozart, Haydn, and later Beethoven. Haydn's first publication of songs was in 1781, Beethoven's in 1783, and Mozart's in 1786, and all were well known by the beginning of the period covered in Alberti-Radanowicz' study. While all three have made significant contributions to the performing repertoire and will be discussed later, the work of other more minor composers was of more importance to the burgeoning interest in song itself, and it is the compositional style of these men that is vital to a full understanding of the milieu in which Schubert moved.

Among the factors that created an artistic atmosphere in which the song could thrive was the happy status of contemporary poetry. Beginning with the publication of Goethe's *Egmont* in 1788, there was a veritable rash of usable material made available to composers, including the same author's *Wilhelm Meister* and his numerous ballads, as well as poems by Schiller (1792–1798) and by Schlegel and Tieck (1802). Mozart's songs and opera arias, in particular their formal and melodic style, and those of Beethoven, in particular their pianistic characteristics, as well as the Singspiel songs of Müller and Hiller all suggested types of compositional approaches that would be appropriate to the short lyric forms. Romanticism itself, with its

2 Editha Alberti-Radanowicz, *Das Wiener Lied von* 1789–1815, Beihefte der Denk-mäler der Tonkunst in Österreich, Vol. X (Wien: Studien zur Musikwissenschaft, 1923).

emphasis upon mood and intense subjectivity, was an equally strong factor. In addition, the song as a genre had received wide circulation and acceptance through the compositions of the *volkstümliches lied* which, in its most ideal form, was easily accessible to a large public, including those who were not themselves trained musicians. Thus all the elements which could encourage a vigorous experimentation in the possibilities of song were ready at hand.

The composers most responsible for the development of forms and styles as well as for the spreading popularity of the song have been largely forgotten; in many cases their names do not even appear in the encyclopedias. Among the dozens who were active, the following might be mentioned as most representative: Johann Braun, Wilhelm Pohl, Moriz von Dietrichstein, Johann Fuss, Niklas von Krufft, Sigmund Neukomm, Johann Hackel, Conradin Kreutzer, and Johann Holzer. The latter was Schubert's first teacher, reason enough for him to assume a position of some significance in the development of song.

In the works of these men was a wealth of song types, all quite highly developed and with individual characteristics. These included the Singspiel song, arietta, ballad, and romance, all developed at an earlier period, and the mood song and *volkstümliches lied*, both of which made their first appearances in Vienna during the period that began in 1789. Likewise at hand were the forms into which song would be cast throughout the succeeding century and beyond: strophic, strophic variation, and through composed. Each had its distinctive features, and within each there was considerable variety of treatment from composer to composer. Melodic characteristics varied according to the song type, the most dramatically vocal and extensive in range being found in the ariettas and ballads. But in all types there seems to have been a wide use of ascending or descending chromatic half-steps, sometimes in a leading-tone sense melodically, but often involving the harmony also. Alberti-Radanowicz identifies them as a stylistic characteristic of Viennese song of the period because of their frequency, but claims also that, like the use of coloratura, there was diminishing occurrence after 1805. As in operatic style, coloratura is partially an accumulation of ornaments and roulades, but just as often a result of motivic manipulation and extension. A further melodic convention was the reliance upon *portamenti*, particularly the "sigh." In the Berlin School these had been avoided on strong beats, but during the period under discussion here they were usually dramatized by being placed on the strong beats.

Harmonically there was a strong reliance upon tonic/dominant/tonic relationships, used as a means of articulating the parts of the strophe or, as in the case of through composition, the strophes themselves. According to the author, a modulation to the dominant always occured, even in the shortest pieces. At the same time, there was an increasingly adventurous use of applied function, in particular the diminished-seventh chord with lowered third (more often referred to as the augmented sixth), which is most commonly associated with a cadence formula involving the subdominant or submediant. The favorite tonality was major, although after 1800 there was wider use of minor in the mood songs and, complementing it, a wider range of modulation upward into sharp tonalities and downward into flat tonalities in connection with text. This culminated in an association of character with tonality (it will be remembered that Beethoven was opposed to transposition of his songs) so that G and C were used for drinking songs, F and B♭ for pastoral lyrics, and A♭ for love and other expressions of sentimentality. Melancholy was usually represented by A minor.

As the period advanced, the accompaniment tended to become more independent with less duplication of the vocal line in the top piano voice. Broken triads of all sorts formed the stylistic basis for piano, independent motives being usually of an illustrative nature, The latter tendency, so important to Schubert's development, is found mostly in the work of Dietrichstein, Fuss, Krufft, and Neukomm.

In most cases the poetic line corresponded to the musical phrase or period, the resulting punctuation of the rhyme scheme imposing a sort of regularity which helped identify the structure of the lyric. However, there was no attempt to match rhyme scheme with melodic motive so the structural concordance between poem and musical realization resided in the cadential character alone. In general, declamation was more careful at the beginning and end of lines than through the middle, so that feminine endings were given with a longer rhythmic value to the penultimate syllable, often in the form of a suspension or appoggiatura. True mood painting was rare; much more frequent was the correlation of musical motives with poetic situation, *e.g.*, the use of horn motives in hunting scenes.

In summation, Alberti-Radonowicz gives the common criteria that had become established by 1815, the date of Schubert's first important songs. In form, the movement had been from purely strophic through strophic variation to the type of through composition represented by *da capo* and two-part songs and eventually into true through composition involving declamatory and arioso passages. Likewise there was a transition from coloratura (of the Mozart-Haydn type) to a more simple diatonic melody. In harmony the main development was the tendency to bring to each degree its own leading tone, thus extending tonal relationships at least in an embryonic sense. The accompaniment gradually gained independence from the vocal melody, first through the use of broken-chord figures and then through the development of illustrative motives and occasionally an independent figure that appeared in introductory or interlude passages.

It is worth noting that the author identifies the songs of Krufft as being the most highly developed of the period and the most influential upon Schubert. In his songs are found the type of sectional declamation-arioso structure that made such an early appeal to Schubert, and in Krufft the blending of one section into another is an important characteristic. Together with the sectional changes of style and some liking for text repetition, there is a concentration upon mood that is not general among Krufft's contemporaries but that leads directly to Schubert. Too, Krufft's accompaniments are highly developed for the period and cover a wide range of figures, including motivic interplay between voice and piano. Also important was his abundant use of minor along with the alteration between major and minor, so strongly correlating to the romantic feeling for change and unrest. The advances in harmony, including altered chords and expressively oriented dissonances, all summed up in Krufft's songs, opened the area of harmonic illustration into which Schubert moved with such assurance. And the author makes the very significant point, quoting from Adler's *Der Stil in der Musik*, that the works of second- and third-rank composers often represent a connecting link of great significance to the historical development of style. To this extent, then, it is necessary to recognize the debt Schubert owed to even his minor predecessors and contemporaries.

At the same time, it is not possible to ignore the importance of Mozart and Beethoven, and to a lesser degree, Haydn, not only because of the intrinsic value of their songs but also because they did strongly influence the work of their fellow composers who were giving perhaps more of their energy to that genre.

Haydn seems to have been unable to harness his forces to deal with the song very successfully. Even in the 1781 publication of *Lieder für das Clavier*, his earliest work of this type, there is evidence that musical considerations take precedence over poetic ones. The first piece in the collection is a setting of Herder's translation of Sedley's folklike poem that Purcell set as the *Knotting Song*. Haydn's treatment can hardly be expected to follow a mid-baroque concept of text setting, of course, but even allowing for a century of change in musical style it cannot be considered a controlled effort musically. A six-measure introduction, complete with trills and turns, presents the material that the voice takes up upon entering. The final two lines of each stanza are given an entirely different musical texture and tempo, changing from the opening Adagio to Allegro. The lacy accompaniment of the first part of the song is altered to a solid chord background. The allegiance to opera is here apparent, and even in this representative piece from his first songs are the seeds that will flower in his later settings of English poetry.

The *Lieder für das Clavier* are so designed that they may be performed by voice and keyboard, or with keyboard alone (with two exceptions, one of which is the witty *Lob der Faulheit*). This is itself an indication that Haydn was willing to do without the poem. They usually include introductory material that presents the coming vocal line. The first set (1781) show a preference for binary or ternary form, the former used for four-line strophes and the latter for longer stanzas. The parts are normally separated by interlude material, sometimes modulatory, sometimes merely reiterative. In almost every case the second part is more chromatic and/or dramatic, frequently involving a mode change and in a closely related key—the dominant or parallel minor is preferred. In the case of ternary form, the return of *a* is practically always given with some modification, and the tendency is to repeat the last poetic line or two within each part. Typical of all these characteristics are *Cupido, Die Verlassene,* and *An Iris,* among many others.

The second set, issued in 1784, show considerably more freedom of structure, a number being through composed within the individual strophes. At the same time there is a generally more elaborate and dramatic approach, even when the texts themselves do not suggest this as appropriate. Typical of this greater intensification of musical content is the *Geistliches Lied,* and *Das Leben ist ein Traum,* as well as the already mentioned *Lob der Faulheit.* The chromaticism, harmonic and melodic, that was present in the first set is here carried even farther, including the extensive use of diminished-seventh chords and abrupt stabs into unlikely tonal areas, as in *O fliess, ja wallend fliess in Zähren,* where a brief but highly chromatic movement moves within the space of two measures from B major to G major and immediately back to B major. In the majority of cases such maneuvering is involved with text illustration.

All the changes that occur between the first and second sets of *Lieder* are intensified in the English *Canzonettas* of 1794. The liking for text repetitions is carried to an extreme but here they are made even more meaningless because they are so often separated by keyboard interludes. Haydn seems particularly taken by the poetry of Anne Hunter and often her lyrics are made still more sentimental by his musical treatment. This is nowhere more evident than in *Fidelity,* but it is still only partially concealed in *Recollection* and even in the beloved *A Pastoral Song* (My mother bids me bind my hair). The movement away from the strict part-song structure of the first *Lieder* is completed in the *Canzonettas,* where most are through composed either within the stanza or totally. An example of the first type is the *Pastoral Song* and of the second, *She Never Told Her Love,* the latter providing a musical realization that is surely in excess of the poetic content. Also represented is the strophic variation (*Pleasing Pain*) where the variations are highly involved with illustration of text.

In general, Haydn is less inclined to declamatory barbarisms in his German texts than in English, where he frequently places ornaments and coloratura on unaccented syllables or inconsequential parts of speech (articles, conjunctions, etc.). It seems clear that beyond a superficial ability to paint the most obvious musical picture of the individual words or phrases, there is little depth in any of the pieces, nor any attempt to capture the subtleties of the poetry. What the songs do show, however, is a growing independence of the accompaniment, particularly as this involves introductory and interlude-postlude material. While the voice is singing, the piano either follows, for the most part, or simply provides a harmonic background of one sort or another. But occasionally, as in *Piercing Eyes,* there is real motivic independence, not yet fully developed but at least indicative of what is to come. The failings of the songs *as songs* is their almost total reliance upon contemporary operatic techniques, techniques that pulled Haydn too far away from the intimacy of the texts. The music simply overwhelms the words.

Insofar as his songs are concerned, Mozart's style does not show Haydn's total preoccupation with operatic device, even in the most elaborate pieces. Nor do his compositions become chronologically more fanciful, as do Haydn's. His earliest songs are in the simplest possible *volkstümliches* tradition, even to the point of supplying merely the melody and bass without inner voices (*An die Freude, Geheime Liebe*). However, as early as 1772, he produced the chromatic and expressive *Wie unglücklich bin ich nit* with its extensive melodic and harmonic underlining of text, and with the chords fully given. In these first pieces as in many of his later ones, he likes to repeat the final poetic line, not as an echo-extension but setting it to a more heightened musical expression. His two favorite devices for introducing the repetition are the deceptive cadence (even when not textually appropriate) and the appoggiatura resolving upward to the mediant degree.

After 1775 the accompaniments are fully realized and under the impetus of his growing interest in the Singspiel and opera, he wrote a canzonetta, *Ridente la calma*, and two ariettas, *Oiseau, si tous les ans* and *Dans un bois*, all of which are quite removed from his *volkstümliches* beginnings. During the following decade he continued to turn out a number of extremely simple pieces, including the *Wiegenlied* and *An die Einsamkeit*. But, as in the latter, he became more and more concerned with text illustration (the song begins with a diminished seventh chord) and more involved with harmonic characterization. At the same time, many of his songs show the encroachment of opera. The introductions, which are short if present at all in his earlier pieces, including the ariettas, become longer, usually presenting the coming vocal melody but often in a highly ornamented form. The rhythms are more complex, the melodies more vocal with extended ranges and more involved coloratura, and the use of chromatic harmonies is frequent. To this period belongs the highly illustrative *Das Veilchen*, probably Mozart's best-known song, and it can hardly be mistaken for anything other than a miniature opera scene in spite of the folkish text.

The songs of the last years continue to include a mixture of styles. *Die Alte,* in which Mozart reverts to an earlier style in giving only melody and bass, is again folklike and uninvolved. More elaborate are songs like *Das Lied der Trennung*, with its departure in the fifth and sixth stanzas from the otherwise strophic format; *Abendempfindung*, in a true through-compositional format that includes sudden changes in accompaniment style, declamatory sections, vocal roulades, ornamentation, and all the other trappings of opera; and *An Chloe*, with its suggestion of rondo-variation and occasional motivic dialogue between voice and accompaniment. The very last songs, published in 1791, are again simple ones, without text repetitions, entirely strophic, restricted in vocal range but nevertheless showing all of the mature Mozart's command of melodic and harmonic imagination.

Despite his growing concern for greater dramatization of text and more extensive musical manipulation, Mozart returned again and again to the simple strophic song. One cannot help feeling that his continuing efforts in this medium exerted a control over all of his vocal writing. Even the most full-blown songs do not display the same embellishment that is so evident in the later Haydn. Mozart's accompaniment style is extremely varied, although he is most strongly attracted to broken-chord figures of all sorts in the style of the period. At the same time he is less inclined than Haydn to indulge in long introductions and interludes. He relies strongly upon the diminished-seventh chord as an illustrative device but beyond this his harmonic range is richer than that of his immediate contemporaries and in the shorter songs it is put to well controlled use in the interest of the text. As might be expected, when he becomes more operatic the declamation suffers. But the more *volkstümliches* pieces are quite faithful to the poetic meter and rhythm while avoiding a pedantic rigidity.

Of all Mozart's characteristics, his melodic style probably exerted the greatest influence on contemporary song. He relies heavily upon appoggiaturas for both musical and declamatory purposes and they are often associated with chromatic or deceptive harmonic movement. His melodic rhythms are unusually flexible for the period and he moves decisively away from a preponderance of melodies based upon broken-chord outlines. He loves dissonant intervals, in particular minor and diminished sevenths and diminished fifths, and frequently intensifies their expressiveness by following immediately with an appoggiatura. In these respects and others he provided models the development and extension of which were to become part and parcel of the melodic vocabulary of the succeeding century.

Like Mozart, Beethoven was occupied throughout his life with a variety of song types. Some, like *Lied (Ohne Liebe lebe)* and *Marmotte*, are presented in the most uncomplex style with only the bass and melody offered. Others, like *Ich liebe dich,* are fully realized pianistically but cling to a simple and intimate lyricism. Again like Mozart, he is given to repetitions of closing poetic lines but those of Beethoven are more apt to be set to short extensions that are exact musical reiterations or at least sequences. His instrumental concern is reflected in, among other factors, his provision of an accompaniment postlude even in the very short strophic songs.

Along with the short, almost folklike type, Beethoven has left a number of extremely extended and dramatic pieces, often in the form of a scene and aria and so indicated (*Ah! Perfido*). Others are in the same operatic format but not identified as such (*An die Hoffnung, Seufzer eines Ungeliebten und Gegenliebe, Der Wachtelschlag*, among others). They are characterized by

numerous tempo changes, interpolated recitatives, accompaniments varying widely in style, and intensely dramatic and illustrative passages in both
voice and piano. At times his love of musical development and motivic
manipulation causes him to overweight a very simple text with a relatively
complex realization, as in *Der Kuss* and *Freudvoll und Leidvoll*, both of which
employ a good deal of tone painting, text repetition, fanciful interludes,
and the like. On occasion this predisposition has the happiest results,
however, as in the cantata-like *Adelaide*, where the text itself is ecstatic
enough to bear the extended musical treatment. It is possible that this sort of
involvement led him in 1816 to produce what is generally conceded to be
the first German song cycle, *An die ferne Geliebte*, cast in the form of a
series of themes and variations and notable for the exceptional involvement
of the piano in the total form and expression. Unlike later cycles, it cannot
be performed except as a unit because each section leads without musical
interruption into the succeeding one. The entire work is given a sense
of completeness through the return, at the end, of the material with
which the composition began, although in a dramatically heightened
form.

There is little doubt that Beethoven's use of the keyboard was an
inspiration to Schubert, who worshiped the older man in every respect.
Not only is there a wide and imaginative range to his patterns, but there
is an unprecedented interplay of accompaniment and vocal motives, sometimes even involving a sense of thematic "working out" that places both on
an equal plane musically and expressively. Often, too, there is a real independence of motivic material (sometimes illustrative in quality) so that the
accompaniment develops a character of its own completely apart from the
voice. *Wonne der Wehmuth* is an excellent example of this, with its piano
motive descriptive of falling tears that functions freely beneath the recitative-like vocal line. The song is, in fact, a forerunner of the sort of lyric
declamation that would be fully realized in the nineteenth century, characterized by the assignment to the piano of a vital part of the poetic suggestion
so that the voice would be left free to deliver the text without an excess of
restrictive melodic responsibility.

From the standpoint of heightened expression, Beethoven's most important contribution to the *lied* was his expanding harmonic range. In view
of the part harmony was to play throughout the romantic century, there
seems to be some justification for Stendhal's statement quoted by Szabolcsi
in his *History of Melody*:

In music, there are two ways of arriving at pleasure, by way of Haydn's style
or by way of Cimarosa's: by sublime harmony or delightful melody. Cimarosa's
style is right for southern peoples. . . . Melody reached its zenith about 1780;
after this date, music changed its nature, harmony won the upper hand, and the
singing line declined.[3]

3 Szabolcsi, *op. cit.*, p. 159. See also p. 128 of this book.

Beethoven cannot be cited for the exquisiteness of his melodic invention, but the impetus that he gave to all facets of harmonic exploitation cannot be denied. The materials he used were not new ones, but even in the songs (never one of his principal preoccupations) he was lavish with his coloration. In *Mignon*, for instance, after establishing A major during the initial period, he moves during the next six measures through the tonic minor to its relative major, C, and from there to F major, which he utilizes as the Neapolitan Sixth of E major in order to return to A major. The abruptness of the movement and the striking coloristic effect is a powerful aid in underlining the climax of the stanza. Again, after a long beginning section in *Adelaide* centering around the tonic B♭ and its dominant, he moves within the space of a single measure from F to D♭ major (one of his favorite relationships and one which Schubert was to exploit) and during the ensuing section of the song to G♭ major. Here again this functions in the large sense as the Neapolitan Sixth tonality to F major by means of which the return is made to the original tonic of B♭.

Often his progressions into unexpected centers are made with no warning at all, as in his setting of the witty tale of the king and the flea, which he entitles merely *Aus Goethe's "Faust"*, where he follows a phrase in G minor with one beginning in F and cadencing in C minor. Even more striking is a passage in the first of his *Vier Arietten*, the very Italianate *Dimmi, ben mio*. Here the tonic is A major and at the close of the first section there is a four-measure pseudo-recitative given over an insistent dominant-seventh chord. Totally without preparation and without resolution of the chord, the next section begins in C major.

Like Mozart, Beethoven loved the diminished seventh. Although he uses it in all contexts as a means of coloring the text (as well as for modulatory purposes), he brings it most frequently to bear upon more serious or profound poetry. Nowhere is it more in evidence than in the *Sechs geistliche Lieder von Gellert*, where it appears in almost every imaginable context. Likewise, he is attracted to the various augmented-sixth chords which, like the diminished seventh, were to serve so meaningfully throughout the nineteenth century. They are to be found in *Neue Liebe, neues Leben, An die Hoffnung*, and even in the relatively simple *An einen Säugling*, and always where they are textually significant.

As in the work of most of his immediate predecessors and contemporaries, Beethoven's use of minor as a device to depict mood is rather unsettled. There are instances when it can be interpreted no other way, as in *Freudvoll und leidvoll*, where the change from A major to A minor illustrates the words "burning and yearning in suspenseful pain." On the other hand, his four settings of *Sehnsucht* include one in E♭ major, although the other three are all in G minor. Undoubtedly the convention of equating minor with sadness was already prevalent but not as solidly entrenched as it was to become even a few years later.

Like composers in every period, Beethoven was drawn to text illustration of all types. The "tear" motive from *Wonne der Wehmuth* has been pointed out above. Other more blatant instances occur throughout his work, among them the rolling of the drum represented by a rolled bass pedal point on F in *Die Trommel gerühret*, the staccato figure that pervades *Aus Goethe's "Faust"*, which can only be a remarkably apt representation of the flea as well as the scratching it inspires, the accompaniment triplets that depict the gentle breeze in *Mignon*, and far too many others to catalogue.

In many ways, and most certainly in his treatment of song, Beethoven stands apart from the trend of the times, which was in the direction of growing lyricism. In the spirit of organic unification that pervades his art in general, he could not avoid the utmost in manipulation of his musical materials. In dealing with larger forms, this manipulative genius stood him in good stead and accounts for much of his mastery, but its application to song composition did not always bring off the happiest results. Alec Robertson has indicated the heart of the matter:

Beethoven so nearly succeeded in making an artistic entity of voice, verse and accompaniment that it appears as if only a lack of the true lyric gift can have prevented him [*viz.*, from succeeding].[4]

But Beethoven's mark was on the musical expression of his time and Schubert was to borrow extensively from his work, adding to it the "lyric gift" with which he himself was so richly endowed.

4 Gerald Abraham (ed.), *The Music of Schubert* (New York: W. W. Norton & Company, Inc., 1947), pp. 150–151.

The Romantic Century

FRANZ SCHUBERT

I T IS abundantly clear that Schubert did not spring from a vacuum, nor can he be considered an innovator in the sense that he changed or invented new patterns of song. Concern for and artistic activity in song composition had reached a high level of intensity, as we have seen, by the beginning years of the nineteenth century. What Schubert brought to the enterprise was an affinity for short lyric compositions of all sorts, a rare melodic imagination, and an unremitting drive, which compelled him to pour his creative energy into the writing of over six hundred songs, many of which have become the embodiment of the best efforts in this genre. Drawing upon the riches of his heritage and adding to it his own special craftsmanship, he turned out a body of work that anticipated most of what was best in the newly awakened romantic temper. To realize the extent of his involvement it is necessary to try to identify the elements which make up nineteenth-century romanticism itself.

Of all the artistic temperaments, romanticism is probably the most complex and the most impossible to tie down in limited terms. Much of this is because one of romanticism's principal characteristics is itself a concentration on limitlessness. As an artistic and expressive medium it attempts to capture and embody the "real living experience" that transcends all categorization and systematization. Thus all of life is open to art—the realm of Nature, individual (and collective) emotion, sensuality, symbolism, sentiment and sentimentality, the known and the unknown, even the longing for those achievements that are beyond man's power to attain or to express. This spirit of boundlessness led to a search for means of blending all the arts in what the romanticists conceived to be a fuller, more complete expressive enterprise. This kinship of the arts is basically what inspired the development of program music as well as the unprecedented concentration upon the art song as one of the principal means of expression.

The interaction between literature and music during the first half of the nineteenth century in Germany has been documented and discussed fully by Linda Siegel in her dissertation.[1] In her study she distinguishes between the sentimentality and irrationalism of the *Sturm und Drang* artists and the same elements in the romantics, who felt that not only the feelings but the contemplation (and thus the rationalization) of them was equally valuable. In the same sense, the symbolism of the baroque was a tangible symbolism while that of the romantics tended to express intangible concepts. Their poetry concentrated on allusions rather than upon direct statement, upon mood and the intensity of the individual experience rather than upon the philosophical rhetoric of previous periods. Of great significance in Siegel's thesis is the effect upon musicians of the heroes and heroines of the novels of Goethe, Tieck, E. T. A. Hoffmann, Novalis, and others, most of whom were either themselves musicians or musically aware. Characters such as Mignon and Gretchen became symbols of the romantic spirit, and composers throughout the nineteenth century turned to them repeatedly for inspiration, not only in song and opera but in programmatic works as well.

So far as song itself is concerned, it is impossible to overestimate the effect of the commingling of poets, novelists, painters, and composers. The concepts that music can reflect color, principally in its harmony, that poetry can itself be musical, that music can serve to express thoughts and feelings that are beyond the power of words—all of these are romantic concepts. And they led to continuing attempts to synthesize the arts, to erase the boundaries between them, and to use all of them to recreate an experience that was not only unique in itself but outside the capacity of any single medium to capture fully.

The themes that attracted the romantics are as limitless as the spirit of romanticism itself. Night, death, dreams, wanderlust, unfulfilled longing, lostness, mystery—all are present. They form the core of both mood and situation in most of the novels, poems, and paintings of the period, and it was inevitable that they should be taken up and given expression in the music. No one medium lent itself so completely to this task as did song. It was not only a very real combination of word and tone, which demanded a synthesis in its very conception, but it was also brief enough to accommodate the greatest intensification of mood and yet varied enough in formal arrangement to allow for the myriad forms devised by the poets. In addition, a public was at hand, a public that was turning more and more to the instrumental counterpart of song, the concise piano piece, with its emphasis upon emotional expression rather than upon expansion and development of musical ideas.

Schubert opened the floodgates. Romantic themes overrun his song output—no other composer has set so many poems dealing with night, death, and dreaming, for instance. The three are symbolically related in their mystical awareness of the unknown. Schubert's involvement with the mystery was to carry over into the songs of Schumann and Brahms, among

1 Linda Suzanne Rogols Siegel, *The Influence of Romantic Literature on Romantic Music In Germany* (Ann Arbor, Michigan: University Microfilms, Inc., 1964).

many others. (Brahms, in fact, used a type of dramatic-lyric declamation that was most unusual for him when he set Heine's *Der Tod, das ist die kühle Nacht,* and his most profound songs are the *Vier ernste Gesänge,* the underlying theme of which is the contemplation of the mysteries of life and death.)

Although composers throughout the nineteenth century were continually drawn to the songs from Goethe's *Wilhelm Meister,* in particular those of Mignon, none gave so much attention to them as Schubert. Among the fifty-seven Goethe poems that he set, eight are lyrics from the novel, and he seemed unable to capture these to his complete satisfaction. Each of them received at least two settings and one, *Nur wer die Sehnsucht kennt,* was given six versions. The themes of lostness, loneliness, and wanderlust occupied Schubert throughout his short life, but never more than during his last years. *Die schöne Müllerin* and *Winterreise* as well as the posthumously collected *Schwanengesang* are filled with the romantic urge to seek in Nature solace for the inability to find fulfillment in the world of real people and things. Even the story of the maid of the mill, with its opening poems full of the exuberance of love and the joy of life, ends with the wanderer seeking from his beloved brook the peace that he needs to heal the wounds received from his encounter with those who inhabit the workaday world.

Thus Schubert is the first of the great romantics in terms of the subject matter that exerted the greatest attraction for him as well as in his individuality in dealing with it. But it would be a mistake to assume that he attained his mastery of song without considerable struggle. There have been so many volumes written about his songs and song style that it would be redundant to add a large body of commentary at this point.[2] It seems necessary merely to indicate some of his early attitudes and the problems they represent, together with a brief synopsis of the factors pointing to his mastery during the final years.

Perhaps the most striking characteristic of the young Schubert is his excess of dramatization. Not only was he drawn to texts of the ballad type that would lend themselves to an extended recitative-arioso-aria setting, but he poured into them all the harmonic and melodic vocabulary of expanding romanticism. Pieces like the 1811 *Vatermörder, Der Taucher* (1813) and others are overburdened with tempo changes, alterations of accompaniment style, and instrumental effects of all sorts. He is especially fond at this time of tremolo effects in the piano, often as a means of accompanying recitative passages but also in interludes and elsewhere. Even when the pieces are not actually great in length (*Der Taucher* is a full twenty-four pages long!) the treatment often tends to be just as sectional and excessive. *Verklärung,* for instance, is quite brief but loaded with harmonic restlessness including enharmonic modulations, movements (often abrupt) into

2 Two excellent studies from recent years are:
   Ernest G. Porter, *Schubert's Song Technique* (London: Dennis Dobson, 1961).
   A. Craig Bell, *The Songs of Schubert* (London: Alston Books, 1964).

distant tonal centers, and fluctuations of dynamics. *Schäfers Klagelied*, one of his earliest settings of a Goethe text, is full of the same illustrative writing, and even though there is a certain attempt to establish motivic unity, this is obscured by the enharmonics, changes of key signature, and overabundance of colorful chords, including one of Schubert's favorites even during these early years, the augmented sixth. *Die Betende* (1814), although cast in a strophic format, shows the same sort of uncontrolled harmonic experimentation, so that the continuity that might have resulted from the form is largely dissipated by the coloristic effects of the accompaniment. In most of these beginning efforts can be found all the musical devices that identify Schubert's fertile imagination. He remained fond of harmonic sequences of all sorts but particularly chromatic ones, enharmonic modulations, deceptive resolutions which were often modulatory in character, sharply dissonant chords, and unlikely key relationships. His early problems were of degree, not of kind. One of the factors which worked against him most strongly at this point was the disservice rendered to his already keen sense of tune, for the erratic and nervous harmony tended, except in rare instances, to draw too much attention to itself and away from the melody.

The materials which most appealed to Schubert at this period were not inappropriate to the dramatic subject matter he so often chose, and there is little doubt that his experimentation was to help in broadening his range of expression, a range that served him well when, in later years, he was able to bring his materials under more control. In one of his many comments on the composer, Porter has this to say:

His early participation in orchestral works and masses, with their extended forms and varied harmonies, [and] the production of Italian arias under Salieri, was not a good school for a budding song composer at the beginning of the nineteenth century. . . .[3]

And again:

When dealing with pure emotion he found that the poet had a great advantage over the musician in that he could make a sudden, even violent change of expression without departing from his metrical framework, for his medium is connotative as well as subjective. The musical equivalents of such changes are alteration of tempo, key, phrasing, or time, and any of these may upset the emotional rhythm and unity of the work.[4]

The real wonder is not that Schubert was able to bring his forces into line within comparatively few years, but that even in the midst of these problems he was able to produce his first great song, *Gretchen am Spinnrade*, in 1814. Although little short of an operatic scene, there is here a sort of motivic control not too much in evidence in most of his contemporary

3 G. Porter, "Schubert's Song Workshop," *Music and Letters*, Vol. XXXIX, No. 2 (April, 1958), p. 143.
4 *Ibid.*, p. 147.

writing, plus the happy choice of an accompaniment motive that is at the same time illustrative and capable of furnishing musical continuity.

The following year, 1815, is a great one, not only because of the astounding number of songs (one hundred and thirty-nine at least), but because the characteristics that were to serve him best are strongly evident. This is the year of *Erlkönig*, as dramatically satisfying as anything he ever wrote but showing the same degree of control as *Gretchen*. But it also brought a host of other more lyrically consistent pieces, among them *Das Bild*, *An Mignon*, and *Nähe des Geliebten*, and many others of similar type. Even the rather fanciful *Als ich sie erröthen sah* utilizes a consistent accompaniment pattern so that the vocal tunefulness can predominate. At the same time, there is a keener sense of harmonic control, and already much in evidence is Schubert's liking for key relationships of a third, particularly those that feature a modal interchange, such as the movement without warning to E♭ major in a tonality that is basically G major.

All the song forms he was to use are present even in the first years. Strophic, strophic variation, ternary, through composed, binary, each with their modifications—all are here. Already, too, there is fairly extensive use of pedal points, motivic interplay between voice and accompaniment, melodic ornamentation both written out and in symbol, and appoggiaturas. His accompaniment patterns range from block chords to broken figures to tremolo to melodic foils for the voice. And also noticeable is his strong penchant for major-minor vacillation.

The years between 1815 and the first great cycle, *Die schöne Müllerin*, in 1823 are marked by a gradual turning away from the pseudo-dramatics of his earliest work toward more concentration on strophic composition and a consistency of musical texture. Throughout, however, he struggled with the problems of declamation and sought a way besides recitative to handle sudden dramatic or expository sections of the poetry. Although there is a gradual rejection of recitative, it nevertheless invades some of the work almost to the end. Of many instances which might be cited, the following list will give an indication of Schubert's continuing resort to the device:

1815	*Der Liedler*
	Hektors Abschied
1817	*Die abgeblühte Linde*
1821	*Der Unglückliche*
1825	*Ein Fräulein schaut vom hohen Thurm*

But during the same period he was increasingly able to work declamatory sections into the songs without impeding the musical movement or disrupting the musical texture. Sometimes these sections occur as vocal statements over a sustained accompaniment chord, as in *Der Wanderer*. Sometimes they are rhythmically vigorous statements interspersed with rests under which the accompaniment pursues its independent movement, as in *Auf der Donau*. And sometimes they simply involve a sharp change of melodic character or a shift of tempo but without any cessation in the forward rhythmical control, as in *Der Alpenjäger*. Many of the later songs show the development of an entirely predominant lyric-recitative style throughout, as in *Die junge Nonne* of 1825 and the settings of the Heine poems from the *Schwanengesang*. It is in songs like *Der Atlas, Die Stadt, Der Doppelgänger* that Schubert makes his most decisive moves toward the synthesis of recitative and aria that became one of the distinguishing features of later nineteenth-century melodic style. Although all his old fondness for harmonic intensity is much in evidence, along with coloristic accompaniment devices such as tremolo, harp effects, exploitation of range extremes and the like, the intense brevity and incisiveness of poetic mood seem to encourage a sort of tightness of musical control which is new to the composer. At the same time, when the poetry suggests it, there is no loss of the old lyricism, still so much in evidence in *Ständchen* and *Das Fischermädchen*.

A good deal of inclination toward the same style can be seen in *Winterreise*, in such pieces as *Der greise Kopf, Im Dorfe*, and the magnificent *Der Leiermann*. The latter is truly one of the masterpieces of the song genre and bears testimony that during his last years Schubert brought his forces under total control. What better way to match the poem's imagery of utter desolation, dejection, and hopeless futility than to provide a harmonic background that is restricted to only two chords, tonic and dominant? Here, too, the illustrative features are completely synthesized with the mood— the open fifths not only representing the grind-organ but the emptiness and lack of direction of both the player and the singer-poet. Never has Schubert used his motivic material more meaningfully, setting up an organ tune as aimless and graceless as the poetic situation. And it belongs entirely to the organ, until the singer echoes it at the question: "Will you grind away on your hurdy-gurdy to my songs?" And over it all, the voice maintains its syllabic, melodically sterile recitation.

One cannot help wondering what would have resulted had Schubert saved some of the more psychologically rich Goethe lyrics for these last years of his life. The 1815 and 1816 settings of the songs from *Wilhelm Meister*, to which he returned occasionally through the succeeding years but without improving them greatly, are indicative of his growing tunefulness but at the same time of his inability to grapple successfully with the depth of Goethe's poetry. The Mignon songs capture a sort of wistfulness, which was certainly a part of the character of the forsaken gypsy child, but they include as well a great deal of exuberance that cannot have mirrored her psychological state. Goethe himself was critical of the aria-like treatment of such pieces as *Kennst du das Land?*

By the same token, the emphasis upon melody led Schubert into expressive difficulty in his treatment of the Harper's songs. The poems are burdened with a boundless loneliness and despair as well as much of the madness that haunted the old wanderer. Almost none of this is reflected in Schubert's settings. The second, in particular, *Wer nie sein Brod mit Thränen ass*, bears little relationship to the text except for a certain pensive quality induced by the use of the minor mode and the gentle arch of the melodic line. There seems little artistic purpose for the changes in mode that occur at the repetition of each stanza nor, for that matter, for the repetition itself. The chromaticism of the harmonic movement toward the final cadence of each strophe and its variant does little to suggest the *himmlischen Mächte* (heavenly powers) or to connect this expressively with the frustration to which these powers have driven the singer. Nor does the "prettiness" of the melody at these points capture the awe and bitterness of the poetic mood. What emerges as a total effect is the lilting, almost saccharine quality of the tune itself and its harmonic treatment in the interest of purely musical color.

Commenting upon the third song of the Harper, *An die Türen will ich schleichen*, Robertson has this to say:

I cannot help feeling that Schubert found the marching tune of the Harper's third song ... before he considered the vocal part. In this case there is not sufficient compensation for the stressing of unimportant words and the forcing of them into an alien rhythm.[5]

He is referring to the accentual importance and rhythmic duration given to such words as *und* and *eine*. The difficulty is not only with declamation (never one of Schubert's strong points) but again with the sheer tunefulness of the piece, which, despite the plodding nature of the accompaniment, fails to capture the brokenness of the Harper's spirit.

Many factors are involved, of course, and it would be doing the composer a grave injustice to insist that his control of musical materials alone was responsible for some of the weaknesses in his early songs, despite some magnificent achievements in others. Certainly one highly important influence was the atmosphere of the times and of Vienna in particular.

As a matter of fact a good many of Schubert's songs—more than has been generally recognized—breathe the characteristic spirit of his age, that mild Viennese wistfulness, that rather lightly-borne sense of the sorrow at the heart of things, that cordial joyousness, in short all the sentimental sensibility of the Biedermeier age, and in particular the sugared and somewhat hypertrophic melancholy of old Vienna.[6]

Still another factor was the psychological change in Schubert himself between the first songs and the last:

After 1822, when his youth was gone and health had begun to fail, and life had become a terrible reality, his thoughts turned inwards. . . .

5 Gerald Abraham (ed.), *The Music of Schubert*, p. 169.
6 Hans Költzsch, "Schubert and the Romantic Problem," *Music and Letters*, Vol. XX, No. 2 (April, 1939), p. 135.

It is very difficult to draw a comparison between the songs of this later period and those of the earlier one, but the difference must strike every one, and it resides mainly perhaps in the subjects themselves. Subjects of romance are natural to the imagination of youth. But in maturer life the mind is calmer and dwells more strongly on personal subjects. . . . After 1822 the classical songs and ballads are rare, and the themes which he chooses belong chiefly to modern life and individual feeling.[7]

The *Wilhelm Meister* settings are the products of Schubert's youth—they represent an impulsive tunefulness that permeated much of the music of the time and that in song composition, had its roots in the work of the Berlin School, and also betray a conscious effort to allow the melody to grow from a sort of natural text scansion. Schubert's grasp of melody served him well throughout his productive years, for his compositions always "sing" most convincingly. On the other hand, the influence of Beethoven's care in construction and his technical mastery of the materials of music made itself felt in the products of Schubert's maturity. Although always a lyricist, in his later period—the period of *Die schöne Müllerin* and *Winterreise* and *Schwanengesang*—his lyricism ceases to be an end in itself and serves more fully the interest of the poetry, frequently as a result of its skillful inclusion of suitable declamatory devices.

Schubert's contributions to both romanticism and the song are immeasurable. He took the forms, the harmonic and melodic devices, the rhythmic possibilities, and the poetic expressiveness of his predecessors and contemporaries and molded them into a heightened sort of brief lyrical exclamation that anticipated most of the song composition of the entire century. Although this did not always produce perfect results, he was often able to free the music from the metrical demands of the poetry, even in his shorter strophic songs, without thereby losing the larger implications of rhythm. When he failed to achieve the ultimate in musico-poetic synthesis, the failure was as often due to his overwhelming melodic sense as to his leaning toward overdramatization, sometimes even diffuseness. In many cases, he relied too heavily upon illustration of textual minutiae that were not even expressively important. But through it all he worked at pulling the forces of words and music into a more compressed and complementary relationship, and because of his imagination, enthusiasm, and productivity the true lyric *lied* emerged as one of the most respected media of romantic expression.

ROBERT SCHUMANN

Any comparison between Schubert and Schumann must take into account several factors about the composers themselves. One of these is the fact that Schumann gave little attention to song composition until he had

7 Sir George Grove, "Franz Peter Schubert," *Grove's Dictionary of Music and Musicians,* Vol. IV (New York: The Macmillan Company, 1948), p. 630.

reached the age of thirty, an age at which Schubert had already produced most of his work. Schumann was already a skillful composer, who had written profusely for the piano and had therefore developed a deep respect for the possibilities of the instrument as an instrument in its own right rather than a mere accompaniment device. Another factor is Schumann's wide acquaintance with and involvement in literary expression of all sorts. The *Neue Zeitschrift für Musik* began operation with the composer as editor in 1834, six years before his first serious attempts at song. Among his many critiques were several devoted to the songs of Schubert as well as to the work of his own contemporaries, including Franz.

The point is that Schumann had already formed a relatively well-thought-out philosophy in regard to a musico-poetic synthesis, and it was one that served him both consciously and subconsciously in his own composition. He was widely read in the poetry of the time and was strongly attracted to the new romantics, Heine in particular, but also to Rückert, Eichendorff, Mörike, and others who placed especial emphasis upon capturing an emotional core of experience in as few words as possible. Schumann did not ignore the greatness nor the possibilities of Goethe and Schiller (two of Schubert's favorites), but he turned to them much less often than to the younger men. Although a great admirer of Schubert, he was nevertheless aware of some of his predecessor's weaknesses, in particular Schubert's tendency to reflect the poetic externals rather than the psychological implications. (In Schubert's defense, it must be pointed out that the difference in the poetry itself was a strong controlling factor. Only late in his life did he come to Heine, whose *Buch der Lieder*, from which so many of Schumann's settings were drawn, was published in 1827, a year before Schubert's death. Among the most psychologically oriented songs the latter wrote are those that are based on Heine and included in the *Schwanengesang*. Thus not only Schumann's own strong literary inclinations but the newly available poetry was of great import to the stylistic differences between the two composers.)

Strangely enough, Schumann's development as a song writer shows an almost inverse relationship to his experience in the medium. The pieces for which he is best remembered and which even now form the bulk of his work before the public are the first things he wrote during the outburst of 1840. It is fashionable to divide a composer's productive years into three periods, and in Schumann's case the division proves an apt and useful one so far as the songs are concerned.[8]

The first period is identified with the years from 1840 to 1847, during which, under the influence of Schubert and the folk song, he tended toward a melodic style marked by the frequent use of sequences and repetition with variation. Like song composers of almost all periods, he was conscious of the possibilities of ballads and ballad-like texts. But unlike many,

8 Rudolf Felber, "Schumann's Place in German Song," *Musical Quarterly*, Vol. XXVI, No. 3 (July, 1940).

including Schubert, he was able to handle the dramatic changes of pace without resorting to a discontinuous musical style. In *Belsatzar*, for instance, there is all the drama one could hope for: tempo changes at appropriate places, changes of accompaniment style to deal with variations in mood, and even considerable variety in vocal melody, which runs from lyricism to declamation. At the same time, the piece is not sectional in the old sense of recitative-arioso-aria; declamatory sections are taken into the general texture and brought into prominence only because of the alterations in accompaniment figure. The composition, although rather extended, holds together much more than most of Schubert's in the same idiom— *Erlkönig* being one of the notable exceptions. A related type of composition which attracted Schumann at this period and throughout his life was the short set of related songs in the manner of a miniature cycle. Perhaps the best-known of these is the three-piece *Der Arme Peter*, but there are others including the tryptich drawn from Heine's *Tragödie*, the last section of which is a duet for soprano and tenor. In most cases such works are quite brief and move without interruption from part to part.

But the greatest works of these years are the cycles: *Myrten*, the two *Liederkreis* on texts by Heine and Eichendorff, *Frauenliebe und Leben,* and *Dichterliebe*. All show Schumann's characteristic ability to establish a central musical texture that reflects the mood of the poem without resorting to illustrative devices and without harmonic or melodic excursions that draw attention to themselves apart from the poem. The role of the piano is well-defined—it suggests, it interrupts, it carries forward the musical movement, it engages in dialogue with the voice, and always it establishes a character of its own with bases in the poetic expression rather than merely furnishing a harmonic support for the voice. The penchant for text repetition which trapped so many composers into disruption of the poetry is largely forsaken by Schumann. Interestingly enough, he tends to lapse from this most often in *Frauenliebe und Leben* where he is dealing with the poetry of the second-rate Chamisso. There is less incidence in the *Liederkreis* and strikingly less in Heine's *Dichterliebe*, rather convincing evidence that Schumann respected the ability of the better poets to make the point without benefit of extended repetitions for musical purposes. This, incidentally, is one of Schumann's greatest contributions in the movement away from the operatic style that still plagued many of his contemporaries,

The second period, from 1847 to about 1851, Rudolf Felber characterizes as intensely subjective in terms of an increased harmonic complexity, a melodic pursuit of more realistic declamation through the use of larger intervals, changes of register, and a more chromatic line which often exploits augmented and diminished intervals. There is also an inclination to place great reliance upon rhythmic elements in the search for greater control of declamation. At the same time, there is even more responsibility assigned to the piano and the demands upon the accompanist become almost virtuosic. Typical of the extended melodic concept is *Melancholie*, with its melisma on *Leben* based on a diminished-seventh chord, phrases that run dramatically over the range of a tenth within the space of half a measure, and declamatory intervals of a tenth and more. These same sorts of jaggedly demanding lines are in *Geständnis*, *Der Kontrabandiste*, and many others. The elaboration of the accompaniment is everywhere in evidence but most strikingly in such pieces as *Geisternähe* and *Aufträge*. This last song features a vocal style that bears an uncanny resemblance to fully developed Debussy, but without the latter's suavity.

It is significant that during this period of concern for the extension of musical materials in an apparent search for broader expressive involvement with the text, Schumann produced the first of his three *Declamations* for a narrator with piano accompaniment. The medium was given some attention by other composers in the nineteenth century, among them Liszt, and it demonstrates two things in particular that are important to the growing concern for music as a handmaid of poetry. The first is a real awareness of the possibilities of the piano as a purely commenting and mood-enhancing instrument in its own right. The second is a companion awareness that the text can almost always be better projected, *as a text*, when it is unhampered by the demands of vocalization. Although the *Declamations* cannot be considered the true forefathers of the lyric-recitative, they are nevertheless closely involved in many of the same motivations and ideologies. Significantly, all of Schumann's *Declamations* (he wrote two more in 1852) are ballads, a form that depends for its effectiveness upon the utmost clarity in delivery of the word.

In the midst of all this emphasis upon dramatic expression, much of which was patently experimental, Schumann was very much aware of the demands for lyricism in song. The *Lieder Album für die Jugend* (1849) is primarily devoted to short strophic songs, many with folk or folkish texts, and most of them are extremely uncomplicated in style. Some, however, even when the vocal melody is relatively straightforward and undemanding, place great stress on accompaniment devices of a quite complex sort, as in *Der Sandmann*. A few of the pieces are quite sophisticated in every way, vocally as well as pianistically. Two of Schumann's most beloved songs from the *Album* which fall into this category are *Er ist's* and *Mignon*. And in spite of the somewhat operatic line with its invitation to *portamento* and relatively wide melodic intervals, *Mein schöner Stern* is unashamedly tuneful, although it comes from an opus other than the *Album für die Jugend*, a fact that testifies to Schumann's continuing need for lyric expression and relative simplicity even when not preparing a work for children.

It is significant that during this period of grappling with the need for psychological intensity in his song writing, the composer turned to the most demanding of the Goethe poems, those from *Wilhelm Meister*. The songs were published as Op. 98a and they include nine of the lyrics in addition to *Mignon*, issued earlier as part of the *Lieder Album für die Jugend*. All of them, but in particular the Harper's songs, are extremely restless harmonically as well as somewhat halting melodically. The poetic continuity is often disrupted by accompaniment interludes, the purpose of which is obviously to provide a musical reflection or commentary on the immediately preceding poetic statement. The difficulty lies both in Schumann's particular problems of style during the period in which he set the lyrics, and in the nature of Goethe's expression. Cooper's comments in this connection, partially given in Chapter 6, are worth quoting more fully here:

The *Wilhelm Meister* songs . . . are among Schumann's most conspicuous failures as a song-writer. Painfully oppressed by the philosophic significance of Mignon and the old harp-player, he rambles on in a portentous, pseudo-symphonic style, with frequent modulations and unnatural vocal phrases, losing the thread of the poem and of his own musical design. . . .
   Goethe's balance and serenity, philosophic depth, and dislike of romantic exaggeration all made him a quite unsympathetic figure to the young Schumann; and later in life his attempt to widen his horizon and to achieve a musical language capable of expressing Goethe's thought led him, at least as a song-writer, to go against all his natural instincts—or rather, since instinct generally gets the better of the artist, to give free reign to the most unfortunate of his natural tendencies, rambling and divagation.[9]

During the last period of Schumann's life he returned somewhat to the melodic and declamatory style of his first period, although retaining the technical achievements typical of the second, *i.e.*, richness of accompaniment and harmonic variety. Some of his most appealing but most neglected works are found among these later songs. Among them are two of the Mary Stuart poems, *Nach der Geburt ihres Sohnes* and *Gebet*, both set in a pseudo-hymn style but harmonically warm and without sentimentality. And even at this date he is drawing upon his favorite Heine for *Lehn' deine Wang'* and *Mein Wagen rollet langsam*, the latter of which includes one of the composer's longest and most reflective accompaniment postludes. The return from the excessive dramatics of his middle years was not without its rewards, therefore, but it must be admitted that his first instincts in song were probably the most valid ones. His own words were prophetic when he wrote to Kahlert in 1842: "I dare not promise better things than I have already accomplished—I mean in song."
   Regardless of the inconsistencies apparent in Schumann's songs, he contributed in a very meaningful way to the evolution of *lied* style. Considerable commentary has been directed toward his emphasis upon the psychological role that music can assume; I have, in fact, referred to this in the preceding discussion. While it may be impossible to fully articulate or demonstrate, certainly one of the important facets is not the description of mood but the involvement *with* mood—with the providing of a musical material that, although it may not be able to project a specific psychological content

9 Gerald Abraham (ed.), *Schumann, A Symposium* (New York: Oxford University Press, 1952), p. 110.

unaided by words, will nevertheless be consistent expressively with the poetic imagery.

Schubert was not totally inept in this regard. The accompaniment style of *Erlkönig* does convey an atmosphere of excitement, haste, even dread—the motivic figure can be felt as threatening. This is the psychological content. It is unfortunate that so often one is reminded that the motive is descriptive of the galloping horse, which is putting the matter on an altogether pictorial plane and one that is not as helpful expressively. What Schumann did was to largely avoid even the suggestion of illustration, choosing instead to direct his materials entirely toward the projection of mood. He is not free of pictorialisms, of course; no composer has been utterly free of them. The accompaniment figure used in *Die Spinnerin* is just about as graphic as Schubert's in *Gretchen am Spinnrade*. And the motive used in *Mein Wagen rollet langsam* is surely meant to represent the turning of the wheels. Yet each, like Schubert's galloping horse, has musical significance also in that their monotony has a direct relationship to the poetry.

Even more telling is the sort of musical mood Schumann can paint when there is no chance to illustrate. In the pair of Geibel lyrics from Op. 138, the accompaniment style of *O wie lieblich ist das Mädchen* is suitably peaceful and lyric, even to the brief flights of ecstasy suggested by the sixteenth-note roulades. And what a vast change for the companion piece, *Weh, wie zornig ist das Mädchen*, where the sharp grace-note dissonances, jerky rhythms, and staccato style sound as disjointed and tempestuous as the maiden herself. If this is pictorialization at all it is certainly of something that has no existence outside the realm of feeling and emotion. There is no way to depict moonlight in sound, and yet Schumann's musical realization in *Mondnacht* creates not only the "feel" of moonlit quietude but also the harmonic striving for release that the poem communicates. In *Widmung*, the abrupt change, not only harmonically but in accompaniment style as well, is entirely appropriate to the change in poetic mood.

In most cases, in fact, Schumann scrupulously avoids a literal illustration of the text. In *Waldesgespräch* there is a real invitation to provide the sound of the horse's hooves, but instead Schumann restricts himself to musical commentary, which can suggest the hastening movement through the forest and is yet adaptable to the various levels of emotion in the poem. Although there are frequent references to birds and other animals as part of the poetic imagery in many of his texts, he seldom is trapped into imitating their sounds in the piano, as Schubert was so inclined to do. In *Frühlingsnacht* there is only the exuberance of joy in love and in *Im wunderschönen Monat Mai* there is only the quiet wonder of first love. No bird calls. Some of his facility in these respects is a direct reflection of the type of poetry. Not only does most of it project a single well-defined mood which can be captured in musical terms, but the poems are short enough to allow for an appropriately concise musical reflection with no fear of the necessity for developing it beyond its capacity. The shifting and often searching content of Goethe did not lend itself well to Schumann's vocabulary, as we have noted. Heine, Eichendorff, Rückert, and his other favorites suited his peculiar abilities perfectly.

The involvement of the piano in projecting the mood is of great significance to song as it was being exploited throughout the century, and Schumann was the first of the great composers to place the piano on a completely equal plane with the voice. But there is a further aspect of his accompaniments that has been largely neglected in commentaries. The period of romanticism was a period of growing concern for synthesis; this has been rather fully discussed earlier. Schumann contributed in some unique ways to this synthesis. The placing of the piano and voice on equal terms expressively is in itself one indication of his concern for creating a richer musico-poetic amalgam. But of similar magnitude was his use of the accompaniment as a structural factor that helped to obscure the seams within the musical fabric. Most poems are designed as a series of strophes, and although there are exceptions, the poems that Schumann used are seldom among them. One of the problems of setting such poems has always been the sectionalizing that takes place from strophe to strophe, even in the process of through composition, where the problem is less acute. A related problem concerns the relationship of poetic phrase to musical phrase. The overwhelming tendency prior to Schumann was to relate the two fairly exactly, so that poetic cadence and musical cadence bore a close correspondence to one another. This is not always bad in itself, but unless carefully handled it can lead to both poetic and musical monotony. Schubert made some gains in a number of his songs, one being the skillful way in which he overlapped poetic line and musical phrase in *Litenei*, for instance. The same piece also demonstrates his capacity for telescoping a musical phrase by musical means so that, although it handles the same poetic line length as the previous phrase, it does not unfold musically at the same rate of speed.

Schumann often uses even more subtle means and they are related closely to the concept of "flowing" form as opposed to crystalline, "static" form. The direction of the century was toward "unending melody" in the Wagnerian sense and despite Schumann's avowed opposition to Wagner's style, there is a good bit of the same technique in the work of the two composers. The tendency in Schumann is to mask the breaks between strophes by interrupting the vocal cadence in various ways, and he frequently gets into his piano postludes by the same means. His *Frauenliebe und Leben* is full of these interruptions and they represent some of his favorite devices.

One is the rather obvious use of deception. This occurs between stanzas of *Seit ich ihn gesehen*, the first song of the cycle, and again between the final vocal phrase and the postlude. Sometimes the deception consists of an unexpected dissonance that steals away the anticipated pause in the music. The addition of a seventh is a favorite device, and this is used often in *Er, der Herrlichste von allen* and elsewhere in order to move from phrase to phrase without sectionalization. In *Ich kann's nicht fassen*, although there are several exceptionally strong cadences, there are also a number of instances of very strong dissonances that occur at phrase endings. Incidentally, this piece is also a good illustration of the use of harmonic restlessness and general accompaniment style in the service of text mood—in this case a hesitancy to believe in the good fortune of reciprocated love, and a fear that it might not really be true.

Another means of binding the musical seams is by overlapping an accompaniment motive with a vocal phrase ending, so that one begins either just as the other ends or even before. This is put to use most consistently in *Er, der Herrlichste von allen* and even more tellingly in *Süsser Freund*. In *Im wunderschönen Monat Mai*, first song of the *Dichterliebe*, the voice enters as a continuation of the thematic material established in the introduction, and at its cadence at the close of the first stanza the piano is already engaged in its own melodic pursuits. This song illustrates another device to which Schumann has recourse from time to time: the avoidance of a definite tone center until the voice has entered and is carrying the song forward. Even more appropriate in terms of text is this same procedure as he uses it in *Mondnacht*, where the avoidance of a strong definition of the tonic at cadential points is particularly effective in terms of the nebulous, ethereal mood of the poem as well as of the searching for something beyond the confines of earth—the image of the eternal outreach of the spirit.

Often the very character of the accompaniment motive is such that it allows for continuous movement despite the vocal phrasing. This is particularly evident in two of the pieces from *Dichterliebe*: *Im Rhein, im heiligen Strome* and *Das ist ein Flöten und Geigen*.

None of these "binding" devices are restricted to his early cycles, of course. They are a vital part of his song style up to the last. *Warnung* from 1851 uses many of them, brief as it is, as does *Mein Wagen rollet langsam*, probably his last solo song.

Thus, although not as fully developed as in Wagner, there is a movement toward real synthesis even within the confines of the musical syntax itself. The tendency is a strictly romantic one in song and has strong roots in the underlying aesthetic objectives of the period.

It should also be emphasized that his increasingly expanding concepts of key relationships and the intensity of his chromaticism place Schumann in the mainstream of romanticism. He is especially fond, like Schubert, of tonal centers a major third apart, and often the movement from one to the other proceeds entirely without preparation or announcement. His chromaticism is almost always in the interest of dramatizing the textual content in some way. There is hardly a poem that has as its expressive core the thought of restlessness, longing, searching, insecurity, or the like, that Schumann has set without recourse to chromatic or unsettled harmonies. If harmony can be equated with increasing infatuation for subjective involvement with text (and I believe it can), Schumann must be considered one of the foremost contributors to the period and the genre.

From the standpoint of melodic style, his work is in a direct line between Schubert and Wolf. In spite of his great concern for declamation, a concern that at times led him into excesses of dramatic writing for the voice, he avoided Schubert's use of recitative. Only once in all his songs (well over two hundred) did he indicate a passage as recitative, and then with the qualification *quasi*, in the 1840 piece *Die Kartenlegerin*. Taking his cue from Schubert's late songs, he frequently composed an entire song in a lyric-recitative style, giving full attention to the accentual and expressive demands of the words but as an entirety rather than by sections. Of many that might be cited, the following are typical and show his application of this technique in a variety of poetic contexts: from Eichendorff's *Lieder-kreis*: *Die Stille* and *Auf einer Burg*; from *Frauenliebe und Leben*: the last song, *Nun hast du mir den ersten Schmerz gethan*; from *Dichterliebe*: *Aus meinen Tränen spriessen, Wenn ich in deine Augen seh'* and *Ich hab' im Traum geweinet*. The list could continue almost indefinitely. What distinguishes his use of this melodic style from Schubert's is the fact that the latter almost always uses it in an extremely dramatic context. The list of songs will show that Schumann was able to use it tellingly in the most tender and poignant situations and in order to point up the subtlest poetic nuances.

It is here that he showed the greatest advances over Schubert's conception of both melody and the interpretation of mood. Schubert declaimed most forcefully and effectively when he wanted pure dynamism. Schumann apparently used the same basic devices when he felt that the textual content was least apt to be enhanced by musical drama but could carry the burden of expression almost unaided. In his command of suitably lyric declamatory devices, then, he was one of the leading figures of the nineteenth century in accomplishing still another synthesis—a close approximation of the best features of song and poetic recitation. And in addition there is his absorption into song style of such operatic devices as dramatic vocal lines and pseudo-recitative, which could serve the purposes of a shorter, more concise lyrical style without at the same time becoming infected with operatic excesses.

JOHANNES BRAHMS

In spite of the respect that Schumann accorded him, a respect echoed frequently since, Brahms does not stand exactly in the center of the developing concern for word and tone that is characteristic of the principal song composers of the century. He is, nonetheless, a figure who must be recognized in any discussion of song, not only because of his prolific output but also because his compositions continue to be such a vital part of the performing repertoire. Nearly two hundred songs for solo voice and piano, plus the lengthy cycle from Tieck's *Magelone* and the *Vier ernste Gesänge* comprise his contribution. Besides these, there are the extensive collections of folk songs that he arranged for solo voice.

If it is possible to generalize about a song production as large and varied as that of Brahms, such a generalization would have to be first and foremost in terms of his melodic gift. His work has been criticized because of the often careless declamation, and such criticism is certainly justified. Misaccents occur throughout his pieces, and often in the course of repeating a poetic phrase or line, which he does in nearly every song, the accentuation will actually change because of the demands of the music. He is seldom at any great pains to illustrate particulars of the text or to shift his established rhythmic patterns in order to take care of rhythmic niceties in the poem. His penchant for text repetition is in itself a clue to his general lack of concern for the poetry as poetry; in almost every case the repetition is merely a vehicle for musical extensions of one sort or another. Again, although there are notable exceptions, the accompaniments tend to provide harmonic interest only, and this despite the almost infinite variety of figures which he utilizes. The primary interest is in the music itself rather than in the shifting nuances of the words. Indeed, many of his poems are of recognizably inferior quality—he seems drawn most strongly to Daumer, surely a poet of no great distinction.

But in spite of these general idiosyncrasies, his songs are probably as readily accessible to performer and public alike as those of any other romantic composer, and a great deal more than some. The basis for this is not very profound. The melodies are gracious and appealing in their own right and the harmonic richness makes an almost irresistible impact on the emotions. Again, if generalizations are possible, it might be safe to suggest that of all the great *lied* composers, Brahms most frequently provides a musical realization in which the particulars of the text are least important. What is needed for the listener (and even for the performer) is merely the most general suggestion of the basic poetic mood. The continuing popularity of his songs is more than enough evidence that this sort of loose musico-poetic relationship can be effective.

Some strong evidence can be offered in support of such general statements. In the matter of inferior poetry, it is notable that a great many of the most revered Brahms songs are based upon the texts of poets of second- or third-rate stature, and this in the face of the flood of truly great lyric poetry in nineteenth-century Germany. The following list is by no means comprehensive, but it does show the tendency.

DAUMER:	*Botschaft*
	Wie bist du, meine Königin
FLEMMING:	*O liebliche Wangen*
HALM:	*Bei dir sind meine Gedanken*

GROTH: *O wüsst' ich doch den Weg zurück*
                          Wie Melodien zieht es mir

ALLMERS: *Feldeinsamkeit*

SCHMIDT: *Sapphische Ode*

LINGG: *Immer leiser wird mein schlummer*

FELIX SCHUMANN: *Meine Liebe ist grün*

The list could be greatly extended. What has been said of the earlier composers of the *da capo* aria is equally true of Brahms—the poetry serves his
purpose best when it is not too demanding as literature but offers instead
a very obvious and general suggestion of mood upon which the music can
enlarge without undue attention to details.

A true romantic in his use of striking harmonic excursions, Brahms
frequently includes these with little or no relationship to poetic statement.
Pieces like *Alte Liebe, Dein blaues Auge,* and *In Waldeseinsamkeit,* lovely and
ingratiating as they are musically, are involved with harmonic byplay that
is entirely out of proportion to the imagery in the text. The composer's
harmonic probings often take him into keys so remote that even the tonic
note itself is erased, and not only is the transition accomplished with great
fluidity (and rapidity) but the return is as graceful as the departure.
Ständchen, for instance, glides smoothly from G major to E major and back
within the space of five short measures. In the same manner, *Therese* uses
D major for the principal tonality, but both of the first strophes cadence
on F♯ major, and the last strophe, set to different music, begins in B major
but finds its way very shortly back to the tonic D major. While there
seems little justification in the poem for the progressions or relationships
of *Ständchen,* in *Therese* one might find a clue to the abrupt movement into
F♯ in that this serves to punctuate the questioning nature of the text, and
into B major because of the promise of an answer. Brahms, like Schubert
and Schumann before him, was fond of moving into the Neapolitan Sixth,
especially when the vocal line was drawing toward a cadence. The effectiveness of the device is apparent in *Wie Melodien zieht es mir.* The same song
demonstrates another favorite means of pointing up a musical climax—the
sudden bringing in of thirds or sixths in the accompaniment to heighten the
lyricism. This is particularly effective also at the climax of the second of the
Vier ernste Gesänge. In the last song of the same set the pattern is employed
throughout as an accompaniment motive, in this case usually moving in
contrary motion to the vocal line.

Like Schubert, Brahms frequently resorts to minor as a means of illustrating one strophe of the poem, as in *Wie bist du, meine Königin, Minnelied,* and
Vergebliches Ständchen. There is, in fact, a good deal of this minor-major
alteration in Brahms, although in many cases it seems more a part of the
harmonic movement than a gesture toward the specifics of the text. But

the mode he chooses for the basic color is almost always an indication of the general expression of the poem, at least in terms of the widely accepted interpretation of major and minor.

Brahms's weakness for putting musical stress, accentually and by duration, upon weak syllables and unimportant words has been so widely recognized that it seems futile to repeat illustrations here. A piece that more fully demonstrates his discomfort with declamation in a general sense is his setting of one of the few really great poems he used, Mörike's *An eine Äolsharfe*. Although he identifies the opening section as *Recitative*, and provides only a series of sustained chords as accompaniment, the melodic character is so stodgy and unrecitative-like in character as to be almost amusing. Later in the piece, unable to meet the abrupt change in poetic direction at *Aber auf einmal, wie der Wind heftiger herstösst* (But suddenly, as the wind blows more strongly), he once more resorts to recitative, this time no more successfully. The line he provides, in fact, is so similar to the rest of the song's melody that one wonders why he bothered to designate it as anything else than pure melody. In other instances (but infrequently) he is more at home in a melodic texture that is primarily declamatory. Apparently inspired by Heine's directness, Brahms comes as close to an ideal combination of lyricism and declamatory excellence as he ever did in *Der Tod, das ist die kühle Nacht*. Even the relatively tuneful singing of the nightingale in the second part of the song does not depart enough from the established style to be distracting. Also worth noting is the fact that in this piece he uses far less text reiteration than is his wont.

In most cases, Brahms does not provide accompaniment motives that are independent of the voice, in the sense that they are not derived from vocal material. When they do appear they are sometimes helpful in masking cadences, as in the overlapping that is characteristic of *Ständchen* and the last section of *O kühler Wald*. This sort of cadential disguise, however, is more apt to occur through the piano's taking over by repetition or sequence the cadential phrase of the vocal line, as in *Serenate* and *O liebliche Wangen*. It is not unusual for the accompaniment to anticipate the voice during an interlude or introduction and then move on to become independent. This motivic byplay is strongest in the *Vier ernste Gesänge*, which are in many ways the most thoughtful of all the Brahms songs. In the second, there is an extremely skillful transition to the section that begins *und siehe, da waren Tränen* (and behold, there were tears), which relies upon this motivic anticipation. The accompaniment states, not the immediately ensuing vocal motive associated with the words *und siehe*, but rather the one that is more expressively assigned to *da waren Tränen*. By the time the voice reiterates the music, however, the accompaniment has moved on to its own material.

Among the other important features of Brahms's song style is his fondness for establishing cross rhythms between accompaniment and voice and using them as a vital factor in promoting the musical movement. In such cases as the interplay between bass and voice, that is a feature of *Liebestreu* and the dialogue effect of portions of *Nicht mehr zu dir zu gehen*, there is no real evidence of accompaniment independence, however, since most of the material is drawn from the vocal line. The functions here are entirely musical—they would serve the same purposes and be equally effective if no words were involved. This is true of most of the characteristics just listed, in fact. It is also true of what is probably the most glorious of Brahms's endowments—his wealth of melodic imagination and inspiration.

The long phrases that have been so often described as the most striking feature of his melodies are certainly there. But the excitement they produce in the listener is quite often a result of their having grown from a background of relative regularity. It is the unexpected extensions that make such a powerful impact. In most cases, the extension results from the sustaining of a word or syllable (often in combination with a melisma) past the rhythmically anticipated length. Such songs as *Erinnerung, Blinde Kuh, Meine Lieder*, and *O kühler Wald* make a typical use of this device. Much of the effect of the musical treatment of *und die einsame Träne rinnt* in *Die Mainacht*, certainly one of the most glorious phrases in all song literature, is a result of the fact that it emerges without warning from the relatively regular set of phrases that precedes it at both appearances. The effect is heightened on the second statement because it is extended even farther by the almost immediate addition of a seventh to the final chord.

When the extension is not just of a single phrase but of a section, it is most apt to be built upon a sequence of the last vocal utterance. In such cases it almost invariably involves text repetition, and is obviously a musically oriented situation rather than one that grows out of poetic demands. There are so many examples of this factor at work that it is pointless to cite instances—the most cursory examination of any of the songs will show the frequency with which Brahms made free use of words in this manner. Because he was so skillful in fashioning phrases of irregular lengths, he was often able to treat irregular poetry in a quite convincing manner. A case in point is Hölty's *An die Nachtigall*, with its alternating eleven- and four-syllable lines. Brahms simply takes most of the short lines in as musical extensions. Likewise he has the good sense to disregard Daumer's linear structure in *Wie bist du, meine Königin*. The third line of each strophe runs into the last, so Brahms simply departs from his regular three-bar phrases, which he uses for the first two lines, and provides a four-bar phrase for the last two, saving *wonnevoll* for separate treatment—an appropriate realization for this word, incidentally. The irregularity is even anticipated in the introduction where his little dialogue between the two top piano voices leads him into a five-measure format. This piece is another fine illustration of his ability to overlap vocal and accompaniment melodies in order to mask the seams between strophes. In all, one would have to admit that the masterful music in this setting does whatever can be done to redeem the inadequacies, structural as well as expressive, in this rather trite poem.

A word should be said about the one cycle that Brahms set, *Romanzen aus Magelone*, based upon Tieck's collection. Although the musical vocabulary is not strikingly different from his normal usage, the songs themselves are considerably more extensive and scenic than most of his other work in this medium. The poems are unusually long ones and Brahms treats them largely by sectionalizing his music, a procedure that leads him into numerous changes of tempo, meter, vocal and accompaniment style, and key. Despite the already considerable length of the individual poems, there is still an astounding amount of repetition of text, as usual in the service of musical needs as Brahms sees them. As in many other Brahms songs the vocal demands are stringent, many passages being operatic in nature. Although they include some of the best things the composer wrote, some of the pieces are musically overburdened. The changes of musical style in the third song, *Sind es Schmerzen*, for instance, seem excessively flamboyant for the poetry.

Throughout his song production, it was unusual for Brahms to make any strong attempt to avoid pulling the poetry into his musical orbit. The result is often more stimulating as pure musical sound than as a meaningful combination of word and tone. It is worth some speculation, however, to wonder whether or not this does sometimes achieve a worthwhile result in a certain expressive sense. Where the musical imagery is readily perceivable, even merely ingratiating, and the poetry is not particularly profound or subtle, it may be entirely desirable to base musico-poetic relationships upon just this sort of superficial basis. This is in itself, after all, a kind of synthesis. In a comparison between Brahms and Wolf, for instance, one would have to admit that the former is considerably more accessible to most musicians (professionals as well as amateurs), a fact that accounts for his greater popularity though it may not contribute to the respect accorded him by scholars as a song composer. There is none of the immense subtlety that can be found in the best things of Wolf, and for that matter in Schumann. At the same time, neither of these men could achieve Brahms's complete freedom of lyric expression except on rather rare occasions. While it may be a disservice to all three composers to attempt a statement that might cover all the eventualities, I cannot help feeling that Brahms makes his basic appeal to the vocalist, whereas Wolf's value is more apparent to the person who is extremely sensitive to both poetry and music—and Schumann stands someplace in the middle. Thus, while Brahms does not contribute markedly to intensifying the ideals of musico-poetic relationships in the nineteenth century, he most assuredly does make a significant contribution to the repertoire of song.

HUGO WOLF

There is little doubt that Wolf represents the highest achievement in German song, certainly during the nineteenth century and quite possibly

for all time. In his work is found the fullest realization of that synthesis
which has been recognized as one of the hallmarks of romanticism. Under
the influence of Wagner's vocal style, Wolf brings to song the best of the
lyric recitative which was becoming more and more a part of late romantic
opera, but it is contained well within the limits of song. In his pieces are all
the vocal demands of opera yet none of its reliance upon the mere drama
of the voice as an instrument. Here, too, is the harmonic limitlessness that
reflects the spirit of the romantic search to erase boundaries of all sorts—
but again put to use in the service of the poetry rather than as a musical
vocabulary complete of itself. It is in the relationship of poem to music
that Wolf reaches the greatest synthesis of all, for in almost every case the
music must be referred to the text in order to be completely fulfilling. The
identifying feature of these songs is the immense care with which declamation is treated but without sacrificing either the musico-poetic mood or
the lyric expressiveness without which a composition cannot really be
considered a song. The interdependence of voice and accompaniment
usually reaches such a high degree that one without the other is greatly
impoverished.

Much of Wolf's success in the dimension of musico-poetic synthesis was
due to his habit of immersing himself in the works of one poet at a time, a
practice that could only result in the establishing of great rapport. In
addition, he was attracted to the greatest poets of his own day as well as
the past. He was the first song composer after Schubert to give great
attention to Goethe, for instance, setting over fifty of the latter's lyrics.
Nor did he ignore the poetry of other nations; many of his finest songs are
based on texts from Spain and Italy, although always in translation.

The range of his subject matter is the widest imaginable, far greater than
any of his predecessors or contemporaries. He treated texts of great nobility
(*Anakreons Grab, Gesang Weylas*), of ecstasy (*Verborgenheit, Er ist's*), of utter
freshness and joy (*Fussreise*), depths of despair (*Agnes*), great religiosity
(*Auf eine Christblume, Auf ein altes Bild*), and impetuosity (*Ich hab' in Penna
eine Liebsten*). But what sets him apart most sharply is his delight in all sorts
of humor and impishness. To Mörike he owed most of this mood (*Zur
Warnung, Der Tambour, Abschied*, and many others) but he used similar texts
from other poets, for instance, Keller's *Das Köhlerweib ist trunken*. In this
respect he represents a turn away from the characteristically romantic
infatuation with soulful self-absorption in the darker moods and back to the
more classically objective level—Beethoven and Mozart were not averse to
setting comic, even ribald, poetry on occasion.

Any attempt to define Wolf's style in concise terms is foredoomed; his
diversity defies generalization. The clue to his song composition actually
lies in his amazing ability to treat each poem in terms of its own individual
demands, so that he has actually as many styles as he has songs to represent
them. The musical vocabulary that was available to him included all the
riches of the expanded expressive resources of the romantic century. What

distinguishes him from his contemporaries, however, is the control with which he put such resources to the service of the poetry rather than using them primarily for their own sake. At the same time he was heir to all the lyric poetry of the century, with a choice of the best material and the sensitivity to exercise that choice wisely. Even in his own day the stream of poetry was turning away from romantic lyricism into channels of experimentation of all kinds. As is so often the case with really great artists, he was in the right place at the right time to take advantage of the very best the romantic period had produced or was to produce.

Wolf's harmonic palette included all the chromatic coloration that Wagner had investigated—*Tristan und Isolde* made its appearance when Wolf was a child of five. His melodic style runs from almost total diatonism (*Der Gärtner*) to extensive use of chromatic passages (*Alle gingen, Herz, zur Ruh*), from extremely speechlike outlines, including many repeated pitches (*Mögen alle bösen Zungen*), through Wagnerian lyric recitative (*Anakreons Grab* and *Zur Ruh, zur Ruh*), to pure tunefulness (*Er ist's* and *Fussreise*). In every case, the governing factor in the style is the poetry itself. As might be expected at the close of a century during which the expressive possibilities of dissonant melodic figures of all sorts, especially the appoggiatura, had been investigated and exploited fully, Wolf's use of such devices is extensive. Drawn as he was to the utmost sincerity and care in declamation, his rhythms are extremely diverse, involving extensive syncopation, cross rhythms, rests—in fact, all the manipulation that can best serve the rhythmic fluctuations of poetry. In these respects, he represents a summation of the greatest advances in song composition.

In terms of the general organization of his songs, he is often quite regular, as in *Der Musikant*, where the phraseology falls into the classic balance of four measures to a phrase, eight to a period. But often the inner structure is most irregular and rhapsodic in nature, as in *Morgenstimmung* and *Bedeckt mich mit Blumen*, although usually this sort of musical realization is associated with somber or reflective texts. In his relationship to the larger view of song development, it is significant that in this rhapsodic freedom especially he bears a close aesthetic likeness to the beginning experiments of the Italian monodists, but naturally with the greater control and discipline that an accompaniment imposes upon the musical movement. This may be seen as one further synthesis—the old with the new, the beginning with its eventual fulfillment. In this sense, then, the song as a type has come full circle after three centuries of sometimes circuitous wanderings.

Nor is Wolf restricted in any way by formal considerations. He is equally at home in the strophic format (*Ein Stündlein wohl der Tag*), binary (*Agnes*), ternary (*Ach, des Knaben Augen*), free (*Das verlassene Mägdelein*—in this case *abca*), and through composed (*Der Tambour, Er ist's*), as well as the wealth of variations within each. Here, as in all other respects, he seems most strongly guided by the demands of the poetry, the relationship between stanzas as well as expressive factors within the stanzas themselves. Almost never is there a shift of structural pattern without a corresponding change in the poetic structure or mood.

Wolf represents no departure from the long-established tendency to illustrate text. His accompaniment figurations suggest all sorts of features —butterflies in *Zitronenfalter im April,* elves in *Elfenlied,* drums in *Der Tambour.* Sometimes the entire texture of a song is involved with descriptive imagery, as in the rhythmic cross-relations between accompaniment and voice in *Nun lass uns Frieden schliessen,* which illustrates the attempt to resolve the strife between the singer and his sweetheart. Often the commentary on mood is given to the accompaniment alone while the voice remains free to declaim the text, as in *Was soll der Zorn.* Likewise the choice of an accompaniment leitmotiv serves a descriptive as well as a musically expressive purpose in *Und willst du deinen Liebsten sterben sehen*; the character of the motive suggests flowing hair but is used musically to reflect the ebb and flow of passion by its melodic and harmonic permutations. Even more general in nature is the tendency in the Spanish songs to provide rhythms suggestive of idioms native to that country, although this device is not carried throughout all the songs. It is worth noting that the Italian lyrics do not exploit the sort of melodiousness that their national source might have suggested. They are, in fact, among the most skillfully designed of all Wolf's songs from the standpoint of declamatory control, which is perhaps a tribute to an earlier Italian style than the operatic excesses of the eighteenth and nineteenth centuries.

Nowhere is the composer more effective than in the musical reflection of text mood, however. He has an almost uncanny ability to create in sound an imagery that lies at the heart of the poetic content. The great setting of Mörike's *In der Frühe* is typical, but as it has been discussed fully in Chapter 7 there is no need to detail it here.

Wolf is skillful in his use of a musical fabric that is referential as well as specific to the individual expressive situation. In *Auf ein altes Bild,* for instance, the pseudo-modal, hymn-like nature of the accompaniment reinforces the religious character of the text and at the same time projects a quiet, reflective mood. The primarily conjunct and undramatic melodic line draws little attention to itself, yet provides a context within which meaningful expressive gestures can easily occur, such as the appoggiaturas on *Knäblein Sündelos* (sinless child). Even the insistence upon major cadences in a basically minor harmonic context is suggestive of an archaic style appropriate to the poetic subject matter. Nor is there need for a departure from the established musical style in order to effectively punctuate by dissonance the reference to *Kreuzes Stamm* (trunk for the cross), although it is so warm and poignant in its treatment. One is struck by the total control which Wolf exercises over his materials, not subjugating them to the text but rather engulfing them in it.

At no point is this control more evident than in *Nun wandre, Maria,* where he provides a syllabic melodic line restricted in range to a fifth and in the best traditions of the lyric recitative style. There is more than enough opportunity for the most subtle inflection of which the singer is capable but almost no invitation for excessive dramatization. At the same time, the steadily plodding movement of the accompaniment bass is relieved by the wonderfully lyric parallel thirds in the treble.[10] As in *Auf ein altes Bild*, it is not necessary to depart radically from the established musical texture in order to heighten the expression at Joseph's plaintive:

Wohl seh ich, Herrin, die Kraft dir schwinden;	I see clearly, my Mistress, that your strength is failing.
Kann deine Schmerzen, ach, kaum verwinden.	Oh, I can hardly bear your suffering.

Translation from International Music Company edition.

All that is needed is the introduction of syncopation, the use of relatively larger and more dissonant melodic intervals (augmented fourths in the phrase, "I can hardly bear your suffering"), and the addition of relatively greater chromaticism.

Wolf's use of interludes is unusual in that they nearly always relate directly to the portion of the text that immediately precedes or follows them. A typical case occurs in *Auf einer Wanderung*, where a fifteen-measure piano rhapsody follows immediately upon the words:

Aus einem offnen Fenster eben,	From an open window nearby,
Über den reichsten Blumenflor hinweg,	Out over a bed of marvelous flowers
Hört man Goldglockentöne schweben,	Came drifting the tones of golden bells,
Und eine Stimme scheint ein Nachtigallenchor,	And a voice like a chorus of nightingales
Dass die Blüten beben,	Made the blossoms quiver,
Dass die Lüfte leben,	The breezes spring to life,
Dass in höherem Rot die Rosen leuchten vor.	And the roses glow in their deep red splendour.

Translation from International Music Company edition.

Only when the voice re-enters is the full significance of the passage made clear:

Lang hielt ich staunend, lustbeklommen.

I stood there a long time astonished, overcome by joy.

Translation from International Music Company edition.

It is not unusual, either, for such purely instrumental material to take on new significance as the poem unfolds. The introductory passage in *Schlafendes Jesuskind* appears at first merely to set the proper musical mood

10 Eric Sams, *The Songs of Hugo Wolf* (London: Methuen & Co., Ltd., 1961). See especially pp. 7–18.

for the poem. When it recurs, however, it gains a greater symbolic richness because of the words that precede it:

O wer sehen könnte,	Could one but see
Welche Bilder hinter dieser Stirne,	What visions behind this brow,
Diesen schwarzen Wimpern,	These dark lashes,
Sich in sanftem Wechsel malen!	Arise in gentle succession!

> Translation from International Music Company edition.

Here, in musical terms, are the "visions" and it is only at this point that we realize how intimately the richly chromatic chorale relates to more than the slumber of the infant Jesus. We see clearly that the chromaticism of not only this material but of the entire song is a forecast of the suffering that the child has yet to face.

The distance between Brahms and Wolf is clear in a comparison of each composer's setting of Mörike's *Agnes*. Although the poetic mood is constant throughout and nowhere suggests a change of imagery, Brahms treats the piece as a set of strophic variations, clearly a principally musical approach. Wolf's song is a quite uncomplex binary form repeated, in which the only alteration is a very slight rhythmic one that occurs at the interlude between the first and second strophes and is retained throughout the balance of the song. It is not clear, either, what Brahms intends expressively by the increased chromaticism of his final stanza. Although his song is entirely satisfactory as a short set of variations, it cannot really be defended as an instance of real musico-poetic synthesis.

On the other hand, the affinity between Schumann and Wolf is made strikingly plain by a comparison of their settings of the same poet's *Das verlassene Mägdelein*. Not only is the general mood practically identical (allowing for increased dissonance in Wolf), but even the declamation is strikingly similar. The structures of the two songs are closely related, Schumann's being a modified ternary format and Wolf's being *abca*. Both pieces project a remarkably consistent musical imagery throughout. The comparison cannot be made except haltingly in verbal terms, but a performance of the two songs, side by side, would prove revealing to even the most unskilled listener. What Wolf adds is almost totally in terms of the fruit of several decades of extended harmonic relationships and this does not relate directly to musico-poetic sensitivity. Both are exceptionally fine songs in terms of synthesis of word and tone.

Since I discussed earlier the treatment given by Schubert and Schumann to Goethe's *Wilhelm Meister* lyrics, a word should be said here about Wolf's settings of the same poems. In the same sense that Schumann differs from Schubert in his greater dramatic intensity, Wolf shows a marked difference from either in both the degree and the extent of his control. It was noted that Schubert's problems were largely with excesses of lyricism, excesses that led him into profuse text repetitions, changes of musical texture, and a number of melodic figurations derived from Italianate opera idioms. Schumann, on the other hand, tended to treat the lyrics as intense psychological challenges (which they certainly are) and to be led into a nervous attempt to capture each individual nuance of the poems. The result is a series of somewhat overdramatic episodes, many of which involve considerably more text reiteration than was habitual with Schumann. In a number of the songs there is even some hint that he was unable to work out a musical solution without providing a series of realizations of the same phrase.

With the harmonic and declamatory vocabulary available to Wolf, it is not surprising that he is able to achieve the psychological intensity that somehow eluded Schumann and that Schubert apparently did not even attempt. At the same time, there is some evidence that too much is being done musically beyond the demands of the poetry. There is certainly in Wolf's treatment all the instability and madness of the Harper, and there is also a sort of motivic relationship between the settings of his lyrics that suggests a continuity of characterization. All the settings of the Harper's songs are exceedingly chromatic, and what they best project is the element of being totally erratic harmonically—a defensible approach to some extent. The Mignon songs, on the other hand, are bent in the direction of passionate longing and supplication, somehow not quite in keeping with the character of the lost child. The most important musico-poetic advance that Wolf makes over either of the other composers is his almost total avoidance of text repetition and his ability to maintain a consistent musical texture without departures for text probing. In this regard there is evidence of more control than in either Schubert or Schumann.

Any comparisons of this sort must take into consideration the changing concepts in song. Goethe himself expressed great concern that settings of his lyrics would become excessively involved with text illustration or operatic device. Much of his concern derived from his personal aesthetic, which was largely oriented in eighteenth-century convention, especially in the notion of the child of Nature as it applied to Mignon. That aspect could not survive, nor could it be resuscitated. It would be anachronistic to attempt to solve the problems of Goethe's texts by renouncing the musical means or aesthetic stance of a later time. One would not want a rejection of Schubert's crowning glory, his lyric gift. Nor would one expect from Schumann a denial of the search, however overinvolved, for musical materials that would most fully exploit the tormented characters of Mignon and the Harper. On the same terms, Wolf could not avoid the exploitation of musical resources that lay at his command, even though they might appear overabundant in the case of the *Wilhelm Meister* songs. Whatever overelaboration is involved in all three composers as they relate to Goethe is very possibly best viewed in the perspective of romanticism itself and its growing emphasis upon emotional intensity. In the case of these lyrics there is a large element of classic understatement and innuendo that did not seem to lend itself to the particular genius of Schubert, Schumann, or Wolf, however outstanding their gifts for song might have been. And it is worth noting, I think, that Brahms set only five of Goethe's poems, none of which was from *Wilhelm Meister*. Prehaps instinctively he was the only one of the great German romantic song writers to fully realize the limitations of the medium.

Wolf's significance for song, then, lies largely in what his compositions represent as the fulfillment of the romantic search for synthesis. In his pieces the opera and *lied* styles come closest to that sort of amalgamation in which one is barely distinguishable from the other. He was able to assimilate the century's ideals of a musico-poetic relationship that would take advantage of the best possibilities of each without undue restrictions to either. Within the context of the songs themselves may be found the synthesis of all the musical elements—melody, accompaniment, rhythms, harmonic implication—closely allied to the text but not subservient to it.

His concern for just this peculiar interrelationship of elements proved detrimental when he turned his attention to the larger vocal canvas of opera. His one completed effort in that medium, *Der Corregidor*, seems strangely like a series of songs rather than a musical drama, despite his admiration for Wagner's ideologies. He was apparently unable to free himself sufficiently from the intimacies of the libretto, a restrictive factor that can hamper the musical and dramatic sweep that is so much a part of opera. But it was this very limitation that served him so well in song and that identifies his work in this genre as the culmination of the German *lied*.

Given the perspective of the nearly one hundred and fifty years that encompasses the song ideals of the Berlin School through the achievements of Wolf, it is possible to establish a scale of development along which the songs of most other composers may be measured. Such measurement should not be interpreted in terms of their individual value *as songs* but more in terms of their relationship to the developing ideals of synthesis. The attempts of the Berlin School to subjugate music to text, the encroachment of operatic device in Mozart and Haydn; the increased involvement of the accompaniment and dramatically illustrative harmony in Beethoven; the outburst of lyricism and later the insertion of declamatory control in Schubert; the increasing attention to declamation and poetic sensitivity of a psychological nature in Schumann; and the final synthesis of tune and declamation in the form of lyric recitative together with the other musico-poetic interrelationships that typify Wolf—even this sort of oversimplification and overgeneralization furnishes a helpful schema to which nineteenth-century song can be related with some meaning.

ROBERT FRANZ

Like Brahms, not all German song composers stand squarely in the mainstream of this developmental scheme. Nor are their songs less valuable for that, of course, although they do tend to represent one or more of the facets of romanticism to the neglect of others. Robert Franz, for instance, is one composer who stands outside the schema I have proposed, although he devoted the major portion of his creative effort to song. Given initial encouragement by such influential men as Schumann and Liszt, he placed himself under such strict ideological limitations that his range of expression was sharply curtailed. Since he was not hesitant to expound at some length on his aesthetics of song, we can find in his own words the boundaries within which he worked. The following excerpt from a letter to Sebastian B. Schlesinger, dated February 11, 1884, is typical:

The modern lyric demands a form as limited as possible, which dispenses with everything that is superfluous, thus leaving more to inference instead of expressing the flow of thoughts to the last drop. This tendency we see not only in modern poetry, but in its sister art, modern music, and in both it is characteristic. When the two arts, therefore, are combined, as in songs, it follows that the music must grow out of the text and must not be wedded to it without having any relation to it. And as every *good* text has a seed from which everything springs, so must the music to it also aim at a gradual developing process; and thus you will find in my songs a certain motive as a ground plan from which all else emanates. Further the melody must be *strictly* in harmony with the words and the rhythm must only in very exceptional cases change; finally, the harmony must be based on the diatonic system. The last I hold especially important because now-a-days it is sought to represent originality by modulations which are forced and foreign. These fundamental principles have guided me in my compositions, and I have never had reason to repent that I have followed them to the utmost of my ability.[11]

The striking thing about this philosophy is its close affinity to the ideals of composers such as Reichardt and Zelter, which had been formulated a century and more before. Franz does, indeed, adhere to his creed. He prefers the strophic and two- or three-part formats, chooses short poems for the most part, poems that avoid dramatic development or suggestion, and in general restricts any tendency for wide-ranging text illustration. His melodies do, as he insists, grow from a basic motive, which is extended usually by sequence or repetition. Key relationships are close to home and there are almost no sudden or illustrative gestures, harmonically speaking. Interesting, too, is the fact that he apparently felt similar restrictions vocally, for all his pieces are composed for mezzo-soprano and he was vigorously opposed to transposition. Very possibly his strongest feature is his sincere approach to declamation, but even this paradoxically tends to restrict his expressive range. He chooses a basic rhythmic figure that usually relates strongly to the poetic meter, and builds his musical rhythm around it. And his accompaniments tend to double the vocal melody with great consistency.

11 I am indebted to Michael Sells for uncovering this revealing statement of the goals and procedures of Franz.

In view of the relative austerity of his philosophy and his assiduous adherence to it in practice, it is surprising that a number of his compositions have a sort of gracefulness and charm not out of keeping with the poems he chose. However, the failure of his pieces to take a place in the repertoire commensurate with the care he lavished upon them and the volume he produced (over two hundred and fifty) must certainly be blamed upon his ideology. He set a large number of poems that had been set by other composers before him and the relative simplicity of his treatment does not really encourage a favorable comparison. Schumann's *Die Lotosblume*, *Die Rose, die Lilie*, and *Im Rhein, im heiligen Strome*, for instance, although they often involve the type of musical illustration that Franz studiously avoided in setting the same texts, strike more sharply into the poetic content. Although Franz enjoyed some success during his lifetime, at least until his hearing failure placed him in an impossible position for continuing his writing, his songs have stood the test of time only in a limited way. Several of them have found their way fairly consistently into collections of teaching pieces, a final tribute to their vocal graciousness if not to their interpretive depth.

FRANZ LISZT

On the other side of the coin is Franz Liszt, as unremittingly attracted by operatic devices as Franz was repelled by them. As might be expected in the compositions of a piano virtuoso, Liszt's accompaniments are astonishingly flamboyant, in many cases actually overpowering the voice. It is typical to find long, florid preludes (many are simply too extensive to be called introductions), interludes, and postludes. It is not surprising in view of his wide travels to find the composer utilizing texts from France, Italy, and even one from England, Tennyson's *Go not, happy day*. Of the French texts, *O, quand je dors* is probably the best known and it is typical of Liszt's inclination toward elaboration. Another piece, *Comment, disaient-ils*, goes so far as to provide an optional vocal line for the climactic portion, a line that is extremely demanding vocally, and even includes an optional cadenza for the close. In another case, *Im Rhein, im schönen Strome*, the composer provides an optional, more difficult, piano accompaniment for those who can meet the technical requirements. A second setting is considerably less dramatic but still rather involved.

Liszt was strongly inclined to treat a poem several times. There are three settings of Goethe's *Freudvoll und leidvoll*, for instance, all considerably more intense than the poem would suggest. Apparently his problem in this case was an inability to accept the paradox inherent in the words without elaborating extensively upon it musically. On those few occasions when he tried to limit his musical resources to some degree, they came under control with great reluctance. His first setting of *Der du von dem Himmel bist* is little short of an operatic scene. A second setting thirteen years later makes some attempt to eliminate the excessive drama by limiting vocal climaxes, setting roulades to longer, less impetuous note values, and cutting back on text repetitions. Nevertheless, the music is still quite overpowering. A third attempt four years later shows an entirely different orientation. The similarities between the first two settings (and they were markedly similar) testify to his difficulty in relinquishing the dramatic intensification of text. But in the third setting this dramatization has all but disappeared. The former virtuosic accompaniment is reduced to block and rolled chords and the vocal line is sharply limited in range. Even here, however, Liszt cannot forego repetition and sequential development of the two most compelling lines of the poem:

> *Ach, ich bin des Treibens müde*
> *Was soll all der Schmerz und Lust?*
>
> Ah, I am weary of striving!
> Why all this pain and pleasure?

Although there is considerable chromaticism throughout the song, the dissonant punctuation is strongest for the word *pain* (an augmented sixth chord), and *pleasure* is illustrated by major.

For an instance of what havoc extremes of musical manipulation can do to a simple, unpretentious text, one should consult *Über allen Gipfeln ist Ruh,* where words cannot adequately describe the altogether unpeaceful mood projected by the restless harmonies and energetic rhythms of much of the piece.

Among Liszt's latest songs, however, there is some evidence that he made a real attempt to provide a musical realization that would not weigh so heavily against the poetry. The very brief and relatively simple *Einst* is in this character, as is *Verlassen,* with its extended and lyrically appealing recitative-like section brought in as the song draws to a close. One earlier (1860) piece does show how effective Liszt could be when he avoided his predilection for overdramatization. It is the entirely lovely *Du bist wie eine Blume* with its gentle and unobtrusive motivic interplay between voice and piano and its wonderfully controlled and expressive harmonic simplicity, entirely in keeping with the poem. It is regrettable that Liszt was unable to content himself more often with this type of disciplined effort, but there is little doubt that both his personality and musical virtuosity could not allow for this. His tendency to re-work settings over a period of time does indicate that he was not entirely satisfied with his efforts. It is significant, too, that he followed in the steps of others of his contemporaries in using *Deklamations* as one means of uniting words and music. His texts in such cases were ballads and his general orientation is indicated by his inscription *mit melodramatischer Pianoforte-Begleitung* (with melodramatic piano accompaniment). As a summation of Liszt's total approach to song, that says it.

Liszt and Franz, then, stand as polemic extremities on either side of the line of song development represented by Schubert, Schumann, and Wolf in Germany. Their songs are neither better nor worse because of that. They simply represent the ebb and flow of varying aspects of the romantic movement, with Liszt drawn to the excessively ornate and operatic end of the scale and Franz drawn as strongly to the *volkstümliches* end.

RICHARD STRAUSS AND GUSTAV MAHLER

The German composers who were involved with song during and after Wolf's most productive years can be seen in much the same perspective as those who immediately preceded him. Of those who carried forward the ideologies of romanticism, Richard Strauss and Gustav Mahler have continued to occupy a place of primary importance in the repertoire. Both are influenced by Wagner and Wolf in different degrees, but by their predecessors too. Neither, of course, gave his fullest attention to song at the expense of other media, and their involvement with the larger forms of composition colors much of their song composition. In both are found the abundance of lyric utterance which is so much part of the nineteenth century.

Of the two men, Strauss tends to follow more closely the tunefulness of Brahms. At his most typical, he does not become overinvolved with accompaniment leading motives nor with the interplay of melodic dialogue between voice and piano. Many of his accompaniments abound in solid repeated chords (*Die Nacht, Wie sollten wir geheim*), many use broken patterns of various sorts (*Traum durch die Dämmerung, Zueignung*), some combine the styles (*Mein Herz ist stumm*). Almost always the statement of important material in the accompaniment is reserved for portions where the voice is resting or when, for dramatic purposes, the melody line is sustaining a long note (*Befreit, Morgen*). To the extent that these generalizations can be applied, Strauss and Brahms share some affinity in their approach to song. As in most cases, however, there are notable exceptions. In *Schlagende Herzen* the accompaniment motive, which is obviously illustrative of the throbbing heart, invades the entire composition, and the same thing is true to a lesser degree in *Nichts*. Among the songs that draw heavily upon a Wagnerian-type declamation is *Ruhe, meine Seele*, and there are a number of others. In general, however, the composer is most gratifying when he is at his most exuberantly tuneful and when, as is often the case, the harmony serves principally to impel the melody forward without great involvement in text illustration.

Although Mahler did compose several sets of independent songs, he is most often represented by his two cycles for voice and orchestra—the *Kindertotenlieder* and *Lieder eines fahrenden Gesellen*, both of which are characteristic of his style at its most full-blown. As might be anticipated in a composer who spent much of his creative energies in the field of symphonic composition, there is extensive developmental manipulation of both vocal and accompaniment motives. While the voice is assigned a role that is as demanding as much of the operatic repertoire of the period, it is seldom put to purely instrumental use. Care in declamation and an especial concern for expressive figurations of all sorts (the long, lingering appoggiatura is a favorite) are hallmarks of Mahler's style. The accompaniment almost never assumes a merely supporting role to the voice in the Straussian manner, but instead seems continually engaged in commenting upon or heightening the emotional content of the text. As in the symphonies, there is sometimes a hint of long-windedness to the songs and in this Mahler is a characteristically and fully developed romantic. Like Strauss, he was inclined to set the texts of the later romantics, avoiding poetry that had already provided material for his predecessors in the century.

There is a wide range in expressive content. Even within the *Kindertotenlieder*, for instance, the second song with its slowly unfolding melody and mood of exalted yearning is in vivid contrast to the stormy, half-mad beginning section of the final song and to the latter's closing section with its gentle rocking motion in simple lullaby style. In some of the shorter independent songs, especially the excerpts from *Des Knaben Wunderhorn*, Mahler tried to scale down his materials to accommodate the folkish texts, but it was with some difficulty. Both he and Strauss, although their individual styles differ to some extent, are illustrative of the inflated concept of all musical media that typifies fully-matured romanticism. Like Liszt, Wolf, and many of their lesser contemporaries, both composers supplied orchestrations for many of their songs, even a number of those that were at first conceived for voice and keyboard. This reaching for an ever larger canvas on which to spread the correspondingly larger expressive range of materials is evidence that the song had emerged from the intimacy of the chamber and taken its place alongside opera as a shorter but equally dramatic vocal form.

SONG IN FRANCE BEFORE FAURÉ

Allowing for the differences in poetic style as well as the basic variations between French musical vocabulary and that of the Germans, the development of song in nineteenth-century France is strikingly similar to that in Germany. The eighteenth-century French counterpart of the German *volkstümliches lied* was the *romance*. A long-range descendant of the troubadour song, it clung tenaciously to the couplet form in verse and the musical realization was simple, nonillustrative, strophic, and in general avoided coloratura effects in the melody. Toward the end of the eighteenth century and during the early years of the nineteenth, there was a gradual infiltration of Italianisms in the melody and, because of the widening influence of the German *lied*, an increase in accompaniment involvement in an attempt to heighten the expression. As in Germany, the end result was a deterioration of the *romance* as a highly controlled type of song and a general reclassification into a variety of forms and styles, primarily identified by subject matter. Although there are a number of charming and melodious songs that are representative of this period, none remain in the performing repertoire and they are actually of little significance in the evolution of what was to become the characteristic French song style.

The first songs of real importance to the stylistic development of the nineteenth-century French song are those of Hector Berlioz. Of these the best-known is the cycle of six pieces on poems of Gautier, *Les Nuits d'Été*. First composed in 1834, these were rewritten in 1841 in the form now in use. Still later, Berlioz scored them for voice and orchestra, although they were originally conceived with piano accompaniments. The composer indicated most of his songs as *mélodies*, and this has become the generic term for French song during and beyond the romantic century. There are some influences of the German *lied*, a natural result of the fact that Schubert's songs had been widely circulated in France. However, the *Nuits d'Été* have a characteristically French flavor, which was to be reflected throughout much of the century in the songs of dozens of Berlioz's fellow countrymen.

One of the factors that was to lead to the fluid and highly sophisticated French vocal style was the romantic relaxation of the couplet form in verse. The end result of poetic lines of varying length is to encourage an irregularity of musical phrase, unless the poetry is to be either rhythmically extended or telescoped in order to accommodate the demands of the music. But not all of the poems in this cycle depart from the standard couplet and as a result much of Berlioz's musical phrasing has an annoying regularity about it. This is particularly true of the first song and it is aggravated a good deal by the rather four-square rhythm, which enforces a metric regularity upon the text that is foreign to the French language of poetry. The second, however, has a much greater pliancy in both the melodic outline and the rhythmic realization, although the verse itself is no less regular. The fifth song, *Au Cimetière*, with its recurring four-syllable line inserted regularly following couplets of eight syllables, presents the greatest problem in flexibility. Berlioz is not entirely successful with it inasmuch as he inclines toward musically extending the short lines. But there is nonetheless a hint of that typical French ability to exploit rhythmic nuance to counteract the metrical relentlessness of music which, unless it is disguised, can destroy the subtleties of poetic rhythm. Although Berlioz provides principally an accompaniment consisting of solid repeated or broken chords only, the harmonic changes are skillfully maneuvered so that they occur at varying places in the measure, in general avoiding the strong first beat. This fluid sort of harmonic rhythm is effective in freeing the musical movement at least partially from the tyranny of the meter.

The songs are typical of the period in France, too, in the relatively restrictive type of accompaniment. For the most part, this is confined to a harmonic support for the voice line, although occasionally there are some slight gestures toward a motivic interaction with the voice. One such is the suggestion of canon between voice and bass in the first song and the exploitation of a sort of leading motive in the third. These are restricted in scope, however, and show no tendency to become highly developed. Unlike the Germans, the French were slow to enter into an accompaniment style that was much more than a harmonic enhancement of mood.

The style Berlioz established for the *mélodie* was to continue well past mid-century. Although there was no lack of song composition, some of it by the leading composers of the day, there was no really insistent pattern of development beyond the best of *Les Nuits d'Été*. Gounod and Massenet, for instance, each contributed about two hundred songs to the great number in circulation, but neither was able to bring to the effort more than a few that have persisted in popularity. Both composers are inclined to do little more than harmonize the melody in spite of the variety of accompaniment patterns they utilize. Only occasionally is there a meaningful gesture in the direction of a declamation flexible enough to erase the predominantly regular rhythms. One of the most notable exceptions is Massenet's *Que l'heure est donc brève*. But there is little doubt that it was the lyric tendencies of Schubert that exerted the most influence rather than the relatively greater subtlety of the Schumannesque style.

There are, of course, good reasons for the general aura of reserve and lack of dramatic illustrative involvement in French song. The poetry itself is much less given to direct statement (present in the most romantic German verse), and the language is more subtly inflected than most. Without the dramatic accents that characterize even the most lyric of German romantic poetry, there is correspondingly less opportunity or invitation to illustrate the text in any but the merest suggestive terms. The occurrence of dissonance in German *lieder* is often deliberately exposed for its effect in punctuating a dramatic poetic expression. French song, on the other hand, tends to cloak the dissonance in innuendo. French poetry, in contrast to German, is a poetry of understatement and a musical language that described the mood in unashamedly overt terms would not only outweigh the poetic imagery but in all likelihood pervert it altogether. To this extent, then, the relatively slow development of a musical texture that could adequately treat the sophistication of the poetic language is not surprising. The problems of early and mid-nineteenth-century song in France were mostly problems that involved the freeing of melodic rhythms so that they could encompass without strain the unusually fluid rhythmic nature of the poetry.

GABRIEL FAURÉ

The first of the great song composers of the century was Gabriel Fauré, and it is important in any comparison which is made between the *lied* and the *mélodie* to recognize that his first compositions were written in 1865, at a time when the *lied* was already a firmly established and highly developed genre, having gone through a period of extended growth and refinement. Fauré's initial songs show no marked advance over those of his French predecessors or contemporaries. In such pieces as *Rêve d'Amour, Dans les ruines d'une abbaye, Mai,* and *Tristesse* there is a consistent tendency to select a rhythm of total simplicity and regularity and to phrase the music almost entirely in keeping with the poetic line. But even in *Mai*, his second song, he shows evidence of having absorbed the harmonic suavity of the century, moving without strain and within the short space of eight measures from G major to B♭ major to F major and back to C major in preparation for the return of the tonic. Not content with this, he resolves the dominant seventh of G deceptively to E minor for the outset of the succeeding phrase. Even in some of these early pieces, however, Fauré was often able to introduce an element of some melodic flexibility when the poem was challenging enough—as in Prudhomme's *Au bord de l'eau.* In this song there is an unusual freedom of phrasing within a relatively static rhythmic framework, a freedom that is helped a great deal by the overlapping dialogue between accompaniment and vocal motives. For the most part, and in spite of these occasional stabs in the direction of greater musical suavity, the composer is inclined to move relentlessly toward the end of the poetic line, pausing briefly to articulate the poetic accent that normally occurs at this point.

In the course of the next two decades, Fauré returned periodically to the song, always gaining in his imaginative use of the keyboard although retaining a primarily harmonic concept of its function. His harmonic fluctuations become more rapid and more unusual without thereby venturing beyond a clear, though extended, tonal compass. At the same time there is considerable gain in melodic fluency and such songs as *Aurore* and *Les Roses d'Ispahan* show his growing use of subtle declamatory variability within the limits of the classic song forms. The former is a modified *aba* and the latter an equally familiar *aaba*. But in both songs, the reappearances of the principal sections are always varied enough rhythmically and melodically to accommodate the changing needs of the text.

The work that best represents the gains Fauré had made is the cycle of nine songs on poems of Verlaine, *La Bonne Chanson.* Some of the poetry itself is extraordinarily ecstatic in terms of the moods that usually attracted the composer, and it is perhaps because of this that they inspire a vitality that is rare in his songs. But even allowing for this, there are numerous purely musical devices that he brings into play for the sake of commenting or expanding upon the implications of the poetry.

Cooper has noticed Fauré's text illustration in the cycle, a practice which occurs infrequently in his work.[12] The rocking nature of *Les Berceaux*, a relatively early song, is not typical of his approach and is not one of his best efforts, because it gets him into serious trouble with declamation. One

---

12 Martin Cooper, *French Music* (London: Oxford University Press, 1961), pp. 86–87.

instance from *La Bonne Chanson* that caught Cooper's attention is the use of a horn motive at the words:

> *La note d'or que fait entendre*
> *Le cor dans le lointain des bois,*
>
> The golden sound which is heard
> Of the horn in the distant woods,[13]

Another instance is in *J'allais par des chemins perfides* where the chromaticism illustrates the stumbling journey of the singer until the words:

> *L'amour, délicieux vainqueur,*
> *Nous a réuni dans la joie!*
>
> Love, delightful vanquisher
> Has united us in joy!

At this point the harmonic movement is to F$\sharp$ major, the tonic, and the melody line of the accompaniment illustrates *joie* with ascending triplets.

They are not the only instances, of course, nor does Cooper imply that they are. The cycle is, in fact, riddled with evidences that Fauré had found ways to get at both generalities and specifics in the text. One is the wonderful enharmonic movement from A$\flat$ to A, which culminates at the words *sourire triomphant* (triumphant smile), in the first song; another is the melodic sunburst at *l'aurore* (sunrise) in the very first vocal phrase of the second song. Later in the same piece the exuberant music of the opening section settles down calmly for:

> *Et comme pour bercer les lenterus de la route,*
> *Je chanterai des airs ingénus,*
>
> And while dreamily walking along the road,
> I would sing simple airs,

In *J'allais par des chemins perfides* the piano plays a role not only in accompanying the textual mood but just as importantly in anticipating it, preparing for it. The opening statement with its sharp chromatic wanderings sets the mood, which the voice need only explain at its entrance. And following the extremely erratic movement that climaxes with the words:

> *Mon coeur craintif, mon sombre coeur*
> *Pleurait, seul, sur la triste voie,*
>
> My fearful heart, my gloomy heart
> Wept lonely on the mournful road,

13 These and succeeding translations from this cycle are taken from the International Music Company edition.

there is the three-measure piano interlude that establishes F♯ major by itself and at the same time introduces the lyric mood that pervades the final two poetic lines. Throughout *J'ai presque peur, en vérité* there is not only the use of an accompaniment style that reflects the fear of the opening and then changes to enhance the more contemplative nature of the second section, but there is an insistence upon musical byplay between voice and piano that is unusual for Fauré. There is hardly an interlude, brief though it be, during which the piano does not introduce either the vocal motive that is to follow or a pattern derived from it. And the insistent repetition of the accompaniment motive as the song draws to its close is surely meant to illustrate the words:

> *Plongé dans ce bonheur suprême*
> *De me dire encore et toujours,*

> Immersed in this supreme happiness,
> To repeat to myself again and again,

In *Avant que tu ne t'en ailles* the alternating *quasi adagio* and *allegro moderato* tempi that accompany the first six poetic lines are in themselves almost as illustrative as is Fauré's choice of a piano motive sufficiently adaptable to the changing text to represent the singing quail and the soaring lark and which can be readily transformed to serve for the joy of the closing section.

And so it goes to the end of the cycle where the texture of the final exultant song is unmatched by anything Fauré wrote for the voice. *La Bonne Chanson* was followed in succeeding years by relatively few songs and they move gradually away from a lyric style toward a much leaner melodic line in which the rhythms are based more closely on speech. At the same time the accompaniments are again less involved in musical interplay and tend to revert to their former role of harmonic support. The harmony in many cases loses its former warmth as Fauré apparently attempted to absorb into his own personal idiom some of the newer experiments in tonality. His last work for the voice, the cycle based upon poems by De Mirmont, *L'Horizon Chimérique* (1922), is illustrative of all these factors.

Most of Fauré's status as a song composer is based upon his work in *La Bonne Chanson* and the style that led up to it. In most of the songs the primary emphasis is upon melodic lyricism, coloristic harmony of a suggestive nature (as opposed to illustrative unless one thinks of harmony in terms of emotional illustration), relatively regular rhythmic patterns that function to outline the poetic form, and an accompaniment style uncomplicated by motivic interplay or development. Of the important French song composers, then, he is related strongly to Brahms and to certain elements in Schubert rather than to Schumann and Wolf.

HENRI DUPARC

Aside from Debussy, the contemporary composer who is most important for song is Henri Duparc, a disciple of César Franck but not an exponent of particulars of his style. Duparc produced only fifteen songs, but practically all of them have taken a significant place in the French repertoire, a tribute to his imagination as well as his creative skill. His songs are so individual in character, much like fully developed Wolf, that it is hazardous and perhaps even pointless to attempt generalizations. What seems clear is a harmonic texture based upon extensive chromaticism, and enharmonic excursions that are based more on the work of Wagner than that of fellow Frenchmen. The opening piano strain in *Extase* as well as the harmonization of it are reminiscent of *Tristan*. Also Wagnerian is Duparc's frequent overlap of accompaniment and vocal material so that there is often a continuously fluctuating texture. The interlude between stanzas in *Extase* is typical of this, as are many briefer maneuvers between phrases. At the same time he is able to provide an entirely coloristic texture that confines the linear concepts to the voice alone, as in *L'Invitation au Voyage*. Here the sensuous play of harmonic nuance serves only to mirror the seductive urgings of the poem. The only melody that intrudes upon the chordal patterns is an occasional reminder of the wish, expressed in the second vocal phrase:

> *Aimer à loisir*   To love without care,
> *Aimer et mourir*   To love and to die

In this song, Duparc's affinity for harmonic nuance and lyrical melodies was a happy match for the thinly disguised sexuality of Baudelaire's poetry. The only other poem by Baudelaire that Duparc set is not nearly so successful—*La Vie antérieure*. He seems drawn off base by the changing chronology in the text and changes his musical styles in accordance with it, but at the expense of the imagery that is so powerfully used in *L'Invitation au Voyage*. Duparc is especially fond of pedal points and, as in the latter piece, they often act as a stabilizing influence on the chromaticism of the harmonic fluctuations that occur so constantly above them.

One of Duparc's most unusual songs is unique to the French repertoire of the period. The strong sense of madness, the vigorous driving rhythms, and the almost melodramatic (but not quite!) climaxes set *Le Manoir de Rosemonde* well apart from his other songs, as well as from those of his contemporaries. There is something quite Germanic in the intensity of the dramatic expression, which is far from being in keeping with the usual French preference for veiled symbolism. The leading motive impelling the song forward, which is confined to the piano, is in itself reminiscent of Wagner's mad-ride motive in *Die Walküre*. Whether the associative symbolism is deliberate or not, the effect is electric. The declamation is as incisively dramatic as any to be found in French song.

Although Fauré and Duparc were instrumental in the establishment of a type of sophisticated harmonic and melodic vocabulary that was peculiarly appropriate to the high stylization of French poetry, their songs are not in themselves revolutionary. Both worked within the limits of the tonal system, vastly expanded as those limits had become. And despite the rhythmic nuance of which both were capable, their melodies are still linear in the older sense of that word—they draw a tuneful line upon which the accompaniment seldom intrudes or asserts its own prerogatives. But the tune, sinuous as it sometimes is, is still structured with principally musical demands as guidelines rather than being derived primarily from poetic inflections. Not until Debussy's *Chansons de Bilitis* did song in France find new directions by which the melody could be given over entirely to *all* the declamatory insinuations of the poetic language and the music as an expressive force could for the most part be confined to the accompaniment.

CLAUDE DEBUSSY

There is nothing in his first song, *Nuit d'Étoiles*, to suggest the direction Debussy was ultimately to take. Even the form is familiar—the long-established and reliable five-part song. He uses the first four lines of the poem as the text for each return of the principal section, and in each case complements it by returning to the home tonality. The accompaniment throughout is studiously harmonic and chordal. In Debussy's earliest songs the melodic interest that creeps into the piano from time to time always quickly recedes at the entrance of the voice (*La Belle au Bois dormant* is typical), and not until the *Cinq Poèmes de Baudelaire* (1887–1889) does the accompaniment come to life and assert its own musical strength. Whatever difficulties are evident in the musical texture of this set result from just this factor, for the "busyness" of *Le Balcon* and *Harmonie du Soir* is immensely distracting. *Le Balcon* in particular strikes me as being perilously close to a musical three-ring circus. *Le Jet d'Eau* with its obvious descriptive motives is hardly less so. But in the last two songs, *Recueillement* and *La Mort des Amants*, it is possible to see the promise of things to come. In these the accompaniments are less assertive, less active in their commentary. Throughout the series, there is evidence of increasing control of melodic rhythms and outlines. Much of the reliance upon tune for tune's sake, so inescapable a part of song vocabulary for so long, has begun to disappear. There is still much of the "singing" concept but there is also a strong sug-gestion of pitch used in the service and in the nature of speech inflection. This is particularly noticeable as a total approach in *La Mort des Amants*, although there are similar more brief excursions in this direction in all the other songs.

These tendencies are apparent also in the *Ariettes Oubliées*, composed during the same years, although here the piano is less preoccupied than in some of the Baudelaire pieces. *L'Ombre des Arbres* is especially impressive in its use of weak beats for phrase endings, a device that is useful in masking the unfortunate metrical strength given by music to the words, a strength that can be disastrous in French poetry. The songs of 1891, in particular *Romance* and *Les Cloches*, are noticeably thinner in texture and the melody returns to a lyric style made up of more even note values and an undulating contour. The harmonic procedures, although still utilizing Debussy's fondness for dissonances of a coloristic nature, are less chromatic than in the immediately preceding songs.

Much of the simplicity of texture and for that matter the tunefulness continues through the first set of *Fêtes Galantes*, dating from 1892. But the *Proses Lyriques*, for which Debussy provided his own texts, are once again relatively full-blown and marred by diverse procedures that confuse the musical effect without adding to the articulation of the words.

During the decade from 1892 to 1902, Debussy achieved full mastery of the musical techniques and procedures with which he is most closely identified—impressionism. It was during this period that he produced the String Quartet, the orchestral *Prélude à l'Après-midi d'un faune* and *Nocturnes*. But in relation to song style, it was his work on the opera *Pelléas et Mélisande* that exerted the most far-reaching effect. The rejection of almost all melodic outlines in favor of a *parlando* manner of vocal delivery, which is the characteristic style of this opera, had been only hinted at in the earlier songs, sophisticated though many of them were in a musical sense. The gestures in that direction had been tentative and relatively infrequent, although they were certainly present in varying degrees from 1887 onward.

But the *Chansons de Bilitis* in 1897, midway through the years during which he was occupied with *Pelléas et Mélisande*, are the first to fully incorporate the undistilled rhythms of speech. For Debussy, this was a point of no return in vocal delivery; never again was he able to concede to the voice anything other than the fullest acquiescence to the demands of the poetry. Never again would he return to the excessive musical manipulation typical of the *Proses Lyriques* and the *Cinq Poèmes de Baudelaire*. The vague and subtle harmonic vacillations of the *Bilitis* songs are only the echo of poetic symbolism, unbridled by the tyrannies of key center. This rejection of the demand for resolution of dissonance and for movement to or away from a tonic is one of Debussy's basic innovations in harmonic function. For him, color is everything and in his vocal music from this period on the color is motivated entirely by the text and not by the musical exigencies as such. In his own words: "Any musical development not called for by the words is a mistake."[14] It is always necessary to bear in mind when trying to understand Debussy's harmonic practice that he sneeringly referred to Franck as a "modulating machine." That sort of tonality-rooted movement he rejected most emphatically.

14 Cooper, *op. cit.*, p. 114.

He does not disown description. The flute is there in the first of the *Chansons de Bilitis* and in the second set of *Fêtes Galantes* in 1904 there is the suggestion of insects in *Les Ingénus*. But for the most part the poetry itself deals with the sort of innuendo that cannot be illustrated by musical figurations nor, for that matter, by musical development in the romantic sense. Debussy in his latest songs never attempts to enlarge musically upon the poetic suggestion, in the style of the *lied*. The restrained insinuations of the words are simply mirrored in the music, not expanded, not dramatized.

The essence of the songs after 1897 cannot be adequately verbalized or put into terms other than their own individual character. A mere description of the musico-poetic vocabulary is self-defeating—it is as though the entire fabric were of such great delicacy and transparency that to attempt a dissection would be to encourage total disintegration. This may account for the fact that all the scholarly volumes on the art of Debussy, in particular those dealing with *Pelléas et Mélisande*, seem strangely impotent in terms of the music itself. It is true that the devices of impressionism are as painstakingly deliberate in music as in the visual arts, but the effect of that art is inexplicable in terms other than its own. While this is true, of course, of all great art, it is more evident where symbolism has replaced statement. It is a large part of the greatness of Debussy that he realized that musical explanation is as futile as verbal explanation when dealing with Louÿs (*Chansons de Bilitis*) and Verlaine (*Fêtes Galantes II*). Although *Le Tombeau des Naïades* from the former and *Colloque sentimental* from the latter are largely in terms of dialogue, never is there a musical attempt at characterization nor an interpretation of the conversationalists and what they say. This essential indissolubility of poetic and musical imagery is unique to Debussy.

It must be obvious that there are definite points of contact between the styles of Debussy and Wolf as they reflect the synthesis of poetry and music. Both men tend to subjugate their melodic style to the requirements of the poetry *as poetry*. The difference between their melodic solutions is grounded in the differences between German and French, both in language and in principles of versification. There is no place in French for the dramatic accentuation and the musical heightening of expression that German poetry not only tolerates but encourages. There is, therefore, a great deal more overt dramatization in Wolf, even within the guidelines, derived from the poetry, that control his music. Nonetheless, there is a certain sense of the esoteric in Wolf as in Debussy, a facet of their art that has made both somewhat less "popular" than other song composers of the century. I have suggested elsewhere that the musical imagery in Brahms functions many times as an actual *substitute* for the poetic imagery, so that the listener who is sensitive to that musical imagery may well derive a general emotional satisfaction and effect comparable to that of the poetry, whether or not he is aware of the specifics of the text. There is an element of this in Fauré, as well, although markedly less evident in *La Bonne Chanson* than in many of the earlier songs. To a lesser degree this is also true of Duparc. But in the Debussy of the *Chansons de Bilitis* and beyond and in the greatest portion of Wolf this is not the case. Only the most intimate acquaintance with the words will suffice, and even given this, only the greatest sensitivity to the deeper symbolic significance of the poetry and to the musical imagery *as it relates to that symbolism* can effect a meaningful response.

As Wolf represents the synthesis of operatic and *lied* styles in Germany, so Debussy is his French counterpart. Everything that can be said stylistically about *Pelléas et Mélisande* can be transferred almost bodily to the late songs, give or take a little for scope alone. Once again the cycle has come full circle, for what Debussy accomplished was the ultimate realization of those ideals toward which Lully had only haltingly striven. The shadow of Wagner looms large here as it did in the last half of the nineteenth century throughout Europe. Debussy was actually an admirer of the great German music dramatist, although his own musical solutions to the same ideological problem took different forms. But it is doubtful that without Wagner's pioneering efforts to bring word and tone into a more integrated relationship Debussy could have achieved the complete musico-poetic synthesis of his late works.

II

The Twentieth Century

Iƒ THE twentieth century is characterized by any one artistic temper it must be identified as an all-embracing experimentalism. The assessment of any era by those contemporary with it is hazardous. The very proximity of its events discourages objectivity and there is not the advantage that can be gained from the seasoning of time and reflection. What can be said with some certainty, however, is that the present century has been marked by the struggle to gain freedom from established patterns. This struggle has not been limited to the arts. It has included political and religious theory, social mores, communications, medicine, and every other facet of human thought and activity. There is ample documentation that bears upon the almost tortured attempt to establish new and different patterns of social behavior, scientific investigation and responsibility, and artistic expression. The purpose of this chapter is not to add to such documentation but merely to indicate some of the effects of poetic and musical trends on song composition, effects that by this point in the century might be expected to have gained some permanency.

Among the welter of new poetic devices inaugurated in the late nineteenth century, perhaps the most influential on the musico-poetic alliance that is song was the tendency away from musical elements in verse itself. Romantic poetry was patently involved with the attempt to incorporate as many musical devices as possible and it was largely due to this orientation that the art song flourished as it did throughout the nineteenth century. But the emphasis toward the turn of the century, strongest in France but spreading rapidly throughout the Western world, was directed away from the "singing" of poetry toward the exploitation of language itself. The increasing use of free verse, the rejection of rhymes or the employment of highly complicated and esoteric rhyme schemes, the insistence upon free rhythms, irregular or totally unstructured meters—all of these, together with the breakdown in France of established principles of versification, sharply restricted the enhancement that music could add in the musico-poetic enterprise.

As early as the 1870's, Rimbaud was turning away from the accepted and time-honored verse structures to produce prose poems such as *Les Illuminations* and *Une Saison en enfer*; at the same time he began exploiting the complications of symbolism to such an extent that interpretation and/or explication becomes virtually meaningless. Equally important in terms of the new directions was the employment by Mallarmé and others of a symbolism so highly intellectual that the attempt to explain it in terms other than its own exact language approaches "the status of exegesis, a term more properly reserved for the exposition of Scriptures and which supposes at least an expert knowledge based on some body of accepted doctrine."[1] In spite of Mallarmé's concern for the pure sonance of the word combinations he employed—their validity as sound apart from and even in ignorance of their validity as denotative elements in language—the results are less musical than verbal. His poetry does not really "sing" in the older, more romantic sense. The attempt to extract all inherent and implied possibilities from language resulted in extremes of obscurity that are still frustrating commentators.

The final breakdown of poetic form in France was a result of the work of the surrealists and Dadaists, led by Breton and Eluard. In the final analysis, their work makes nearly impossible any real distinctions between poetry and prose. Although the backgrounds are those of symbolism, the extremes of free expression to which they carried those backgrounds and the abandonment of all contextual logic except that which might be implied from Freudian psychological interpretations resulted in an almost total negation of the communicative possibilities of poetic language—or at least of a type of communication that allows for paraphrase or explication.

In Germany, the source of so much of the nineteenth century's poetic lyricism, the rejection of established patterns and ideals was equally severe and decisive. Rilke, the poet of Hindemith's *Das Marienleben*, for instance, turned toward a sort of spiritual expressionism in which his reflective use of language leads him to the brink of a mysticism whose symbolism is too remote and elusive for any but the most sensitive initiate. The work of Stefan George goes even further in the same direction. Aside from the obscurity of the spiritually grounded imagery, George's work is characterized by heavy rhythms, often the result of insistence upon one-syllable words that impart chant-like texture to the poetry. Fifteen of the poems from his *Die Bücher der Hirten und Preisgedichte der Sagen und Sänge und der hängenden Gärten* have been set by Schoenberg, whose abstruse style serves not to clarify the verse but merely to add its own confusing dimension.

Echoing the disenchantment that followed World War II, Gottfried Benn articulated the aims of the modernists.[2] The four areas of rejection of

1 Geoffrey Brereton, *An Introduction to the French Poets* (London: Methuen and Co., Ltd., 1956), p. 213.

2 August Closs, *The Genius of the German Lyric* (London: The Cresset Press, 1962), p. 350 ff.

past poetics that Benn and his disciples believed to be necessary include the romantic address to Nature, the excessive use of similes, the romantic use of color, and the "seraphic tone" designed to transport the reader to "heavenly spheres." Much of the new poetry, experimental in both mood and form, was patterned on the work of T. S. Eliot and his followers. Among the facets that identify the style of these revolutionaries are the emphasis placed upon the shock value of words and images, the bitterness of the satire, and the reliance on words as purely verbal entities within themselves rather than upon their denotative or connotative validity within the poetic context.

English and American verse has reiterated the patterns of change that are evident elsewhere. Although some poets like A. E. Housman and Thomas Hardy reaffirmed much of the older lyricism and warmth of the romantics, others have forged ahead on more adventurous paths. Among those who have attracted song composers of the present century are symbolists such as T. S. Eliot, James Joyce, and Ezra Pound, mystics like W. B. Yeats and Hart Crane, and those with a strong metaphysical bent like Gerard Manley Hopkins. As among the Europeans, there are strains of harsh realism and a fascination with earthy images delivered in the language of the street and the rugged countryside. Possibly most typical of such emphases are Carl Sandburg and Archibald MacLeish, both of whom have had settings of their poetry by leading English and/or American song writers. Among others who have been in the forefront of highly experimental movements in verse are Gertrude Stein and E. E. Cummings, with their almost painful contextual vagaries and their use of language for its value as sound alone.

In Italy the growth of a contemporary poetic expression was not unlike that in other European countries. Because of the peculiar political situation, marred by divisiveness and a struggle for a national image, much of the subject matter was devoted to engendering a patriotic fervor. What was not directed toward that end was heavily oriented in religious devotion, a natural result of Rome's being the seat of worldwide Catholicism. The break from the traditionalism of the nineteenth century was marked by the verse of men like Giuseppe Ungaretti, Eugenio Montale, and Salvatore Quasimodo, and it took forms similar to those in France—a rejection of established syllabification and metric principles, a deepening awareness of the possibilities of the word as symbol in the most obscure and often indeterminate sense, and also an entity within itself as a projection of sound. Although directed toward what might be considered peculiarly nationalistic problems in Italy, the poetry is derivative in style, echoing much that can be traced to Mallarmé in France or Eliot in America. Despite the extensive poetic activity of the Italians, however, there has been no widespread dissemination of their work outside of their own country. It is notable that, although there are a number of fine commentaries in English that treat in some detail the contemporary poetry of France and Germany, there is only one volume of significance dealing with Italian verse. And even in this, the comments are included only as a portion of a discussion which deals with the entire Italian literary output in all media.[3]

In music there has been a rash of idioms that counterpoint those in poetry. Following the breakdown of tonal underpinnings that was fostered by the extreme chromaticism of Wagner and the coloristic harmonic devices of Debussy, there was an inrush of polytonality, atonality, and dissonant counterpoint, along with an interest in thinning of musical texture often to the extreme of pointillism—experimental probings that led almost inevitably to the serial organization of Schoenberg with its denial of functional tonality in the established sense. Accompanying these harmonically and melodically revolutionary adventurings, there arose a considerable interest in the exploitation of sound combinations purely for their own sake. The interest was an almost exact parallel to the efforts of the poets to extract the ultimate sonant character from word clusters and even from individual words themselves. Ultimately, the investigations led in some quarters to a complete abandonment of traditional instruments and into the realms of sound phenomena created and reproduced electronically and organized into astoundingly intricate complexes with the aid of computers.

The many idioms in music were reflected in song to some extent, without concurrently focusing upon a discernible stylistic trend comparable to the development of the nineteenth-century *lied* in Germany or the *mélodie* in France. Nor can such a trend be anticipated. The entire musical scene has been in a continuing state of flux from which no dominant directional tendency has emerged, other than the negative one of movement away from most nineteenth-century ideologies, which at this point are viewed largely as decadent. Among the generalizations that might be suggested, however, is that the factor that looms largest in the song of this century may be the tendency to use the voice as an instrument and to exploit it in combination with other instruments principally for its color rather than as an idealized focal point for the text. In some ways, this is a restatement of the ideals of the baroque, but there is an attempt in much modern song to utilize *all* the sound-making possibilities of the voice rather than concentrating only upon its capacity to sing beautifully. From the standpoint of the voice in its role as a significant element in the musico-poetic endeavor, there is a hazard inherent in utilizing the more experimental types of poetry. The obscurity of such texts is difficult enough to cope with in even the most careful and leisurely reading. They become all but incomprehensible in song, where the fleeting nature of the delivery creates an insurmountable barrier to assimilation by the listener.

It would be tempting, particularly in view of the proximity of their work, to deal in some detail with the many song composers of the twentieth century. As in the other eras with which this book has dealt, however, an

3 Sergio Pacifici, *A Guide to Contemporary Italian Literature* (New York: World Publishing Co., 1962).

exhaustive commentary and description would serve no better purpose than to catalogue. In general, song composition has inclined toward one of two directions. The majority of the songs that have consistently appeared in recital have been those that retained at least a minimal portion of the tunefulness and lyric declamation of the last century while at the same time incorporating enough of the contemporary "isms" to provide them with a certain currency of sound. Pursuing a different bent is a body of song, less frequently performed, that has been turned out by composers whose allegiance has been directed insistently toward the new.

The French provide the strongest link with the past, so far as song style is concerned, while continuing to add those elements that strongly identify their efforts as forward-looking.[4] The composer who most clearly provides a liaison between the *mélodie* style of the mature Debussy and those who followed him is Maurice Ravel. Although his earlier pieces, of which *Sainte* is typical, rely upon the sensuously colorful harmonic vocabulary of Impressionism with the chromaticism entrusted most consistently to the accompaniment, the later songs move toward what was to become a more characteristic twentieth-century idiom developed under the influence of *Les Six*. During the first decades of the century, the period of *Histoires Naturelles* and *Cinq Mélodies Populaires Grecques*, there is a noticeable thinning of texture and a growing concern for meticulous declamation. Despite this, however, Ravel adds his own sense of melodic continuity so that there is less rejection of vocal line, less insertion of almost fragmentary inflected speech, than is typical of Debussy's work during the same period.

The relative sparseness of the texture and the clarity are perhaps the two most important features that were carried into the work of *Les Six*. Of the group, which included Louis Durey, Germaine Tailleferre, Georges Auric, Arthur Honegger, Darius Milhaud, and Francis Poulenc, only the last three have left a body of song that has proved of continuing interest to present-day recitalists. In addition to their rejection of the overripeness and sensuality of their immediate predecessors, they exploited a rhythmic complexity fostered by several factors. The first was the influx into France of Negro jazz musicians, an influx that was simply an international extension of their migration out of New Orleans. Related to this was the work of Stravinsky with its striking rhythmic innovations, and the lack of superfluity in the compositional style of Erik Satie. Also involved was the development of a new interest in musical dialogue and with it a trend toward polyphony, with its emphasis upon linear movement rather than upon the vertical implications of harmonic color. The combination of influences, insofar as they converged upon song composition, resulted in a far more concise and objective expression than that which had typified the late nineteenth century in either France or Germany.

4 Among the best discussions of early twentieth-century French musical style is Cooper's in his *French Music*. My own descriptions of French song during this period have been somewhat guided by that treatise.

Many of these characteristics are evident in one of Arthur Honegger's earliest song groups, *Six Poèmes*, excerpted from Apollinaire's *Alcools* (1916–1917). All six pieces show a high degree of purely musical organization, from the *ostinato* figure that pervades *A la Santé*, the first, through the reiterated pattern used for text illustration in the last song, *Les Cloches*. In *Automne* there is the rhythmic complexity brought about by the use of $\frac{4}{4}$ in the accompaniment treble against $\frac{12}{8}$ in the bass, over which the voice intones the text in melodic recitative. And although there are brief gestures toward polytonality in several of the songs, the most consistent use of it is in *L'Adieu*. In general and throughout his later song compositions, Honegger was not bound to a restricted type of musical style. In much of his work there is a fascinating mixture of impressionistic effects always highly spiced with penetrating dissonances (often a result of his penchant for mixed tonalities), as well as frequent gestures of a modal nature. Honegger was drawn most strongly to contemporary poets (Apollinaire, Claudel, Cocteau), and the cleanliness of his musical palette is as kind to their verbal niceties and obscurities as music can be expected to be.

The most prolific song writer of *Les Six* was Darius Milhaud, although he brought no significant change of direction from the general objectives of his fellows. Because of his continued interest in song, his selection of poets covers a wide range in both time and style, from the sixteenth-century Ronsard to the Bengali Tagore, and includes most of the French contemporaries of importance. His accompaniment style is inclined to be more chordal than either Honegger's or Poulenc's, although there are many exceptions. One of the most striking is in the second of his set of *Trois Poèmes* on texts by Jean Cocteau, where the single treble and bass lines that sketch a haunting bitonal background create an atmosphere perfectly suited to the "foggy" text. Most of his songs utilize a completely tonal melodic line, often even totally diatonic, which is sometimes contradicted by the harmonic implications of the accompaniment. The result is a piquantly dissonant effect but one that places no unreasonable burden upon the vocalist or the listener. For the most part Milhaud avoids the statement of a key signature, so that much of his music appears visually to be more chromatic than it turns out to be aurally. The range of his musical vocabulary is evident in a comparison of his *Cinq Chansons de Charles Vildrac*, with their almost folksy settings in keeping with the poetic language to the very recent *Adieu*, based on the esoteric poems of Rimbaud taken from *Une Saison en enfer*, an immensely sophisticated group in every way. The latter piece is also illustrative of the twentieth-century inclination to return to the baroque use of the voice as part of a chamber ensemble. The songs are scored for voice, flute, viola, and harp. Although none of *Les Six* were innovators in the reawakening of interest in vocal chamber works, they are solidly in the mainstream of the current favoritism for this medium.

Almost equally productive in song has been Francis Poulenc. Like his companions he was partial to the poetry of his own time, in particular that of Paul Eluard, but did not wholly ignore earlier works. He set verses by Charles d'Orléans and Ronsard, for instance, as well as a number of anonymous pieces, some from the seventeenth century. His strongest attraction was to the surrealists, and perhaps because of this his musical realizations are a good deal more fanciful than either Honegger's or Milhaud's. Of the three, he is the most apt to provide a vocal line which is often meandering in its harmonic implications and likewise more rhythmically bound to the text—the _Deux Poèmes_ on texts by Apollinaire are illustrative of both facets of his style. Despite his harmonic fluctuations, however, there is always a decided sense of tonality, including departure from one center and satisfactory arrival at another. He is able, too, to scale down his materials when the occasion demands (as in _Priez pour Paix_ on d'Orléans's poem) so that an entirely appropriate simplicity is present, in this instance strongly colored by hints of modality. Among more recent works that illustrate his facility with a relatively sparse supply of musical material are the group of seven songs, _La courte paille_, on poems by Maurice Carême. In this case the extreme directness of Poulenc's approach is a wonderful foil for the witticism of the verses.

While other French composers of stature in the twentieth century (Henri Sauguet and Erik Satie among them) have contributed a considerable body of song that is performed with some consistency, there has been no real evolution of style, indicating a change of direction from that inaugurated in the works of _Les Six_. The retention of the most usable devices of impressionism and a return to the linear clarity of earlier periods have been the identifying factors. If there is a revolution of style that will culminate in anything as "progressive" as the dodecaphonic adventures of the Germans, it has not yet become evident. The high sophistication that has always marked French music in general and its song in particular is still very much a part of the picture. If there is less establishment of rapport between the twentieth-century French song composer and his audience than between the latter and the _mélodie_ composers of the previous century, the basis lies not as much in the musical vocabulary as in the poetic language. The texts demand extensive reflection and even then they often remain elusive and ambiguous. In performance there is little opportunity for reflection, so that the response is almost always in terms of the music alone. Such a response is not a negligible factor, but it has not promoted the richness of musico-poetic sensitivity that was characteristic of earlier centuries, nor can musical device and poetic device be as closely correlated except in the more blatantly satirical works like Satie's _Ludions_. Nevertheless, it seems reasonable to state at this point in time that many of the songs of Honegger, Milhaud, Poulenc, Sauguet, Satie, and others of their general persuasion have found a reasonably substantial place in the performing repertoire. The reasons may well lie principally in the fact that their styles, while dissimilar among themselves, share a common interest in the retention of enough of the past to accommodate recital-goers who are, whether justifiably or not, attuned to the nineteenth-century concept of song. And they are certainly in the mainstream of what appears to be the twentieth-century return to a deepening concern for musical strength as the dominant role in vocal composition.

In England, a renewed interest in song marked the dying years of the last century and the birth of the present one, and it was patterned for the most part on the German *lied*. The harmonic vocabulary, the subject matter, the often overabundant sentimentality, and the concern for a sort of melodic sweetness—all these elements are present in the work of Ralph Vaughan Williams, the most significant of the English song composers before Benjamin Britten. The qualities are most apparent in his earlier works, *Songs of Travel* and *The House of Life*, but the addition of modal parallelisms in the *Five Mystical Songs* do not really obscure the underlying evidence of the composer's romantic heritage. Lesser composers like Cyril Scott, Roger Quilter, John Ireland, Gerald Finzi, and Peter Warlock move only tentatively away from an aesthetic orientation toward the previous century. Of these, perhaps Warlock and Finzi took the most definite steps in establishing a more linear texture with a greater contrapuntal interest between accompaniment and vocal line. The latter's *A Young Man's Exhortation*, one of his many sets of songs on texts by Thomas Hardy, is notable in this respect. And both were somewhat more adventurous in their gestures toward an accommodation of the new tolerance for dissonance.

Benjamin Britten is the English composer who most closely approximates the inclination to thinner, crisper, more clarified statement that typifies the French style of the present era. It is true he arrived at his first really important songs (the *Seven Sonnets of Michelangelo*) in 1940, when the century was well advanced and the musical concepts of the world had been set in new directions by Stravinsky and Schoenberg, among others. Nevertheless, there is a relatively wide gap which separates these early efforts of Britten's from pieces by Finzi and Vaughan Williams that are of the same date or later. His melodic imagination is already apparent, including his ability to structure tunes that make extensive use of chord outlines without falling into harmonic stodginess. A complementary sensitivity for declamatory excellence and a corresponding skill in pseudo-recitative (factors that are of great service to his musical works for the stage) are evident also, particularly in *Sonetto XVI*, where the declamation grows out of a starkly illustrative piano figure, and *Sonetto LV*, where it is completely independent of the *ostinato* accompaniment motive. It is indicative of his approach, too, to find the musical realization descriptive without being obvious. In *Sonetto XXX*, for instance, the juxtaposition of triads in F♯ major and G major not only reflects the contemporary fascination with extension of tonality but serves to mirror the paradoxical text as well.

By the year of *A Charm of Lullabies* (1947), the texture had become even more sparse and the dissonance even more piquant. All of the songs are illustrative to the extent that they use motives which rock rhythmically, but this pictorialism is so skillfully woven into the total musical fabric that it is not obtrusive. The growing reliance upon melodic independence in the accompaniment is also evident, the first lullaby being structured entirely on a continuing flowing melody in the piano treble that never runs parallel to the voice. Despite the sharpness of much of the dissonance, the vocal lines are still quite tonal, often even diatonic over relatively long stretches, as in *The Highland Balou*.

The contrapuntal emphasis is even more marked in the more recent (1965) *The Poet's Echo*, on texts by Pushkin. The first song of the group is, in fact, a straightforward three-voiced canon, which employs many of the standard canonic techniques—augmentation, diminution, etc. The form is thus a reflection of the poem's subject matter (*Echo*), a far more sophisticated type of text illustration than is normally found in even the best of nineteenth-century song composition, and one that is indicative of the strong inclination in the present century to utilize purely musical techniques to get the point across.

More austere are the *Songs and Proverbs of William Blake* from the same year, which incorporate a number of musical devices from a much earlier musical period—free barring, recitative sections, parallelisms, and the like. Both the Pushkin and Blake sets employ a considerable amount of vocal melisma, again a Britten characteristic that identifies his fascination with the distant past. Too, his tendency to employ text illustration when the occasion suggests is as much a clue to his ties with Purcell as are many of his other characteristics. The opportunities are rife in the Blake poems (*The Fly, Proverb VI* which refers to the bee and the clock, *The Tyger*, and others) and Britten does not pass them up. The harmonic treatment is extremely contemporary, however, and the later songs make extensive demands upon the vocalist in terms of melodic complexity. Thus, although many of the musical devices are drawn from a past era, the framework in which they appear is undeniably twentieth century.

Of the composers in England, Britten is far and away the most significant in terms of vocal music. Already his work seems destined to occupy a place of permanence alongside that of the lutenists and Purcell. His interest in the music of England's past is evidenced in his imaginative arrangements of folk songs, as well as in his realizations of a number of Purcell's figured basses. At the same time, his assimilation of present-day harmonic techniques while eschewing the more esoteric vocabularies assures him a public able to respond without developing the aural resources of a cultish devotion. He is extremely catholic in his choice of texts, setting the Russian of Pushkin, the French of Rimbaud, and the Italian of Michelangelo with an ease equal to his treatment of the English poets. And if the trend of the present century is toward a greater utilization of the formal devices of music as an anchoring principle to provide the ear with a sense of security amid the onslaught of dissonance, Britten is very much in the forefront. The use of *ostinato*, passacaglia-like figures is frequent, as is a reliance upon rhythmic, melodic, and harmonic sequence, all of which are aids to structural clarity.

In America, the links with the past have been similar to those elsewhere in that there are some song composers who have assimilated much of the subject matter and harmonic-melodic approach of the previous century without entirely denying their own. Typical of this type of carry-over is the work of Charles Griffes and John Alden Carpenter, with their empathy for the impressionistic vocabulary. Of a less categorically derivative nature are the songs of John Duke, David Diamond, and others of a like persuasion. Nonetheless their work is characterized by a retention of many facets of romantic harmonic style together with an emphasis upon lyricism in the role of the voice. To the extent that the performing profession and the listening public are appealed to by this type of song, the compositions have won at least a temporary place in the repertoire. Perhaps of greater significance is the work of Samuel Barber, whose more recent songs absorb a good many of the rhythmic, melodic, and harmonic techniques of the century without at the same time eliminating the tunefulness of the vocal line. Like so many of his contemporaries, his greatest attention has not been given to song, and it is therefore worth noting that even his relatively few efforts in the medium have gained considerable currency. The thinning out of his texture and the growing assimilation of twentieth-century techniques are evidenced in the change of style between his earliest pieces (*Dover Beach, With rue my heart is laden*, and others) and the 1953 *Hermit Songs*. The metric diversity and sometimes jagged vocal lines of the latter pieces are entirely in the idiom of the present, although the harmonic undergirding retains a sense of tonal security.

Possibly the most prolific song composer in America during the present era has been Ned Rorem. In any consideration of song he is important, not only because of the unusual attention he has given to it but also because of his several books in which he has shared some of his ideologies. Because of his associations in France with the members of the group, *Les Six* and their immediate associates, it is not surprising that many of their techniques turn up in Rorem's pieces. There is the same concern for linear construction, usually of a relatively sparse nature, and an accompanying interest in contrapuntal techniques. He is fond of *ostinato* figures (rhythmic as well as melodic) of all sorts, and in fact they frequently supply the principal structural material for many of the songs. There is a corresponding use of purely imitative passages involving accompaniment and voice, often in a strict canonic sense. At the same time, on those occasions when the texture is oriented in vertical (as opposed to linear) harmony, the vocabulary is often quite contemporary, utilizing chords in quartal harmony in the manner of Hindemith, and even sometimes of a polytonal nature. This is particularly

appropriate in his *Visits to St. Elizabeth's*, where the contradictory key
feeling relates to the paranoia of Ezra Pound whose incarceration in St.
Elizabeth's inspired the text by Elizabeth Bishop.

There is considerable variety in Rorem's songs. Some, like *Early in the
Morning*, are obviously in the "pop" tradition; others, like *I am Rose* and
O You Whom I Often and Silently Come, are mere vignettes; some, like *My
Papa's Waltz*, are wonderfully witty musico-poetic caricatures. Among his
most thoughtful compositions is the song group, *Poems of Love and the Rain*.
Perhaps more than any of his other songs, this cycle evidences Rorem's
concern for musical virtuosity on a small scale. The group consists of eight
poems, each of which is set in two contrasting styles, plus one that serves
as an interlude and is set only once. In his explanatory notes, the composer
sets forth his objectives: to provide the utmost difference between the
musical realization given in each pair of settings while at the same time
maintaining a motivic continuity. Although there is no rash departure from
his general linear style, the cycle is more than usually inclined toward
sharpness of dissonance and in some cases (*Love's Stricken "Why"* and
Interlude in particular) a dramatic approach to declamation. One of Rorem's
most striking characteristics, in these as in his other songs, is his care
in the treatment of the word. This is a surface characteristic, however,
involved with accentuation and rhythmic pace rather than with any interpretive subtlety. The composer himself seems inclined away from any
excessive aesthetic rapport with the poetry as literature. In one place he
writes:

A student contralto asks: "Before I sing this song of yours, Mr. Rorem, could
you explain what the words mean?" "The words mean what my music tells
you they mean." What more do I know about poetry?[5]

In another context he states a similar thesis:

Any good song must be of greater magnitude than either the words or music
alone. I wouldn't mind if this piece were played in concert on the violin; or,
omitting the vocal line, as a piano solo.[6]

Although the contradiction is obvious, the point is clear that for Rorem
the music must carry the burden of justification expressively. His admiration for Poulenc may be partly responsible for this philosophy, since he
writes in the same book:

André Dubois tells us that Poulenc has no awareness of the meaning of poetry
(or literature) as an art. This is no doubt why he (Poulenc) writes such marvelous
songs; he is concerned with words *only* inasmuch as they are connected with
music. Auric, a real intellectual, on the other hand, does not write successful
songs.[7]

5 Ned Rorem, *The New York Diary* (New York: George Braziller, 1967), pp. 197–198.
6 Ned Rorem, *The Paris Diary* (New York: George Braziller, 1966), p. 11.
7 *Ibid.*, p. 133.

For Rorem, as possibly for most song composers, there is a recognition that what might be called purely musical inspiration cannot be articulated in terms other than its results *as music*. In *Music from Inside Out*, an invaluable commentary on current music and musicians by one who is intimately involved, the point is made quite succinctly:

> Any competent craftsman can fabricate an impeccable song in which every note is justified by some sort of musico-prosodic logic. One composer will undertake the writing slowly, with controlled manipulation not requiring "inspiration. . . . " Another will produce his song in a fever of impulse with music spilling out all at once; . . .
>
> A professional has only a subconscious inkling of his working methods once they are ingrained. He is in the happy position of not being obliged to give himself an explanation for his individual choices if their sum total seems logical. It is for the theorist to inquire later into the reasons of choice; they may not necessarily jibe with those of the composer who may even have forgotten them.[8]

Whether or not Rorem's songs will assume the status of "greatness" is a question that time alone will determine. Already his work is receiving some attention in critical commentaries and there is some reason, therefore, to believe that at least a number of his compositions will persist in the repertoire. It is possible that a portion of his appeal lies in his ability to incorporate twentieth-century idioms while avoiding the extremes of the avant-gardists, an ability he shares with Barber, Britten, *Les Six,* and numerous others.

A word should be said about Italian song of the present century. Although there has been considerable interest in its composition, only a few composers have gained even a minimum of attention on the recital stages of this country. It is perhaps indicative that Miller gives the translations of only six songs in his anthology of song texts and that three of these are by the impressionistic Respighi.[9] While Respighi's songs (the *5 Liriche* on texts by Shelley, Fersen, and others and the *4 Liriche* on poems by Zarian are typical) are not lacking in intrinsic value, they make no significant advances upon the harmonic vocabulary of Debussy. Nor is their melodic style particularly distinctive, although there is considerably more Italianate tunefulness than is found in the late songs of the great Frenchman, as well as many of the pseudo-recitative effects which are typical of the late nineteenth century in general. Other composers such as Cimara, Paul Vellucci, and Giulia Recli follow much the same general approach, Cimara being more inclined to exultant lyricism than some of his contemporaries. More recently the compositions of Luigi Dallapiccola have had some circulation outside Italy but the style is based on serial techniques under the influence of the Germans, Alban Berg in particular. If there is a movement beyond these extensions of an essentially borrowed sort of idiomatic expression,

8 Ned Rorem, *Music from Inside Out* (New York: George Braziller, 1967), p. 54.
9 Miller, *op. cit.*

it has not made itself felt with any strength nor have its results taken a place of prominence in the recital repertoire. Perhaps the most meaningful comment that might be made on the resurgence of interest in Italian song following the neglect of centuries is the fact that even this far into the century, one of Italy's most reactionary song writers, Stefano Donaudy, continues to enjoy a certain currency despite the patently archaic nature of his lush romanticism.

Even this brief survey indicates that all the countries that supplied the bulk of the song literature of the past are continuing in the present century to provide a substantial repertoire, which has moved only cautiously into the more experimental areas of musical manipulation.[10] The most representative composers among those discussed above have continued to allow the voice a true singing role as opposed to a mere sound- or pitch-making one. Most have returned to linear concepts in reaction to the overabundance of vertically organized harmonic illustration that typified high romanticism. With this has come a complementary return to many of the contrapuntal procedures of the baroque and a corresponding thinning out of musical texture. National styles, if there are such phenomena, have differed somewhat in the amount of text illustration, the French tending to avoid it more sharply than either the English or Americans. Some of this has its basis in the differences in poetry. Britten, Warlock, Barber, Finzi, and others have been attracted to poets of past eras whose work speaks more directly to the senses in a literal way and within a context that not only allows but encourages tone painting. The French composers, on the other hand, have leaned rather heavily upon poets of their own generation and the imagery and symbolism is often too delicate and obscure to allow for the intrusion of definitive musical representation. Rorem, of the Americans, has more consistently used the poetry of his contemporaries, but most of what seems to appeal to him is material that is neither excessively abstruse nor given to artistic mysticisms of any sort.[11]

What nearly all of the "nonexperimental" song composers of the present century have carried almost intact from the nineteenth-century traditions is a healthy respect for careful but not fussy declamation. The musical demands that linear procedures have imposed upon their styles have not intruded adversely upon their treatment of the word. Nor have their indulgence in dissonant fabrics, their forays into polytonalities and sometimes even their approach to atonality, or their adventurous use of rhythmic and metric complexities blinded them to the basic need in song for at least a minimum of tunefulness appropriate to the innate capacities of the voice.

10 The Germans, not yet mentioned in this chapter, are represented by Strauss and Mahler, the former having remained interested in song composition into the 1940's. The Americans, not significantly active in song composition before the present century, must be considered in company with the English in any discussion of twentieth-century song.

11 For an articulate exposition of his aesthetic in this regard, it is worth consulting Chapters 3, 4, and 5 of his *Music from Inside Out*.

They have been, in other words, the heirs to some of the best of the past without at the same time becoming anachronistic to their own time.

In respect to the forms into which the songs have been cast, it is impossible to identify preferences. The increasingly free formal style of poetry itself is one of the controlling factors at this point, of course. The widespread abandonment of end rhyme and the tendency to utilize lines of unequal length have combined to eliminate the regularity of cadence that might be echoed in the musical phrasing. The declamatory advances that are identified with late romantic lyric recitative have been invaluable in providing a means for realization of poetic irregularities. In general, the tendency is to allow the poetic language to flow in a steady movement from beginning to end. Repetition of words is unusual, an indication of the contemporary composer's respect for the adequacy of the poet's statement as it stands. The insertion of interludes is likewise curtailed for the most part, although the composers in English (Finzi and Barber particularly) are more apt to indulge in them than are the French. The exceptions to this generalization are most often found in songs conceived for voice and chamber ensemble, where much of the musical interest is entrusted to the instrumental group. In some cases where the work is sectional, an entire movement will be given to the instruments alone, as in Poulenc's *Le Bal Masqué*, which includes three rather extensive interludes and a *Préambule*, none of which involves the voice at all.

But there have been and are song composers who cannot be seen as primarily traditionalists, for they have brought into play musical devices the end result of which is not yet fully clear as far as song style is concerned. Perhaps the composer whose songs best represent a mixture of the old and the new is the American, Charles Ives, whose experimentation in all musical media was far in advance of his time. The significance of his work has only recently been fully realized and performances of his instrumental and vocal pieces.have at last received the blessing of the creators of musical fashion. Certainly no other composer of his time (the turn of the century) matched the fertility of his imagination nor were any of his contemporaries as daring.

Most of the devices which have become identified as "contemporary" can be found in his songs—metric and rhythmic complexity of the severest type, polytonality, atonality, unbelievably dense sound clusters resembling nothing so much as sheer noise, a welter of poetic types ranging from the traditional through hymn excerpts to St. Bernard and including many of his own authorship as well as by such established writers as Goethe, Rossetti, Whittier, and others of similar caliber. A description of Ives's work would involve consideration of each individual composition since he was so diverse in his methods. Alongside his most experimental songs, for instance, there are pieces of the utmost lyrical simplicity like *The Children's Hour* and *A Christmas Carol*. At other times he abandons vocalization altogether and gets into sheer recitation over a descriptive accompaniment (*Charlie Rutlage*). Some of his songs are admittedly satires on what he considered to be decadent styles, like *On the Counter*, to which he appends the note: "Though there is little danger of it, it is hoped that this song will not be taken seriously, or sung, at least, in public." As in his instrumental works, he is fond of quoting familiar tunes (often from hymns) but presenting them in disjointed rhythms and providing them with unfamiliar and often outrageous harmonic backgrounds (*At the River*, *His Exaltation*). As in these two pieces, the material is sometimes drawn from his instrumental works—these are derived from two of his violin sonatas, for example.

Among his most adventurous songs is *Majority*, the dissonant nature of which, often the result of huge tone clusters, leads him to suggest that the voice part is nearly impossible for a single voice and needs the support of a unison chorus. Again he often composed a song completely without bar lines (*from "Lincoln, the Great Commoner"*) and frequently when the bar lines are present, they serve merely as an aid to orientation rather than to articulate the meter, which is so irregular as to be virtually nonfunctional. The extreme complexity of his rhythmic imagination does no service to the declamation in many cases. Pieces like *Tom Sails Away* and *General William Booth Enters into Heaven* and even the far-from-esoteric *Christmas Carol* tend to distort the natural speech rhythms simply through an overabundance of musical manipulation. The problems for the performer and listener alike are immense by any standards of difficulty. Ives's stature as an avant-garde composer is borne out by the fact that his songs present obstacles to performance even for a generation that has become more or less acclimated to dodecaphonic and aleatoric procedures. One wonders if some of the complexity presented by his music is a result of the inadequacy of notational practices to handle his imagination—whether, indeed, what appears on the page is really what he intended.

Although Ives did anticipate most of the musical "isms" that have invaded the present century, he did nothing to organize them nor to develop what might be thought of as a systematized vocabulary. Schoenberg must still be recognized as the leading composer of the century in this regard, for it was out of a chaotic conglomeration of experimental types that he evolved a completely different but immaculately ordered conception for the organization of musical material in a nontonal context, or at least in a context that departed from the tonal implications of the past. If one single factor in the establishment of a new musico-poetic concept in song can be isolated at this point in time, it must be the influence of dodecaphonic compositional techniques. None of the other developments of the century has placed such a burden upon the performer nor has any other "system" so sharply controlled the relationship between word and tone to the end that musical considerations almost completely override poetic ones. Although Schoenberg's disciples did succeed in evading some of the original arbitrariness of twelve-tone organization, their work remains, for the most part, oriented toward the voice as a pitch- or sound-producing mechanism rather than as a medium for the emission of ingratiating melody. Despite the disadvantages it enforces on song as a lyrical expression, however, the dodecaphonic methodology has so permeated all musical media that some of the literature of the school must be recognized as having taken an important place in the literature of song.

Schoenberg himself has contributed a portion of that repertoire. It is worth noting that the first volume of his collected works is given to his *Lieder*.[12] Within these songs can be seen the composer's development from the Brahmsian romanticism of *Dank* (1897) through the rejection of tonality in the fifteen songs from *Das Buch der hängenden Gärten* to the fully developed twelve-tone *Drei Lieder*, Op. 48. This very evolution of Schoenberg's creative methodology has been so completely documented in the numerous volumes devoted to his genius that there is no need to recapitulate it here. His own remarks, and those of his editor, however, are important for their implications about song style. In his introduction to the volume of songs,[13] the editor quotes Schoenberg as having written in 1920:

... I had composed many of my songs right through to the end, intoxicated by the sound of the opening words and without concern for the subsequent course of the poetic action—indeed even without grasping this at all in the exuberance of composing—and only some days later came to examine the text to find out what the poetic content of the song really was. I then discovered to my great astonishment that I have never done greater justice to the poet than when, led on by the first direct contact with the opening sound, I had foreseen everything that obviously with necessity had to follow this initial sound.

Schoenberg is attempting to verbalize here his instincts as a composer, which insist that the nature of artistic creation is of itself organic, to the extent that its parts cannot be separated from the whole either before or after the fact of creation. The editor adds:

They [Schoenberg's statements] correspond to and define Mozart's postulate that poetry should be the obedient servant of music. It loses its sole power of expression and becomes structural material for the composer when he assimilates the poetic substance and gives it new form and shape in terms of his own language of music.

The editor continues to defend the composer's ideology in terms of the absorption of the poetry by music as being merely the same expression cast in a different mold and employing different materials. And once again he quotes Schoenberg:

... the external correspondences between music and text as manifested in declamation, tempo, and volume (in other words in merely illustrative composition) have little to do with those that are internal, and are on the same level of

12 Arnold Schoenberg, *Sämtliche Werke*, Vol. I (Mainz: B. Schott's Söhne, 1966).
13 *Ibid.*, pp. xvii–xx.

primitive imitation of nature as the copying of a pattern. And that an apparent divergence on the surface can be necessary because of parallels on a higher level.

The points are well taken and have gained considerable support from aestheticians of the persuasion of Langer and others. It is something of a mystery, however, how even a composer of Schoenberg's stature can "assimilate the poetic substance" without reading the poem.

The difficulty for both performer and listener lie not in justifying the method of composition but in the practical area of reproduction and assimilation. In so many cases what appears to be completely logical to the eye is incomprehensible to the ear. In addition, the choice of material to be utilized in the tone row inevitably places melodic restrictions upon the music, restrictions to which the words must yield at least in large part. The fact that such a wealth of explanatory literature has already sprung into being in defense of dodecaphonic techniques is evidence that, although Schoenberg's aesthetic may be defensible on his own terms, it requires a huge amount of intellectualization in order to meet with understanding and acceptance by a large segment of the public.

But the "system" has attracted numerous first-rank composers and some of its methodology has appeared in song. As might be expected, an eclectic artist like Igor Stravinsky could not but be drawn into serial composition, at least spasmodically. His *Three Songs from William Shakespeare* (1953) utilize the techniques. The first of the set, *Musick to heare*, is a rather strict application in which the voice line picks up the basic material after it has been presented by the flute. The other two pieces are more freely organized but are nevertheless serial in their conception. The group is typical of Stravinsky's approach in other ways, including his sparseness of texture and the extreme freedom of his rhythms. A more recent piece cast in the serial format, *The Owl and the Pussy-Cat* (1966), is even more austere in texture. The accompaniment, entirely in octaves, although limited like the melodic line to the material of the row, never duplicates the voice. And all the contrapuntal devices of the idiom are here—retrograde, augmentation, diminution, etc., although with a considerably less fussy approach to rhythm than is usually the wont of Stravinsky or row composers in general. Evident also is the relaxation of Schoenberg's early dictum against tonal suggestion, so that portions of the vocal melody suggest varying key centers for brief periods, a suggestion that is often contradicted by the accompaniment, however. It might be argued that this sort of clever and ingenious musical realization, which draws so much attention to itself, is well advised to employ a text both familiar and lacking in profundity.

Among the other composers who have applied Schoenberg's principles to song are two of his most avid disciples, Ernst Krenek and Anton Webern, along with Alban Berg, Milton Babbitt, Gunther Schuller, and too many others to catalogue. It seems safe to say that with but a few exceptions,

Ned Rorem among them, the younger composers of the century have been drawn at some time to serial composition or one of its close derivatives, and that when they have been at all interested in song, some of the techniques have appeared in that medium. The most obvious result has been a startling increase in the emphasis upon linear texture and upon the almost arbitrary brashness of dissonance. An accompanying factor has been the extended concept of the possibilities of the human voice. Jagged outlines, extreme demands of range, astounding complications of rhythm—all are part and parcel of the vocabulary of the school and all have taken their toll in performer participation. Although their intrinsic merit may not be in question, depending upon the aesthetic orientation of the individual, there are certainly inhuman demands made upon the human instrument in such pieces as Babbitt's *Sounds and Words* and Krenek's *The Flea*, to isolate merely two songs from the many in this idiom. It is not surprising to find a work such as Jeanne Hericard's *Zoo en do*, a series of studies in serial song that take the student on a guided tour of all the paraphernalia of serialism, including the virtually indecipherable performance directions that accompany the species. One is tempted to suggest that a lifetime devoted to a study of the score could not assure successful mastery by the singer not equipped with perfect pitch, a superhuman voice, and a built-in slide rule. Nor could such mastery really be expected to transfer wholesale in meeting the demands imposed by such works as Krenek's recent *Sechs Lieder nach Gedichten von Emil Barth*, any more, in fact, than familiarity with the German language could insure an understanding of the poet's statement.

Even more *outré* are the compositions, usually for voice and chamber ensemble, of the more advanced of the avant-gardists. Compositions such as Poul Olsen's *A L'Inconnu*, with its absence of words and its elaborate directions for emission of vocal noises in combination with an almost incomprehensible score for the instrumentalists, approach faddist proportions, interesting though they may be as pure sound. Even the Italians are joining in the fun, despite their heritage of sumptuous vocalization. A 1964 *Cantata da Camera* by Boris Porena for soprano, soprano chorus, and chamber orchestra is as "far out" as similar pieces by the German, French, or American probers into the unknown. The acoustical effects of much of the composition along these lines are undeniably fascinating. Whether they constitute a genre that can be classified as either music or song is a decision that will have to await the passage of time and the development of more skilled performers and listeners than are available in any significant numbers at present. Like so many of the contemporary ventures, this type of interest in vocal and instrumental sound production can be traced to Schoenberg. His *Pierrot Lunaire* was the first of the latter-day attempts to extract the unusual from the human voice and put it to use in a musical context. His experiments in *Sprechgesang*, inaugurated in that work, have at least nominal roots in the *Deklamations* of Liszt and Schumann in the previous century, to say nothing of their counterparts in the eighteenth century, even further removed in time. If this is a link with the past, however, it is a hazy one and hardly worth belaboring either musically or aesthetically.

What seems clear is that some features of contemporary society and the contemporary musical scene have been favorable to the encouragement of avant-gardism in general. One is the increased emphasis during the past half-century on the development of academic programs in music. The end result has been a sharp upswing in the number of trained, often highly skilled musicians who are not only willing but eager to investigate new musical materials in an environment where their commercial success is not at issue. It is, indeed, within the colleges, universities, and conservatories that much experimental music has found its most consistent production and public. Those agencies that depend for their prosperity upon a wide and diversified market have been more reluctant to depart from the more standard fare. Thus, opera houses tend to emphasize the reliable works of the past, inserting only sparingly those works from the present century that seem most palatable to large audiences. The recording industry, too, inclines toward the tried and true repertoire, edging tentatively into the newer areas most enthusiastically when there is support from foundation grants of some sort. But the very existence of such grants has proven a boon to the avant-garde. The financial generosity of many of the available sources assures a number of the composers a living for not-inconsiderable periods of time, and enough subsidy for performances and recordings into the bargain. It is doubtful, were the academic sanctuary and foundation support to be withdrawn, along with the performers and audiences that come with the academic environment, whether the production and dissemination of most of the advanced musical experimentation would be possible at all. In song, as in all music, this would be of some loss to the future. While it is patently foolhardy to assess the present trends in relation to their lasting value (or even their immediate value in some cases), there is no reason to believe that future directions will not in large part be dependent upon freedom of investigation, which appears to be looming on the contemporary artistic scene.

As for song itself, only a few generalizations about the present and future seem supportable. The tunefulness of past centuries is less apparent in the twentieth, although portions of it are surviving in the songs of *Les Six*, Britten, Barber, Rorem, and the like. Even in the work of these more traditional composers, however, there is less evidence of deep involvement with musico-poetic principles and more exploitation of musical interest, often as a substitute for poetic expression rather than as a commentary upon it. The same emphasis is more evident in the more esoteric compositions, of course, but an element of it is present in all song. The truth is basically that this is not a lyric century, nor does it seem to be a century in which the song ideal can find its best expression. The simplicity of metric organization and the relative regularity of structure which were characteristic of the lyric poetry of the eighteenth and nineteenth centuries offered a perfect foundation for similar elements in the music of the time. The poetry suggested song, not only because of its surface but because of the intimate, reflective idealism that was its subject matter. On the other hand, the vagaries of all sorts that have invaded the poetry of the twentieth century are not conducive to lyrical reflection. And the complexities of rhythm, melodic style, and harmonic reorganization of present-day music tend to draw attention to themselves and to present performance and auditory problems, which inhibits the full and immediate absorption of the text even in those cases when the text might itself allow for such absorption.

An additional factor is the increasing availability of larger forms of vocal composition. The proliferation of local and touring opera companies during the last quarter of a century has been phenomenal in America. The result is a widening and deepening interest in that medium. One of the side effects has been the tendency to feature on recitals the leading personnel of the opera houses. In many cases where the inclusion of songs is involved in the programming, there is some disservice simply because the singers are more at home and more capable, vocally and interpretively, with the literature of opera than with the more subtle and intimate song.

Again, the renewed interest in group performance is taking its toll in compositions for voice and piano. The ready availability of instrumentalists who are willing and eager to participate in chamber works that include a vocalist has encouraged the composition of hundreds of pieces for such combinations of musicians, many of which have taken an important place in the performing repertoire. They cannot be considered songs, of course, and many of them treat the voice as an equal to the other instruments rather than building the compositions in such a way as to spotlight the vocal line and with it the words. This is decidedly healthy in many respects. There is a far greater ensemble balance in these pieces than in the baroque chamber cantatas, for instance, where the instrumentalists often furnish nothing more significant than a kind of harmonic support for the featured soloist. It has nevertheless been a factor that has exercised a certain amount of control over the type of composition being offered to singers by contemporary composers.

At least to this date, there has been no development comparable to the outburst of *lied* composition in the early years of the romantic century. It is significant, I think, that a number of the nineteenth-century composers are identified entirely with song—Franz, Duparc, Wolf, for instance. And others of first rank in other media—Schubert, Schumann, Brahms, Fauré, Debussy, and countless others—devoted much of their best effort to song composition. In the present century, only Ned Rorem has forged a reputation on the basis of his songs, although he has produced a considerable body of literature for chorus and for instrumental combinations as well. For other composers of stature, the song has been a largely subsidiary part of their output and a part that cannot be thought of as having contributed strongly to their status.

There is something to be said for the fact that the vast bulk of the performing repertoire continues to be drawn from the past, in song as in other media. This is, of course, a normal and healthy situation, because it is only against the heritage of the past that the contemporary scene can be viewed with any perspective at all. At the same time, many of the apologists for the most experimental types of twentieth-century music have defended its highly dissonant and often chaotic nature as being a reflection of the same characteristics in present-day culture. Regardless of whatever truth there may be in such a postulate, there is much evidence that performers and public alike are still consistently drawn to the artistic expression of less tormented periods.[14] It seems likely that the creators of an art that is most rejective of the past may be creating it at the risk of disenchanting a large segment of the public, which continues to find stimulation from the very aesthetic against which so much current expression is directed. There must be, and probably always will be, room in the musical repertoire for the present and the past together. It must remain for future generations of performers and listeners to decide what portion of twentieth-century song will endure, as well as which of the many stylistic types will emerge as most stable and idiomatic.

14 One might even suggest that the medium that seems to be speaking most forcefully to the violent and tormented 1960's is the popular folk-rock and protest songs. At least in these the music is uncomplex enough to allow the focus of attention on the words, which certainly address the situation in as direct and powerful a manner as possible.

Toward a More Realistic Criticism

ONE OF the besetting problems of critical discussion of any artistic expression is the establishment of reasonable criteria. It is entirely possible that neither the establishment nor the application of such criteria will ever reach an ideal state where total agreement among writers and readers will be attained. It is even possible that such a state would not, indeed, be ideal because it might well carry with it the dangers of stereotyping in both creation and response. Nevertheless, a very imposing body of commentary does exist and much of it is marred by evaluations that are given without qualifications of any reasonable sort and without reference to or defense of criteria. The following three quotations, chosen at random, are illustrative:

[Schumann's] cannot compare with the setting, however faulty, by Liszt or the magnificent one by Hugo Wolf, but it is very much better than the rest of the *Wilhelm Meister* songs.[1]

It may be said that if he [Schubert] failed, Schumann and Wolf did no better; their settings are altogether too elaborate.[2]

If Schumann's setting is too elaborate, certainly Liszt's offenses . . . are greater.[3]

In each case, the song under discussion was *Kennst du das Land?* The incongruities are not only because individual tastes differ and what is apparently "too elaborate" for one may be "magnificent" for another. One of the basic fallacies in this sort of comparative criticism is the fact that it ignores the distance in time between Schubert, Schumann, Liszt, and Wolf, and that it fails to take into account the varying forces active in the artistic environment of each. The composers were not heirs to the same influences

1 Martin Cooper in *Schumann, A Symposium*, edited by Gerald Abraham, p. 118.
2 Alec Robertson in *The Music of Schubert*, edited by Gerald Abraham, p. 169.
3 George Edward Luntz, *Musical and Literary Expression in Songs from Goethe's Wilhelm Meister.* Unpublished Ph.D. dissertation, State University of Iowa, 1953, p. 163.

nor ideologies nor devices, and to expect their compositions to lend themselves to evaluation by the same criteria is foolhardy and manifestly unfair
to all.

This book has been an attempt to define more clearly some of the varying
concepts that have been brought to bear on effecting a synthesis between
word and tone, and to show the gradual evolution and fluctuations of the
principles governing that synthesis. A discussion as severely selective and
limited as this one has of necessity been cannot provide a set of evaluative
criteria that can be applied with real depth. Only the most profound awareness of the aesthetic ideologies underlying the poetry and music of the
past three centuries would be sufficient for an in-depth study of musico-
poetic synthesis. Such profundity is dependent upon scholarly research of
the richest sort and I can lay no claim to such an accomplishment. What
has become abundantly clear in reading about and discussing song, however, is the fact that in many cases judgments are based on a preference for
one style over another, for one harmonic or melodic vocabulary over
others, or even on a preconceived set of standards for song composition
in general that fails to recognize either the possibilities or limitations of the
medium.

It would seem that any critique of song from any period must consider
the musical and poetic milieu out of which the compositions emerge. One
very elementary consideration should be the function the song is expected
to serve. The purposes for which lute songs were written were not the same
purposes for which Purcell composed his songs, for instance, and they
cannot therefore be subjected to the same criteria. The intimate, chamber
character of the lutenists could not have supported the exposure to display
at state occasions and other public gatherings to which Purcell's songs were
often subjected. It may well be a disservice even now to program Dowland
in a large recital hall and to present his songs in an environment more
compatible to Strauss. Similarly, Wolf was composing for a public that had
become enamored of the extravagancies of high romanticism and at a time
when the presentation of songs in recital was a common practice. On the
other hand, Schubert was composing during a period when there was little
likelihood that his songs would be given performances except at small
gatherings or, at best, as incidental inclusions in more elaborate musical
offerings. The function, then, accounts for much of the difference in scale
between the works of various composers.

Similar variations are, or should be, anticipated in all facets of the songs
from differing periods. Duparc should not be evaluated in terms of
Debussy's harmonic vocabulary, nor Schumann in terms of that of Strauss.
By the same token, one should not search for a Brahmsian sort of melodic
exuberance in the pieces of Alban Berg. And the rhythmic complexities of
most of the moderns cannot be disallowed just because they often frustrate
the performer and listener to a greater extent than do the relatively simpler
rhythms of Mozart. Each era develops its own artistic objectives and its

own means of achievement. And, similarly, different composers working within a given time span must be granted their individuality. It is certainly to be hoped that, aided by the present wide dissemination of music by recordings, radio, television, and public performance, one does not expect Liszt to sound like Schumann, and dismantle him critically because he fails to.

The only reasonable means by which a critical analysis of song can be supported is through the discovery of word-tone relationships. This implies, of course, a considerable degree of awareness in regard to both poetry and music. A lack of sensitivity to the rhythms of verse can lead only to confusion in assessing the role of musical rhythm in song. On a far deeper level, only an unusual insight into the musical and poetic imagery can serve as a guiding force in recognizing the synthesis of the two elements in those cases where a synthesis exists. Nor can such synthesis be expected to operate at the same level for all periods. The often cavalier treatment of the text that is typical of the baroque period is the result of a certain concept of the role of music in vocal composition, a concept that involved the devising of a musical fabric capable of imitating in its own terms the most obvious suggestion of the text. From that point on, the responsibility was in the music—and the words usually came along principally as vocalization tools for the voice. There is a real parallel between this concept and the approach that Schoenberg defends in his own composition—the admission that in writing a song a few words from the text might furnish a sort of inaugural point that can be grasped without even a complete reading of the poetic details. Thus it is not only the structural devices of Schoenberg that recall the baroque (imitation, retrograde, inversion, and all the other paraphernalia of contrapuntal technique) but the very ideology behind musico-poetic relationships. The application of nineteenth-century criteria to either Purcell or Schoenberg, then, is insupportable in terms of either the musical fabric or the synthesis of word and tone. On an entirely different plane, Schoenberg and his followers may be justly criticized because what they write is often highly unvocal from a purely mechanical standpoint. But this must be sharply separated critically from a consideration of the music *as music*, unless there can be a very clear establishment of the role of the voice. For the baroque composers it was conceived as a vehicle for the projection of beautiful and luxuriant sound, quite apart from its possibilities in the enunciation of the text. For Schoenberg it is obviously a vehicle for projection of pitches, which are of immense significance to the structure but relatively unimportant so far as beauty or magnificence of vocal sound are concerned. And one suspects, as well, that there is a comparable baroque disregard for an impeccable enunciation of the text.

The same interrelationships, dichotomies, and even paradoxes that must govern critical evaluation of Schoenberg and Purcell should undergird a consideration of song from any era, and should certainly take precedence over such factors as simple melodic or harmonic appeal, which are valuable enough in their own right but hardly a basis for criticism because they are meaningful only in terms of subjective response. It is heartening to find a growing body of comment that is based upon an awareness of musico-poetic possibilities and relationships.[4]

Since performers are themselves critics by virtue of the fact that they decide what material is worth the effort of preparation, it is to be hoped that they will become increasingly involved with seeking out correspondences between word and tone that will allow for a meaningful presentation on more than simply the vocal level. There should be a corresponding awareness, too, that differences in style demand differences in approach to text. In a general sense, Italian song of the baroque period can be successfully projected on the basis of glorious vocalization alone, as can much of the operatic repertoire of the eighteenth and nineteenth centuries. The same approach to Debussy's *Chansons de Bilitis* would be a catastrophe in every way. There is good reason for Joan Sutherland's astonishing success with the sort of repertoire that has made her justly famous, because the words carry relatively little of the expressive responsibility. In view of the meager role of the text, it matters little that one is hard put to identify even the language in which Miss Sutherland is performing. But it is to be hoped that this concept of the role of the voice will not be extended to include vocal literature that is not amenable to such disregard both for verbal clarity and for sensitivity to the implications of the words.

The search for musico-poetic synthesis as it relates to an understanding of stylistic variation can be a rewarding one. In this book I have attempted merely to suggest some avenues of investigation that might prove fruitful. A great deal still needs to be done in terms of individual composers and highly particularized styles like the serial techniques. The end result will be successful only to the extent that it encourages involvement by the literally thousands of students and teachers of singing as well as interested commentators and critics, each of whom can bring his own insights to bear on more fully understanding the many-faceted value of the song as an expressive force.

4 Much of this sort of commentary is to be found in journals and in the theses and dissertations that are pouring forth from academies. Three recent examples from readily available periodicals and of widely differing types are:

Bennie Middaugh, "Poulenc: Tel Jour Telle Nuit. A Stylistic Analysis," *NATS Bulletin* (December, 1968).

Jack Stein, "Poem and Music in Hugo Wolf's Mörike Songs," *Musical Quarterly* (January, 1967).

Carlisle Floyd's *The Mystery* and Benjamin Britten's *The Poet's Echo*, reviewed by Francis Monachino in *Notes*, the journal of MLA (September, 1968).

Bibliography

THE following Bibliography is not the usual sort that accompanies a discussion of a particular type of composition. The normal procedure is to offer an exhaustive listing of books and articles that treat of the type—in this case song—and its principal composers. I have avoided that sort of listing simply because it is available so readily elsewhere. Reference shelves are full of just such material. What I have tried to do is to suggest works that include the sort of reading which might stimulate further investigation into the nature of song, the interrelationship of its parts. Included are many standard volumes, a number of them in the German language, primarily because the scholarship from that country has continued to be unusually rich. There are literally dozens of periodical articles of value that I have not even hinted at. And there are many studies of the work of individual composers, all of which are helpful to some degree. Additional sources have been given as footnotes to the text and are not repeated here. The invitation that accompanies this Bibliography is simply to use whatever of it strikes the fancy and to branch out from there—as widely and vigorously as possible.

ABOUT POETRY

ALDRICH, PUTNAM, *Rhythm in seventeenth century Italian monody* (New York, 1966).
BRERETON, GEOFFREY, *An Introduction to the French Poets* (London, 1956).
CLOSS, AUGUST, *The Genius of the German Lyric* (London, 1962).
DEUTSCH, BABETTE, *Poetry in Our Time* (Garden City, N.Y., 1963).
DREW, ELIZABETH, *Directions in Modern Poetry* (New York, 1940).
MCAULEY, JAMES PHILLIP, *Versification—A Short Introduction* (Michigan State University Press, 1966).
MUSSER, FREDERIC, *Strange Clamor* (Detroit, 1965).
PACIFICI, SERGIO, *A Guide to Contemporary Italian Literature* (New York, 1962).
SHAPIRO, KARL JAY and ROBERT BEUM, *A Prosody Handbook* (New York, 1965).

ABOUT MUSICAL PHILOSOPHY AND PSYCHOLOGY

BARZUN, JACQUES, *Classic, Romantic, and Modern* (New York, 1943).
COOKE, DERYCK, *The Language of Music* (London, 1959).
COOPER, MARTIN, *Ideas and Music* (London, 1965).
COPLAND, AARON, *Music and Imagination* (Harvard University Press, 1952).

EPPERSON, GORDON, *The Musical Symbol* (Ames, Iowa, 1967).
FARNSWORTH, PAUL R., *The Social Psychology of Music* (New York, 1958).
FERGUSON, DONALD N., *Music as Metaphor* (Minneapolis, 1960).
KEYS, IVOR, *The Texture of Music* (London, 1961).
LANGER, SUSANNE K., *Feeling and Form* (New York, 1953).
———, *Philosophy in a New Key* (New York, 1942).
MEYER, LEONARD B., *Emotion and Meaning in Music* (Chicago, 1956).
———, *Music, The Arts, and Ideas* (Chicago, 1967).
PRATT, C. C., *The Meaning of Music* (New York, 1931).
RÉVÉSZ, GÉZA, *Introduction to the Psychology of Music* (London, 1953).
SCHOEN, MAX, *The Effects of Music* (New York, 1927).
SESSIONS, ROGER, *The Musical Experience* (New York, 1965).
WINCKEL, FRITZ, *Music, Sound, and Sensation* (New York, 1967).

ABOUT MUSIC IN GENERAL

BOYD, MORRISON COMEGYS, *Elizabethan Music and Musical Criticism* (Philadelphia, 1940).
BUELOW, GEORGE, *Thorough-Bass Accompaniment according to Johann David Heinichen* (Berkeley, 1966).
COOPER, MARTIN, *French Music* (London, 1951).
EINSTEIN, ALFRED, *Essays on Music* (New York, 1962).
EVANS, WILLA McCLUNG, *Ben Jonson and Elizabethan Music* (New York, 1965).
MATTHESON, JOHANN, *Der volkommene Capellmeister* (1739) (Kassel and Basel, 1954).
MÜLLER-BLATTAU, JOSEPH (ed.), *Die Kompositionslehre Heinrich Schützens in der fassung seines Schülers Christoph Bernhard* (Kassel, 1963).
NORTHCOTE, SYDNEY, *Byrd to Britten* (London, 1966).
NOSKE, FRITS, *La mélodie française de Berlioz à Duparc* (Amsterdam, 1954).
ROREM, NED, *Music from Inside Out* (New York, 1967).
SCHOLES, PERCY A., *The Mirror of Music, 1844–1944* (London, 1947).
SIEGEL, LINDA SUZANNE ROGOLS, *The Influence of Romantic Literature on Romantic Music in Germany* (Ann Arbor, 1964).
STRUNK, OLIVER, *Source Readings in Music History* (New York, 1950).
SZABOLCSI, BENCE, *A History of Melody* (New York, 1965).
TOVEY, DONALD FRANCIS, *The Main Stream of Music and Other Essays* (New York, 1949).
WILSON, JOHN (ed.), *Roger North On Music* (London, 1959).

ABOUT SONG IN PARTICULAR

ALBERTI-RADANOWICZ, EDITHA, *Das Wiener Lied von 1789–1815* (Wien, 1923).
BRESLAUER, MARTIN, *Das deutsche Lied, geistlich und weltlich bis zum 18. Jahrhundert* (Wiesbaden, 1966).
BROWN, CALVIN S., *Music and Literature* (Athens, Georgia, 1948).
CLINTON-BADDELEY, V. C., *Words for Music* (London, 1941).
DUCKLES, VINCENT and FRANKLIN B. ZIMMERMAN, *Words to Music* (Los Angeles, 1967).
FRIEDLAENDER, MAX, *Das deutsche lied im 18. Jahrhundert* (Wiesbaden, 1962).

GIBBON, JOHN MURRAY, *Melody and the lyric from Chaucer to the Cavaliers* (New York, 1964).

GREENBERG, NOAH, W. H. AUDEN, and CHESTER KALLMAN, *An Elizabethan Song Book* (Garden City, N.Y., 1955).

HAAS, HERMANN, *Über die Bedeutung der Harmonik in den Liedern Franz Schuberts* (Bonn, 1956).

HALL, JAMES HUSST, *The Art Song* (Norman, Oklahoma, 1953).

IMBERT, CHARLES, *Histoire de la chanson et de l'operette* (Lausanne, 1967).

KNEISEL, JESSIE, *Mörike and Music* (New York, 1949).

KRAMARZ, JOACHIM, *Das Rezitativ im Liedschaffen Franz Schuberts* (Berlin, 1959).

KRETZSCHMAR, HERMANN, *Geschichte des neuen deutschen Liedes* (Wiesbaden, 1966).

MELLERS, WILFRED HOWARD, *Harmonious Meeting* (London, 1965).

MILLER, PHILIP, *The Ring of Words* (New York, 1963).

MOSER, HANS JOACHIM, *Das deutsche Lied seit Mozart* (Tutzing, 1968).

MÜLLER, GUNTHER, *Geschichte des deutschen Liedes vom Zeitalter des Barock bis zur Gegenwart* (Hamburg, 1959).

RONGA, LUIGI, *The Meeting of Poetry and Music* (New York, 1956).

SCHWAB, HEINRICH WILHELM, *Sangbarkeit, Popularität, und Kunstlied* (Regensburg, 1965).

STEVENS, DENIS WILLIAM, *A History of Song* (New York, 1961).

SYDOW, ALEXANDER, *Das Lied: Ursprung, Wesen, und Wandel* (Göttingen, 1962).

THOMAS, RICHARD HINTON, *Poetry and Song in the German Baroque* (London, 1963).

UPTON, WILLIAM, *Art Song in America* (Chicago, 1930).

Index of Names and Subjects

Index of Songs

DATE DUE